D1647510

CREATIVE TEACHING:

HISTORY IN THE PRIMARY CLASSROOM

Also available:

Unlocking Creativity by Robert Fisher and Mary Williams (ISBN 1 84312 092 5)

Creativity in the Primary Curriculum by Russell Jones and Dominic Wyse (ISBN 1 85346 871 1)

CREATIVE TEACHING:
HISTORY IN THE PRIMARY CLASSROOM

Rosie Turner-Bisset

 David Fulton Publishers

David Fulton Publishers Ltd
The Chiswick Centre, 414 Chiswick High Road, London W4 5TF

www.fultonpublishers.co.uk

First published in Great Britain in 2005 by David Fulton Publishers
10 9 8 7 6 5 4 3 2 1

Note: The right of Rosie Turner-Bisset to be identified as the author of this work has been asserted by her in accordance with the Copyright, Designs and Patents Act 1988.

David Fulton Publishers is a division of Granada Learning Limited, part of ITV plc.

Copyright © Rosie Turner-Bisset 2005

British Library Cataloguing in Publication Data
A catalogue record for this book is available from the British Library.

ISBN 1 84312 115 8

All rights reserved. No part of this publication may be reproduced, stored in a retrieval system or transmitted, in any form or by any means, electronic, mechanical, photocopying, or otherwise, without the prior permission of the publishers.

Typeset by RefineCatch Limited, Bungay, Suffolk
Printed and bound in Great Britain

Contents

Acknowledgements

Several people have helped either through inspiration or practically in the creation of this book. The first people to acknowledge are three heroes of mine from the Nuffield Primary History Project: John Fines, Jon Nichol and Jacqui Dean. The late John Fines was a wonderful teacher and storyteller: the source of much inspiration for the way I teach now. He is greatly missed but lives on in the memories of those fortunate enough to have experienced his teaching. Jon Nichol has been a colleague, mentor and friend for the past ten years, and without him I would not have learned so much about high-quality history teaching so quickly. Jacqui Dean is a marvellous innovative teacher, from whom I have also learned a great deal. All three have been instrumental in my development as a teacher and teacher educator. It was a privilege to be asked to research with them, and to work with these colleagues on in-service courses for teachers. I extend my thanks to teachers on these courses, many of whom were excellent examples of creative teachers. I also thank the teachers who allowed me into their classrooms to carry out curriculum development and action research. One of the factors that has made this book possible has been the award of a National Teaching Fellowship, which has given me time to work on projects such as this. I thank my colleagues at the University of Hertfordshire for their support during the process of application and award. In particular I would like to thank Mary Read for her continuing support over the years. Much practical support has been given by the publishers, especially by Tracey Alcock. Finally, thanks go to my family for enduring the writing process.

Preface

'Only connect!'

(E. M. Forster, *Howards End*, ch. 22)

Possibly this quotation is well used to the point of becoming a cliché: yet it is completely apt for a book about creative teaching. The concept of creativity presented in this book is one of connecting different frames of reference to create humour, discovery or works of art. It is about opening the mind to perceive things in alternative ways. The concept of creative teaching similarly is about using those connections to help children learn through a range of representations, teaching approaches and activities, which enable children to be active agents in their own learning. Through being in role in approaches such as storytelling, drama, simulations and songs, they experience aspects of past historical situations as 'players in the game'. In this sense, both children and teachers are being creative.

All this happens within the structures of history as a discipline: the combination of historical enquiry, interpretation and exercise of the historical imagination to recreate the past while remaining true to the surviving evidence. In faithfulness to the umbrella nature of history, concerned with all aspects of past societies, examples of curriculum history are given, not merely integrated by theme or topic, but by concept, process, skill and content. There are more connections, between aspects of different subjects, which those subjects have in common, such as enquiry in history, geography and science, or sequencing in history, English, maths, PE and dance.

The book is structured around the pedagogical repertoire for teaching history: all those approaches and activities which teachers can use to connect their learners to the subject matter to be taught. The intention is that each teaching approach receives more than a few lines: usually a whole chapter is devoted to each approach. Through the detailed narratives for each approach, teachers can gain access, for example, not only to the practicalities of how to do storytelling, but also to underpinning theory and to the pedagogical reasoning of planning for such teaching.

Finally the book is by way of homage to those three great heroes of creative teaching: John Fines, Jon Nichol and Jacqui Dean. Their work was illustrated in the excellent *Teaching Primary History* (Fines and Nichol, 1997) which is now alas out of print. If you can get hold of a copy of this book, you will find it an invaluable source of teaching ideas and approaches for history in primary schools. In the meantime, I offer up this book as emulation and adaptation, and as a source of understanding creative teaching. I hope you enjoy it and find it useful.

Rosie Turner-Bisset
September 2004

CHAPTER 1

Creative teaching

Examples of creative teaching in history

Cameo 1: Local study

A teacher working in tandem with a colleague is doing the local study unit. They have recently taken their classes to St Albans Abbey for combined history, geography, religious studies and art work. At the Abbey the children undertook history/RE trails and art workshops with Abbey staff, and drew maps of the Abbey's layout. Back in the classroom, the teacher gathers her Year 3 class on the carpet. She tells them the story of Athelstan, the medieval peasant with a problem, and the Abbey tax collector who upset his plans by calling for his tithe (see Chapter 6). Just before the end of the story, she pauses and asks the children where Athelstan might have hidden his money. They have one minute to discuss it in pairs. She takes feedback quickly from the pairs, praises the children for good ideas, and finishes the story. She shares with them some documents from the Abbey which list the different goods sold in the market: butter, cheese, vegetables, apples and pears, meat, fish, leather goods, wool, linen, silk, clothing, basketry, jewellery, pottery and glassware. She divides the class into groups to make paper versions of these goods. There are three or four children to each stall making goods. All children have access to a loan collection from the library on medieval times so that they can make their goods look 'right'. They have access to paper, pens and crayons. When they have made enough, they rearrange the room as a marketplace and the groups set out their stalls. They may carry on making goods while selling them. The children can take it in turns to go around and barter goods with other stall holders, while other children in their group mind their stall and make more goods.

Suddenly the teacher announces that the tax collector will be coming around in a moment to collect his tithe (one-tenth of all they have made or sold). The children frantically search for places to hide some of their goods, just as Athelstan did in the story. Some put them in storage trays, in folders, or in exercise books. Others, despairing at the last minute, sit on them. As the teacher comes around, each group has worked out one-tenth to give to her. There is much 'innocent' talk of 'It's been a bad week, sir, haven't made much' or 'One of my cows has been ill'. After this the teacher signals that the market is over. The children groan: they were having fun! Everyone helps to tidy up and restore the classroom to its normal layout. The teacher settles the children on the carpet and ask what they have learned. Hands shoot up:

- They didn't use money in medieval times: they bartered instead;
- The Abbey took money from ordinary people to pay for building;
- What they ate in those times;
- What they wore in those times;
- They had pottery and glass;
- Shoes were made of leather;
- A tithe means one-tenth;
- People traded goods and swapped, say, fish for clothing; or meat for pottery;
- People worked hard for themselves and their family, then the tax collector came around and took some of their money;
- What houses were built of.

Cameo 2: The Victorians

A teacher is studying the lives of people at different levels of society with a Year 6 class. She gathers the children on the carpet and tells the story of Martha, from *Lark Rise to Candleford*, going for her first job as a housemaid at the age of 12. After the storytelling, the teacher asks for volunteers to make a freeze frame of part of the story, the moment when the door is opened to the children, and they confront the lady of the house. She then reads with them a typed section of the chapter from the book from which this comes and asks them to highlight in one colour all the words which are to do with time, and in another colour all the words which are the jobs Martha would have to do. She tells them that this is a source of primary evidence: it comes from a book of memories written by the grown-up who was Martha's friend as a child. They are going to look at two more sources. She asks them what they would do if they were going to cook a meal and needed to know how. The children suggest using one of Delia Smith's cookery books. She tells them that in Victorian times, if a newly married lady wanted to know how to run a house and treat her servants, she would use a manual of household management: an instruction book similar to the recipe books of today. She reads with them the next source of primary evidence: an extract from Cassell's *Book of Household Management*. The extract outlines the duties of a housemaid. She asks the children to tell her words they do not understand and explains them. She asks also if they could get up at 6 a.m. every day without being called. Most of the children who were bussed to school thought that 6 a.m. was not a problem, but getting up without being called was! They then carry out the same exercise of highlighting words to do with time and jobs.

The third source of evidence is a song, 'The Serving-maid's Holiday', which tells of all the jobs a housemaid had to do before her half-day holiday when she would go out and meet her young man. The teacher sings it twice, with the children learning the tune the first time and singing all together the second time. The same highlighting exercise is carried out. The teacher gives them a grid with three columns, one for each source of evidence. She checks that the children understand chronological order, and asks them to write down in each column the jobs each person in the evidence had to do, in order of time. During this time she works with the two least able groups who can do the task since it has been carefully structured, but who need encouragement to complete it. When the grid has been completed, she asks the children to write about 'What was it like to be a housemaid in Victorian times?' Some children adapt the title; all produce some writing (an example of children's work is given in Figure 1.1). The main historical learning from this lesson included:

- for the children to have some understanding of what it was like to be a house-maid in Victorian times;
- for the children to carry out historical enquiry and interpretation of evidence using primary sources;
- for the children to select and organize material for presentation of their interpretation in the form of writing.

The main literacy objectives were:

- for the children to read collectively some challenging texts in different genres;
- to make sense of them;
- to produce high-quality pieces of extended writing.

The lesson also involved music in singing the song, and drama in creating the freeze frame of part of the story. This work occupied one whole afternoon and part of a literacy hour the following day to finish the stories.

Cameo 3: Games and simulation

A teacher has been studying the Tudors with her Year 4/Year 5 class. They have done some work on analysing a portrait of Drake and are now discussing Drake's voyage around the world. The teacher puts a large map of the world on the board, and gives the children a sheet with a chronicle of the voyage. They read this as a shared text,

<u>A day of my life as a maid</u>

"I wrench myself out of bed at 5:55 am and start getting dressed. I start my morning chores at 6:00 am, and start sweeping the floor is my first job. I can't see the point of it because I just disturb the dust, let it settle and do it again after I am cleaned up. But complaints call punishment, and punishment means no supper. Then the grates have to be cleared, for seven o'clock. Then I go and get cleaned up to take the mistress's water to her room. Then I disturb the dust and fluff. By nine the breakfast dishes must be cleared, and I have to strip the beds and get rid of the mess in the chamber pots. It is always best to try not to look or smell it, so you don't throw up. Then the bedrooms must be tidied. Eleven, all the upstairs work has to be done, but today there's extra cleaning. Then it's up to my elbows in soapy water, where I wash the china and glass. Then dust down my throat when I dust the drawing room. Then I light all the fires and lamps.

After mid-day I'm ok. All those jobs aren't dirty jobs, but I have to be dressed to answer the door, wait on the family. (shore, Miss Louisa's reading) and needle work.

When the sky starts to darken, and the winds start to get colder, it's my job to see that all the windows are shut in the upper. My last chores before bed are to turn down all family beds, get the hot water bottles, empty slops again. (it's fine in the dark, but the smell's still there.) and put everything to rights. Master dismisses me at ten, when I drop into bed, dreading the next day of torture".

My account is true, because I took my ideas from several sources of information, and they all said the same sort of things for instance the diary, the song and the manual.

Figure 1.1 Children's work: Victorian maidservant

one child reading each line. For each location in the world that Drake went to, she asks for a volunteer to come and point to the place on the map. The child then puts a marker with the name of the place on the map and the date he was there. After this, she tells the class that, working in fours, they are going to design and make board games of Drake's voyages, but first they have to do a little planning and thinking. She has ready a number of board games: Monopoly, Game of Life, Journey Through Britain, Explore Europe, Scotland Yard, and Cluedo. She asks for volunteers to explain each game briefly. They discuss what the games have in common, and, with the children contributing, the teacher draws up on the board a list in two columns:

(1) those items their game must have; and (2) those items their game might have. Each game must have a board, playing pieces, dice or spinners, a set of rules, and a set of playing instructions. They can have 'chance cards', 'treasure cards', 'captured ships' or any other extras they need for their game. Their board can be highly decorated and they can design a box for its storage. Later the games will be trialled and tested by other classes.

There is a buzz of excitement as the groups settle with their list of items, and start to plan and allocate roles and tasks. The teacher hands out a prepared sheet which gives a timescale for completion of the game, working one afternoon a week. At the end of the period, she has a reporting back session: one child from each group has to report back to the class. She has already trained the class in group work: each child is ready to be the resources manager (who fetches and tidies all resources), a time/order keeper (who keeps an eye on time and sorts out disputes), a recorder (who records in writing what is done) and a reporter/observer (who reports back to the class and observes the group work, achievement and behaviour, giving a score for each of these). The work continues over the half-term unit, occupying design technology time. In history they move on to considering the question: 'Was Drake a hero or a pirate?', using their knowledge from the board game work and documentary sources provided by the teacher.

The scheme of work described in this cameo represents learning over a period of six or seven weeks. It is a complex period of learning and presents an opposite view of learning to the kind detectable in official government documents or in Ofsted guidance for inspectors, which suggests that learning is simple, uncomplicated and almost mechanical in nature. The official view would seem to indicate that the teacher writes down the learning objectives on the board, ensures the children know what they are, the children do the learning activities, and hey presto, they achieve the learning objectives! Doubtless some learning occurs in single lessons, but, just as often, complex learning occurs over a period of time. In the Drake activity, clearly one learning objective for history would be to deepen the children's factual and conceptual knowledge of Drake's voyage (range and depth of historical understanding) before moving on to judging his achievements and whether he could be considered a hero or a pirate (historical enquiry and interpretation of evidence). This was to be achieved via knowledge transfer from one genre of text (the timeline) to another (the board game). There are also learning objectives one can write for geography (the use of maps), design technology (the design and making of the games), literacy (writing in the instruction genre) and PHSE (co-operation and collaborative group work).

All of the above cameos are examples of creative teaching. What makes them so will be explored in this chapter, which is in two sections. The first deals with the nature of creativity; the second moves from there into defining creative teaching. There is an analysis of how the three cameos are examples of creative teaching in history. Through an understanding of creative teaching one can aim to teach high-quality, challenging history, which exercises proper historical skills and processes and promotes the engagement of the historical imagination. The remainder of the book deals with how to achieve this aim.

An explanation of creativity

Creativity is a concept which needs some explaining. This explanation starts with a joke:

During the French revolution, hundreds of people were guillotined. One day, three men were led out to die. One was a lawyer, one was a doctor, and the third was an engineer.

The lawyer was to die first. He was led to the guillotine, the attending priest blessed him, and he knelt with his head on the guillotine. The blade was released, but stopped halfway down its path. The priest, seeing an opportunity, quickly said, 'Gentlemen, God has spoken, and said this man is to be spared; we cannot kill him.' The executioner agreed, and the lawyer was set free.

The doctor was next. He was blessed by the priest, then knelt and placed his head on the guillotine. The blade was released, and again stopped halfway down. Again the priest intervened: 'Gentlemen, God has again spoken; we cannot kill this man.' The executioner agreed, and the doctor was set free.

At last it was the engineer's turn. He was blessed by the priest, and knelt, but before he placed his head on the guillotine he looked up. Suddenly, he leapt to his feet and cried, 'Oh, I see the problem!'

This joke acts as a kind of representation of the interpretation of creativity presented in this book, and as a playful summary. How this joke works and what it has to do with creativity will be explored briefly in this chapter.

Currently creativity seems to be something of a buzz-word in educational discourse. Some people think creativity is synonymous with designing and making things, or expressing oneself through the arts (e.g. Abbs, 1985, 1987, 1989). A survey of teachers and lecturers found that there was 'a pervasive view that creativity is only relevant to the arts' (Fryer, 1996, p. 79). While there may be creativity in these activities, this is too narrow a conceptualisation of the whole business of creativity. A broader definition is given in the Report by the National Advisory Committee on Creative and Cultural Education (NACCCE, 1999) entitled *All Our Futures*. This Report concentrated on creativity in children's learning and curriculum experience, and offered some useful definitions. One problem is that the word 'creativity' is used in different ways and in different contexts. Thus, as the authors of the Report point out, it has an elusive definition:

> The problems of definition lie in its particular associations with the arts, in the complex nature of creative activity itself, and in the variety of theories that have been developed to explain it.
>
> (NACCCE, 1999, p. 27)

They favoured a more comprehensive scope to creativity, believing in its importance in advances in sciences, technology, politics, business and in all areas of everyday life as well as in the arts. They did not regard creativity as an elite activity and believed that it could be taught. Their definition of creativity is: 'Imaginative activity fashioned so as to produce outcomes that are both original and of value' (NACCCE, 1999, p. 29). In their account of using imagination, one useful notion is that of imaginative activity being a form of mental play – serious play directed towards some creative purpose. They refer also to analogy and unusual combinations of ideas:

> Creative insights often occur when existing ideas are combined or reinterpreted in unexpected ways, or when they are applied in areas where they are not normally associated. Often this arises by making unusual connections, seeing analogies and relationships between ideas and objects that have not previously been related.
>
> (NACCCE, 1999, p. 29)

The NACCCE states that creativity is purposeful and that creative activity must have some value. There are dead-ends in the creative process: ideas and designs that do not work. It also stresses the importance of originality, whether that may be judged as original, as against a person's previous work, relative, in relation to a person's peer group, or historic, in terms of outcomes within a particular field.

Books aimed at encouraging creativity in the primary sector (e.g. Beetlestone, 1998a; Duffy, 1998) do embrace the notion of creativity across arts and sciences, and offer much in terms of how to achieve creative teaching, yet they are less clear as to the nature of creativity, preferring multi-stranded definitions or constructs. For example, Beetlestone argues that creativity involves:

- The ability to see things in fresh ways;
- Learning from past experiences and relating this learning to new situations;
- Thinking along unorthodox lines and breaking barriers;
- Using non-traditional approaches to solving problems;
- Going further than the information given;
- Creating something unique or original.

(Beetlestone, 1998b, p. 143)

There are also official views of creativity. The QCA has a website devoted to creativity. Its sections include:

- What is creativity?
- Why is creativity so important?
- How can you spot creativity?
- How can you promote creativity?
- Examples of creativity in action.

It adopts the definition of creativity given by the NACCCE, focusing on imagination, purpose, originality and value. This is helpful as far as it goes, but it still does not define creativity very clearly. The emphasis of this website is on promoting creativity in children, rather than creative teaching. For how to spot creativity, it suggests: 'When pupils are thinking and behaving creatively in the classroom, you are likely to see them:

- Questioning and challenging
- Making connections and seeing relationships
- Envisaging what might be
- Exploring ideas, keeping options open
- Reflecting critically on ideas, actions and outcomes
- Thinking independently.

(http://www.ncaction.org.uk/creativity/index.html)

It also gives suggestions for promoting creativity in children, teams of teachers and teams of managers. Some of the suggestions would apply to any good teaching; others are closest to some of the teaching approaches suggested in this book, but there continues to be a fundamental vagueness about creativity on this site.

Koestler's book on creativity, *The Act of Creation* (1964), explored a concept of creativity based on studies of creative people across all varieties of human endeavour. His analysis dissects humour as a route to understanding the act of creation. In this major study, he advanced the theory that all creative activities including artistic originality, scientific discovery and comic inspiration have a basic pattern in common. He called this 'bisociative thinking' – 'a word he coined to distinguish the various routines of associative thinking from the creative leap which connects previously unconnected frames of reference and makes us experience reality on several planes at once' (Burt, 1964). The best way of understanding this is through the analysis of a joke, in this case the joke at the start of this section (see p. 6). The two frames of reference for this joke are: the religious belief which assumes that if the guillotine does not work, then God is telling us the men deserve to live; and the natural tendency of an engineer to try to solve technical problems, ultimately at the expense of his own life and possibly those of the doctor and lawyer too. In a joke, 'the ascending curve (or narrative tension) is brought to an abrupt end … which debunks our dramatic expectations; it comes like a bolt out of the blue, which, so to speak, decapitates the logical development of the situation' (Koestler, 1964, p. 33). The connection of the engineer looking to see where the problem is with the guillotine is totally unexpected. The tension is relieved and explodes in laughter. The humour lies in the unexpectedness of the outcome or linkage between two different frames of reference. One frame of reference is God's will; the other is the nature of engineers. It is the clash between the two mutually incompatible, yet logically self-consistent frames of reference which explodes the tension. The connection of one of the victims being an engineer and behaving as engineers do enables us to experience reality on two planes at once through the bisociation of thinking on two planes simultaneously.

Koestler wrote a great deal about these frames of reference, using a variety of terms to describe them, such as 'frames of reference', 'associative contexts', 'types of logic', 'codes of behaviour' and 'universes of discourse'. He chose to use 'matrices of thought' (and 'matrices of behaviour') as a unifying formula. 'Matrix' denotes any ability, habit or skill, any pattern of ordered behaviour governed by a 'code' of fixed rules. Koestler stated that all coherent thinking is equivalent to playing a game according to a set of rules; in disciplined thinking, only one matrix is active at a time. When one's mind wanders across to other matrices, it happens through bisociation of the two different matrices, that original creative jokes, acts or discoveries are made. Koestler shows this bisociation as two planes at right angles to each other, M1 and M2 (as shown in Figure 1.2).

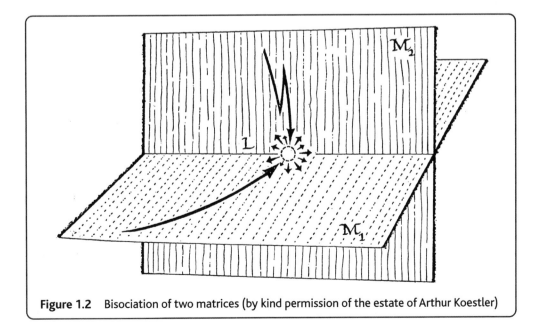

Figure 1.2   Bisociation of two matrices (by kind permission of the estate of Arthur Koestler)

The event (L) is the creative act, the joke, or the discovery at the intersection of the two matrices. The grouping together of jokes, creative acts and discoveries needs further explanation. Koestler presented a triptych of creative activities as a starting-point and unification of ideas for his exploration of creativity (see Figure 1.3). He

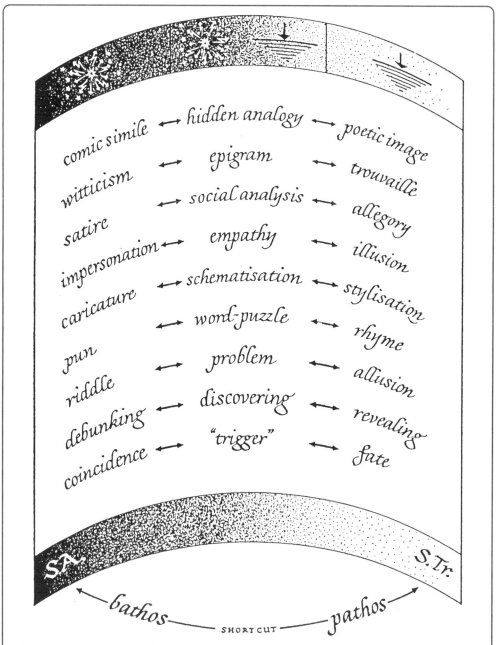

Figure 1.3   The triptych of domains of creativity (by kind permission of the estate of Arthur Koestler)

states that these domains of creativity shade into each other without sharp boundaries: humour, discovery and art. The Sage is in the middle, flanked by the Jester on one side and the Artist on the other. Each line across the panel stands for a pattern of creative activity: in the first column to make us laugh; in the second to make us understand; and in the third to make us marvel. Koestler stresses that the logical pattern of the creative process is the same in all three cases: the bisociation of ideas from different matrices of thought. The emotional climate of each of the three panels is different however, moving fluidly from slightly aggressive or self-assertive in the left-hand side, through neutral in the central panel of the scientist's reasoning, to self-transcending, sympathetic or admiring in the right-hand side. Seeing the joke and solving the problem are thus related: the 'Eureka' cry of Archimedes in its explosion of energies is the same effect as laughter following a joke. Koestler gave examples of jokes, scientific discoveries and originality in art as examples of the creative act within each domain. There is room for only one example in this chapter, so a historical/scientific one is presented:

'Hero, tyrant of Syracuse and protector of Archimedes, had been given a beautiful crown, allegedly of pure gold, but he suspected that it was adulterated with silver. He asked Archimedes' opinion. Archimedes knew of course the specific weight of gold – that is to say, its weight per volume unit. If he could measure the volume of the crown, he would know immediately whether it was pure gold or not; but how on earth is one to determine the volume of a complicated ornament with all its filigree work. Ah, if only he could melt it down and measure the liquid gold by the pint, or hammer it into a brick of honest rectangular shape, or . . . and so on' (Koestler, 1964, p. 105). Blocked situations produce stress: one's thoughts run round and round within one matrix without finding a solution. Archimedes was in the habit of taking a daily bath: he knew from several years of climbing into baths that the water level rises owing to its displacement by the body, and there must be as much water displaced as there is body immersed. He did not think to connect the two matrices, until he was under the stress of finding a solution to Hero's problem (see Figure 1.4). M1 was the matrix of the problem of the crown, M2 was the train of associations related to taking a bath. The link (L) may have been a verbal or a visual concept: perhaps a visual impression in which the water level was suddenly seen to correspond to the volume of the immersed parts of the body and hence to that of the crown, an image of which would have been lurking in Archimedes' consciousness as a result of the continued stress of trying to find an answer to the problem. As Koestler put it: 'The creative stress resulting from the blocked situation had kept the problem on the agenda, even while the beam of consciousness was drifting along quite another plane' (Koestler, 1964, p. 107). The tension built up by the creative stress was released in the famous 'Eureka' cry.

Creative teaching

As with creativity, some vagueness surrounds the notion of creative teaching. The NACCCE Report (1999) defines creative teaching in two ways: teaching creatively;

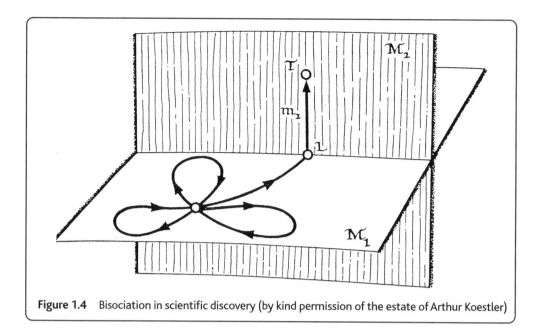

Figure 1.4 Bisociation in scientific discovery (by kind permission of the estate of Arthur Koestler)

and teaching for creativity. The first of these is dealt with briefly in the Report, namely teachers using imaginative approaches to make learning more interesting, exciting and effective. There is nothing here with which one can take issue, only that it is rather nebulous and does not go far enough. In teaching for creativity, the Report states that there are three related tasks: encouraging, identifying and fostering. This is not to reject the importance of these activities, but they tend to cast the teacher in the role of facilitator. That this is part of the teacher's role is undeniable, but I would argue that there is more to creativity in teaching than this. A clue lies in the following sentence: 'Teachers cannot develop the creative abilities of their pupils if their own creative abilities are suppressed' (NACCCE, 1999, p. 90). Thus we need to understand what might be meant by teachers' creative abilities, and what a deeper, more informed understanding of creativity might have to offer towards our conceptions of creativity in teaching.

Some of the literature on creative teaching offers insights such as the depiction of creative teachers being innovative, having ownership of the knowledge, being in control of the teaching processes involved, and operating within a broad range of accepted social values while being attuned to pupil cultures (Woods, 1995). Apart from the first of these, innovation, there is nothing peculiar to creativity. I would expect the other three attributes to be present in all good teachers. Beetlestone suggests that: 'Creative teaching can be seen as the same as good practice, yet good practice is not necessarily creative teaching' (Beetlestone, 1998a, p. 7).

Presumably creative teaching has some extra dimension which distinguishes it from mere 'good practice'. Beetlestone states that the creative teacher demonstrates commitment, subject knowledge, knowledge about techniques and skills, and involvement with the task. The attributes listed by Beetlestone (1998a) encompass many of the qualities of 'good' teaching, but still leave vague the definition of creative teaching. By defining creativity and creative teaching in vague terms, educationists sidestep important aspects of both, and leave themselves open to vague statements which do not help us to understand the real nature of creative teaching.

Koestler's theories of the act of creation seem to me to be the most complete account in the literature of how creativity works across all fields of human activity. His analysis of the creative act across the three domains of humour, discovery and art moves us much further forward in our understanding of creativity than do vague notions of innovation and being highly imaginative. The concepts employed by Koestler – of the matrices of thought or frames of reference; the bisociation between two or more frames of reference, which provides the creative leap; the notion of blockage while one operates, stuck, within one frame of reference; the notion of experiencing reality on several planes or frames of reference simultaneously; and above all the central importance of analogy in making the creative leap – may serve to explain some of what happens at the moment of creation. The same notions can also explain what occurs in creative planning and teaching, and in learning. They also serve to explain the importance of analogy or representation in teaching and learning, and how, in true learning, there is an 'act of re-creation' as the learner strives to make that creative leap first made by others long ago.

This kind of analysis may be applied to acts of creative teaching, such as those cited in the cameos which opened this chapter. In Cameo 1, the teacher decision is made to tell a story of a medieval peasant and re-create a marketplace of that period. The children become engaged with the historical situation as actors, and learn from this enactive representation what it is like to trade and barter, and to have the taxman come around to collect a tithe. Instead of 'trade', 'barter' and 'tithe' being mere words on a page, they are lived experiences. Children learn concepts through such experiences, as well as stepping briefly out of their own shoes and understanding what it was like to live in those times. In this sense Cameo 1 involves creative teaching in connecting universal concerns (a son getting married, the need to build a house for him and his wife, and the taxman's demands), to a particular historical situation. The drama is both re-creation and recreation.

In Cameo 2, three disparate pieces of evidence, documents of different genres, are brought together for the children to read and interpret: an extract from a book of memories; an extract from a household manual; and a folk-song. Instead of the children reading a factual account of a day in the life of a housemaid, they are guided towards reconstructing their own account. Domestic service was a major form of employment in Victorian times, particularly for women, and the texts give clues as to the reality of that employment. The texts engage the emotions and, through the teaching approaches used, the storytelling and freeze frame, and singing the song, the children become imaginatively engaged with what it was like to be a housemaid in Victorian times: to rise at 6 a.m. and work until 10 p.m. every day, to work on your half-day holiday, and to long for that half day. The creative teaching here lies in the assembly of disparate sources, the teaching approaches, and the connection of the frames of reference of the children's own lives and the lives of people in Victorian times.

Cameo 3 shows complex learning over a period of time. The teacher takes the material on Drake, presented as a timeline or a simple chronology, and connects it to another frame of reference: the board game, one which is familiar to all the pupils. To make the activity a success she builds in a further frame of reference of the co-operative groups. This kind of learning involves knowledge transfer, as the children take the new knowledge presented to them (Drake's voyage around the world as a chronicle) and re-present it in another genre: the board game. Through working with the information to put it into a new genre, they make it their own knowledge.

In these cameos the creativity lies both in the juxtaposition and connection of different frames of reference, from subjects, teaching approaches, the teacher's self and interests, and the interests and concerns of the children. Teachers who teach in this way make 'creative leaps' to connect children with subject knowledge in the broadest possible selection of ways, drawing on a wide pedagogical repertoire. I have defined expert teaching as a creative act; however, this creative act is not always teaching in new ways, and what may be innovation for one teacher may be part of the daily repertoire of another. Rather, the concept of creative teaching presented in this book is based on Koestler's notion of creativity:

> The creative act is not an act of creation in the sense of the Old Testament. It does not create something out of nothing: it uncovers, selects, re-shuffles, combines and synthesises already existing facts, ideas, faculties, skills.

> (Koestler, 1964, p. 120)

In this sense, one is being a creative teacher even when one reconstructs or re-creates successful teaching done by others. We have all watched, as learners or colleagues, wonderful teachers at work and wanted to emulate them. But through the act of re-creation, we add ourselves and our own frames of reference to an activity. Creative teaching is good for teachers and it is good for children. Through creative teaching, teachers open themselves up to all sorts of possibilities for communicating their knowledge and experience. It is enjoyable and helps to renew the teacher both personally and professionally, a renewal much needed in the current culture of performativity and accountability. Children too benefit from creative teaching, which fosters their own creative abilities through the kinds of activities and approaches in this book. Of central importance is the notion that planning for teaching in the ways presented here is a genuinely creative act, in Koestler's terms. Teachers who work in this way draw together ideas, materials, activities, analogies, representations and the whole of the pedagogical repertoire to generate activities which will enhance children's learning, making it both memorable and enjoyable. Planning in this book is not a matter of filling in boxes and ensuring 'curriculum coverage'; it is instead an act of creation and celebrates what teaching is really about.

CHAPTER 2

History in the primary curriculum

Chapter 1 introduced a number of cameos of creative teaching in history and set out a concept of creativity and creative teaching which informs the presentation of teaching history in this book. History however is not an isolated subject. There are connections to the whole of the primary curriculum. Cooper (1992, 2000) remarked that history is an umbrella discipline, embracing, through the study of past peoples and cultures, all their art, science, design technology, religion, philosophy, music, dance, song, geography and values. Some understanding is needed of the nature of the primary curriculum, and of the discipline of history, to inform teaching approaches and the design of learning activities. There follows a brief discussion of the primary teaching context and the primary curriculum, touching briefly on the history and nature of primary teaching, and on curriculum integration and topic/thematic work. Next the focus is on history in the primary curriculum, its nature and structures. Finally there is an introduction to the pedagogical repertoire and how it may be used to teach high-quality, challenging history, which exercises proper historical skills and processes and promotes the engagement of the historical imagination. The rest of the book deals with how to achieve these aims.

The primary curriculum and subject integration

The current primary curriculum is probably one of the most prescriptive in the short history of primary education in the United Kingdom, in some ways as prescriptive as the 'Payment by Results' curriculum of 1862 to 1897. Between the beginnings of primary education there was the revised Code of 1904 which was far less prescriptive, and gave teachers much more autonomy both in content and pedagogy. This lasted until 1926, when the removal of the elementary code resulted in the unregulated curriculum (Richards, 1999), also referred to by Richards as the 'lottery curriculum', of 1926 to 1988. Prior to the introduction of the National Curriculum in 1989 to 1991, primary school-teachers were allowed comparatively enormous freedom in their work. The impact of the Plowden Report (CACE, 1967) created a myth of 'progressive education' of which a prominent feature was the topic or theme, a structural and organisation device for planning an integrated curriculum. The introduction of the subject-based National Curriculum in 1989 marked a major change from freedom to prescription in curriculum content, and from topics to subject-based teaching. *The National Literacy Strategy* (NLS) (DfEE, 1998) and *The National Numeracy Strategy* (NNS) (DfEE, 1999b) further codified the content of maths and English and prescribed pedagogy. There are further changes afoot however, and the new Primary National Strategy (DFES, 2003) suggests a relaxation of prescription, increased teacher autonomy on curriculum content and pedagogy, and the restoration of a broad and balanced curriculum. One of its key points is: 'Empowering primary schools to take control of their curriculum, and to be more innovative and to develop their own character.' Thus the opportunities are there, potentially at least, for teachers to take control of the curriculum, and to be much more creative and innovative in how they organise the curriculum and in how they teach it.

One feature which is apparent in the cameos presented in Chapter 1 is that of curriculum integration. Creative teaching is not synonymous with curriculum integration, though it can involve it. A teacher can be creative in teaching only one subject through her connection of different frames of reference through a wide range of teaching approaches which offer children multiple opportunities to connect with the subject matter. It is important to be clear about both curriculum integration and the nature of history.

Curriculum integration

Integrating the curriculum is a controversial issue, involving teachers' deepest beliefs and understanding about subject knowledge, about how children learn, and about the nature of 'real life' outside schools. During the 1970s and 1980s the prevalent view was that young children should not be exposed to subjects. It was argued that they saw the world in a seamless kind of way and imposing subjects on them was unnatural. Research and writing from the late 1980s and early 1990s challenged this view (e.g. Mortimore *et al.*, 1988; Alexander *et al.*, 1992). They suggested that multi-focus curricula tended to produce less effective teaching. Curriculum integration used to be applied to thematic or topic work, and indeed, during the 1970s and 1980s there were many tenuous links made between subjects in an attempt to tie everything into the topic, often without due regard for the nature of each subject.

An important distinction needs to be made between integration that brings together quite different subjects, which none the less have some characteristics in common with other subjects, and non-differentiation which is a way of thinking about subjects that does not admit their separate identities (Alexander *et al.*, 1992). In this book it is the first way of characterising curriculum integration which is employed. To integrate and do full justice to each subject being taught, we need a very clear understanding of the distinctive nature of each subject, and of what may be integrated. In Turner-Bisset (2000a) there is an analysis of curriculum integration which suggests for the future, integration by concept, by skill or process, or by content.

Each of these deserves some explanation, since those teaching activities presented in this book which involve integration use these alternative forms of integration.

Integration by concept means taking the concept as the unifying factor in linking subject matter or teaching activities. All subjects have their concepts, and history is awash with them. There are overarching concepts such as time or chronology, cause and effect, change and continuity, evidence and enquiry. There are concepts such as democracy, monarchy, power, authority, which are abstract in nature. Finally there are concepts specific to history such as the Black Death, the Reformation and the Blitz. Thus one might teach about scale as a sub-concept for understanding timelines, through maths and geography. There are some skills and processes which are common to a number of subjects. Sequencing is found in maths, English, history, PE, dance and music. Observation is found right across the curriculum, in art, history, design technology, science, music and geography. Comparing and contrasting are found in several subject areas. Reasoning from evidence is intrinsic to maths, science, history and geography, as are enquiry and interpretation of evidence. Interpretation is used in English in the understanding of literature. Some analysis of the various skills and processes across the curriculum can reveal ways of linking subjects through the key concepts, skills and processes. There is yet another way to integrate: by content. This means using one subject as a vehicle to teach another. One example might be using music and dance as evidence of the past, and for imaginative reconstruction of the past through performance of music.

The nature of history

To teach history well in schools requires a deep understanding of history as a discipline. Without an informed understanding of the nature of history one can teach history inappropriately, without due regard for the structures of the subject. Schwab (1964, 1978) argued that an understanding of the disciplines was fundamental to teaching subjects in school. He stated that disciplines had two kinds of structures: substantive and syntactic. This distinction resembles Ryle's (1949) propositional knowledge and procedural knowledge, or 'knowing that' and 'knowing how'. Substantive knowledge is essentially the substance of the discipline, which has two aspects. The first of these comprises the facts and concepts of the discipline (for example, in history, that the Battle of Waterloo was fought in 1815). Concepts are more complex, since there are different orders of concepts. The first order concepts are over-arching concepts which define the ideas with which history is concerned. These are:

- Chronology (time)
- A sense of period (historical situations)
- Change
- Continuity

- Cause
- Effect (consequence)
- Historical evidence
- Interpretations of evidence or points of view

There are also second order concepts such as society, monarchy, democracy, class and the Church which we use to understand historical situations. Finally history is packed with third order concepts peculiar to history which we use as a kind of shorthand for periods of time, events, systems, major changes or ways of thinking: the Middle Ages, the feudal system, the Renaissance and the Enlightenment, to give a few examples. The second aspect comprises the organising frameworks or paradigms which inform historical enquiry. In history, competing frameworks have waxed and waned over the years, shaping the kinds of enquiry carried out. At one time history was thought of as the working out of God's purpose in the world, or as a kind of moral illustration, as a science or as an art (Evans, 1997). Later it was conceptualised both as an art and as a science.

Just as important and perhaps more significant for intending teachers of history are the syntactic structures of a discipline. An understanding of these structures can fundamentally shape one's notions of the nature of history and what it means to teach history in the primary classroom. Syntactic structures are the processes by which new truths become established in a discipline. In history these are the processes of enquiry: the search for evidence; the examination of evidence; the recording of evidence; the interpretation and weighing of different sources and kinds of evidence; and the synthesis of historical narrative or argument. In these processes there is always the exercise of the historical imagination, since evidence from the past is nearly always incomplete, in some cases fragmentary. We speculate and hypothesise about the past. We imagine how it might have been and we fill in the gaps left by the evidence. Thus history is a combination of three aspects: the scientific aspect in enquiry and interpretation of evidence; the imaginative or speculative aspect in the exercise of the historical imagination; and the literary aspect in the presentation of history or histories to others (Trevelyan, 1913).

To achieve excellence in the teaching of history one needs a full understanding of these structures. This may seem to be a bold claim, or too far removed from the concerns of primary teachers. However, one only has to consider what happens, or what might happen, when history (or any other subject) is taught without due regard for its substantive and syntactic structures. If history is presented to children as definite facts about the past, recorded in books as secondary evidence, then children miss out on part of the essential nature of history. They have no understanding that history is about enquiry and interpretation of evidence. History at worst can become the meaningless copying out of information from topic books, and the production of pleasing work and artefacts for display. Of course children will learn something about the past but they will be deprived of a full understanding of history. They will also be deprived of the skills of enquiry, of interpretation, of detection of bias and of the synthesis of argument. All these skills are arguably of major importance for adult life.

There is a tendency in schools (and sometimes in universities) to treat the fruits of disciplines as if they are uncontested facts or literal truths instead of interpretations of evidence. Schwab (1978) argued that we have tended to simplify the findings of scientific, mathematical or historical enquiry to the point where such knowledge can be correctly understood without reference to the structures which had produced it. This was done in the interests of effective teaching, because we tended to think that what was taught would not be affected by presenting knowledge in this way. These ideas are difficult, but an example of Schwab's point is the cramming of scientific facts for SATs. Schwab further argued that to teach without due attention to both substantive and syntactic structures was, in terms of teaching and outcomes, 'a corruption of the discipline' (Schwab, 1978, p. 243).

Over long years of observing history lessons taught in primary schools, I have witnessed many occasions of corruption of the discipline. One common example is for children to do comprehension work on historical texts, or cloze tasks on paragraphs prepared by the teacher. Another common example is for teachers to gather children on the carpet, tell them factual information, and ask them to draw pictures and write about what they have heard. Video is often used as text, with the children answering questions on the video. This variant I call 'video comprehension'. There is often an emphasis on the production of work for display or for topic folders, which seems to be an example of the 'production line' classroom described by Cockburn (1995) in which there is an atmosphere of business and productivity. There is also the ubiquitous 'research' or 'finding out' from children's topic books, encyclopedias, CD-ROMs and the internet, which is not genuine historical enquiry, being rarely fuelled by questions. More often it is guided by a general instruction to 'find out about', and can lead to copying of information, or the modern equivalent of copying, cutting and pasting to produce historical writing which contains nothing of the child's understanding. All these are examples of the corruption of history as a discipline.

A third strand to subject knowledge is our set of beliefs and attitudes towards the subject. What we believe history to be has considerable impact on how we teach it: this is why a proper understanding of substantive and syntactic structures is so important. There are still widely held views that, for example, history is about learning facts and dates and about kings and queens. One's beliefs about a subject can influence one's attitudes towards it, being shaped by perception and experience. Many beginning teachers come to primary history with negative attitudes, based on their own experience of it as a school subject. Negative attitudes are hard to alter in any subject; however, it is of vital importance to change them. To teach history well one needs enthusiasm born out of understanding. It is not easy to communicate enthusiasm for a subject which one does not understand or even like. Enthusiasm is a vital element in

HISTORY

Substantive knowledge	Syntactic knowledge	Attitudes and beliefs
CONCEPTS time (chronology) historical situations (a sense of period) change continuity cause consequence (effect; result) interpretations (points of view) historical evidence: source types	PROCESSES historical enquiry interpreting evidence questioning using and applying existing knowledge SKILLS evaluation sequencing observation and senses hypothesising reasoning and deducting extrapolating reflecting/ remembering predicting classifying comparing and contrasting	history is enquiry-based discipline history involves both interpretation of evidence and imaginative reconstruction of the past history is enjoyable, interesting and exciting history involves important literacy and numeracy skills

Figure 2.1 Map of history (reproduced with permission from *Teaching History* (Historical Association, 2001))

teaching: crucially, beginning teachers need to understand the nature of history, and to enjoy and value it. Figure 2.1 presents a 'Map of History' which may be used as a guide to understanding its nature and an aid in planning.

This 'Map of History' should be used in conjunction with the History National Curriculum document. The present *History National Curriculum* (DFEE, 1999c) is a revision of two earlier versions (DES, 1991 and 1995). It is important to understand that this is a 'framework' curriculum comprising two parts. The first part, numbered 1–5 in the document, comprises the knowledge, skills and understanding which are to be developed through the history curriculum. The second part is the breadth of study, which comprises the content to be taught. The really important point is that only information printed in purple or black ink has statutory force. There is no legal requirement to teach all the suggested content, which is in grey ink. Teachers may select from these suggestions, or substitute their own areas of content within the framework of the breadth of study units offered. Readers should compare the 'Map of History' with the curriculum document, and pick out key concepts, skills and processes.

Definitions of history for primary teaching

Four key definitions are used in this book, along with key ideas from the Nuffield Primary History Project (Dean, 1995; Fines and Nichol, 1997; Nichol and Dean, 1997). These definitions are those of Trevelyan (1913), Collingwood (1946), Turner-Bisset (2000b), and Hexter (1972). It is practicality rather than delusions of grandeur which encourages me to place my rather basic definition next to that of three eminent historians. Trevelyan's concept of history as the combination of science (enquiry), imagination and literary activity has already been mentioned. Collingwood suggested that historical evidence had something in common with the evidence used in a murder enquiry: historians are like detectives, working out what might have happened from a range of clues and sources. In trying to define history simply as a summary of the activity students had been engaged in, playing at detective with a suitcase from lost property, I devised the following definition:

> History is the imaginative reconstruction of the past using what evidence we can find. We can state what we definitely know from the evidence. We can hypothesise about things we are unsure of, and we can use other knowledge and experience to inform our interpretations.
>
> (Turner-Bisset, 2000b, p. 171)

This definition leads us to Hexter's work which is extremely valuable for understanding history teaching in the primary classroom. He showed that history is a process. From him one can take the idea of 'doing history' (Fines and Nichol, 1997). Rather than children studying history as do professional historians, it can mean that we try to engage children in tasks which see them acting as historians. They follow the syntactic structures of what historians do, and understand how history differs from other subjects. Fines and Nichol (1997) gave a very clear outline of the study of history in the primary classroom:

- First, we must be examining a topic from the past and raising questions about it.

- Second, we must search for a wide range of evidence to help us answer our question.

- Third, we must struggle to understand what the sources are saying (and each source-type has a different language) so that we can understand them in our own terms.

- Fourth, we must reason out and argue our answer to the questions, and support them with well-chosen evidence.

- Finally, we must communicate our answers for the process to be complete.

(Fines and Nichol, 1997, p. 1)

These are the processes of historical enquiry: of 'doing history'. Interpretation is central to this process, as evidence may be viewed from a multitude of perspectives. Historical evidence takes many forms: archaeological remains, artefacts, pictures, photographs, paintings, engravings, cartoons, clothing, buildings, sites, the landscape and the environment, music, song and dance, literature of a period, historical fiction and film, and documentary evidence of all kinds: newspapers, magazines and books, diaries, memoirs, journals, eyewitness accounts, census returns, trade directories, letters, inventories and advertisements, to give only a few examples. It is the task of historians, and of children acting as historians, to collect (with the aid of the teacher), analyse, organise and interpret the evidence, weighing its validity and reliability against other evidence of the same event, person or period.

According to Hexter (1972), the available sources are history's 'first record': the raw material of primary sources and the secondary sources of later interpretations. In examining and interpreting these sources, we bring to bear upon the 'first record' what Hexter called the 'second record'. This is all our rich experience and knowledge of life to date. This 'second record' is usually private and personal, as well as individual. For example, a teacher who had grown up in the Middle East would have a very different second record with which to interpret news of the war in Iraq than someone born and raised in England. Children do not have such richly developed second records as adults do, though they may have experienced hunger and hardship, racism and violence. One of the roles of the teacher is to extend the children's second records by sharing her or his own second record with them; and through providing opportunities for them to pool their knowledge through pair, group and whole class discussion. Hexter's ideas of the first and second record are most useful for teachers: for understanding the processes of historical enquiry; and informing their planning for teaching history. The notion of interpretation needs to include the exercise of the historical imagination, since this is vital both as a part of the historical process and as a process of learning in the primary classroom. Hexter's ideas can also partially illuminate our understanding of how children learn in history.

Children's learning and history

Teaching a subject involves understanding its substantive and syntactic structures, and what makes it distinctive from other subjects. In addition, knowledge and understanding of the psychology of children's learning are essential for excellent teaching of history. There is not space in this chapter for a full exposition of theories of children's learning, but a brief outline is given below of those most relevant to learning history. These theories are: schema theory; theories of conceptual change; Bruner's (1970) ideas of different modes of mental representation; and Vygotsky's theories of social learning.

The key notion in schema theory, which originated in the Genevan School with Piaget (1959) and his colleagues, is that thought processes depend upon our ability to create mental representations of objects and people. The experience of these, including the way they relate to each other, is stored as schema: internal representations which can be quite complex patterns. Adaptation is the process by which schemas are changed, and it has two aspects: assimilation and accommodation. Each time a person has a new experience, he or she makes some sort of image or internal representation of it. This alone is not enough for learning. To become part of a schema, accommodation is required. It is not simply a process of adding new knowledge. The new ideas, knowledge, mental images or experience need to be worked on in some way so that the schema is altered to accommodate the new material, concept or understanding. A state of disequilibrium is experienced during the process of accommodation, which may be accompanied by emotion. Such emotion may be pleasurable (e.g. laughter or surprise). Interestingly, these emotions accompany humour in Koestler's exposition of creativity. The intersection of two different matrices or frames of reference can provoke laughter, insight or wonder depending on the position in the triptych (see Figure 1.3, p. 10). Learning is thus linked to creativity. Sometimes less comfortable emotions accompany accommodation, such as fear, anger, or of not being able to cope. There are various ways of coping with cognitive and emotional dissonance or conflict. One possibility is to ignore new information or experience which does not accord with our existing schema. Another is to live with the conflict or disequilibrium, but this can be rather uncomfortable. Alternatively, people can restructure their schemas to accommodate new information, knowledge and experience. The learner has to take an active part in this process of accommodation or restructuring. In history, through the activities designed and led by the teacher, the children's existing second record, which forms part of their schema, is altered through the process of studying history.

The second set of theories about learning is that of learning as concept acquisition and conceptual change. When young children first encounter creepy-crawlies, they might call them all spiders: only later might they learn to distinguish spiders from beetles and flies. The understanding of 'dog' comes through repeated experiences of a wide range of creatures, from miniature poodles to Labradors, to eventually produce a concept which embraces all these different varieties of the same kind of animal. Abstract concepts, for example those concerned with emotions such as happiness, or systems of government such as democracy, likewise are acquired over a period of time. When Laurie Lee was asked to 'Sit there for the present' by his infant teacher, he learned by the end of the day (with some uncomfortable emotions) that 'present' meant something to do with time as well as something to do with gifts. History is packed with concepts, many of which are abstract. They must be taught actively to ensure that children's understanding of concepts matches that of adults. The concept of the 'Church' as a powerful organisation (and not just the building the children pass every day on their way to school) would need to be actively taught. Stones (1992) argued that much learning was conceptual and that teachers had to plan for the teaching of concepts and sub-concepts. Thus in carrying out historical enquiry on the Palace of Knossos, for example, the teacher would have to actively teach the concept of 'palace'. This may be done by showing OHT images of palaces, colour-photocopied from coffee table books, asking the children to point out their characteristics, and then getting them to design their own plan of their palace.

The third set of theories come from Bruner (1970), and I have found his ideas extremely powerful in understanding learning and teaching, and finding a language with which to discuss both. Bruner states that there are three characteristic ways of mentally representing the world. Enactive representation is understanding by doing. Iconic representation is understanding through pictures, diagrams, drawings, maps and plans. Symbolic representation is understanding through some kind of symbol system. Examples of symbolic systems are language, both spoken and written, mathematical notation and musical notation. Young children tend to use enactive representations first, then iconic ones, finally moving to symbolic representations. A child might learn to use a slide by watching other children in the playground. Later in reception class she might draw herself playing on the slide. Later still she will write about her weekend visit to the playground as part of her class journal. The spoken symbol system of language accompanies all these experiences. As adults we move back and forth between these forms of representation. The younger one's children, the more useful enactive representations are for learning, although children across the whole primary age range will gain a great deal from teachers using them. One can, for example, learn about the intricacies of Tudor dance through doing it, by looking at pictures of it, or by reading about it. Of these options, performing the dance will be the most powerful form of learning: through dancing and hearing some of the Tudor music one will begin to understand their pastimes, their highly sophisticated nature and something about the Tudor people.

The final set of theories come from Vygotsky (1962, 1978), who generated ideas of social learning. Two ideas are drawn upon here. The first is the notion of the zone of proximal development: the potential for learning, understanding, knowing and doing which is not yet reached, but which can be realised through interaction with more knowledgeable, experienced others. Social interaction is the second idea of great importance for learning. A child may not be able to achieve something on his own, but, through social interaction with others, he may do so. Such social interaction can take the form of teachers' whole class questioning and dialogue, or through peer interaction with others in pairs and small groups. In this way, children can pool their ideas, test them against each other in open debate, and deepen their understanding. If one relates theories of learning to the ideas of Hexter (1972), they provide a powerful justification for the kind of whole class, pair and group teaching which characterises best practice in history teaching. It is possible to trace examples of these theories at work in the cameos presented at the start of Chapter 1.

Knowledge and understanding of a number of theories about learning can inform our teaching approaches. Schema theory would indicate that we need to provide a range of activities which allow children to work on historical material in very active ways, not merely reading words on a page, but engaging physically, mentally and emotionally with facts, concepts, skills and processes to make the new material part of their mental map of the world. Conceptual change theory emphasises the acquisition and modification of concepts. If one harnesses this theory to Bruner's ideas of enactive, iconic and symbolic representation, we can see the need for a wide range of teaching approaches, using all three forms of representation. Vygotsky's ideas of social learning and the zone of proximal development can help us to understand the importance of language, in particular of speaking and listening, in learning: for sharing, exploring, challenging and shaping ideas and understanding through discussion. If one understands teaching and learning history to be partly a matter of altering, enriching and enhancing children's second records through 'doing history' in Hexter's terms, one has moved a long way from merely giving or exposing children to historical information and expecting them to remember it.

Important principles in the teaching of history

These principles were devised and used by the Nuffield Primary History Project Team, who, in a major research and curriculum development project, spent five years teaching the new *History in the National Curriculum* (DES, 1991) to children in a huge variety of primary schools. The principles are underpinned by the ideas of history set out in the previous section. History teaching based on these principles is excellent practice. The central tenet is that history in schools should be taught in terms of investigation and discussion. Children should investigate primary sources, question them rigorously, set them into context using their imagination and experience of life, and each produce their own history in some form, spoken or written: a play, a poem, a drawing, a piece of writing, a display, an assembly, a dance or expressive movement, or a song. The seven principles of the Nuffield Primary History Project are:

1 Challenging the children

2 Asking questions

3 The study of a topic in depth

4 The use of authentic sources

5 Economy in the use of such sources

6 Making the sources accessible to children

7 Pupil communication of their understanding to an audience

(Fines and Nichol, 1997)

Challenge

A key factor in studies of effective teaching is having high expectations of children (see e.g. Mortimore *et al.*, 1988; Hay McBer, 2000). This is as true in history as in other subjects. If you give children challenging (but accessible) materials, they respond well. Children can often surprise and delight us with their response to 'difficult' work or ideas, as long as we make the materials and ideas accessible to them (see principle 6).

Questioning

Questioning is so vital a part of the historical process that it is difficult to envisage studying history without it. Questioning is the force that drives historical enquiry. A unit of work should ideally start with a key question from which may spring other questions. From open, speculative questions which may spring either from the children or the teacher, the children can generate further questions which refine the focus of the enquiry or open up further themes. Although questions should drive topics of study, one might not always start with a question. In selecting from the pedagogical repertoire (see p. 28), a teacher might choose to start with a story, a role-play, a film-clip or an OHT of a picture, and then move on to questions arising from the sources or imaginative reconstructions.

Study in depth

Dean (1995) and Fines and Nichol (1997) argued powerfully that real historical knowledge means knowledge in depth. It is quite usual to see medium-term plans in which children spend their weekly hour or so on several different aspects of a period. For the Victorians they would attempt to 'cover' transport, inventions, houses and homes, the Great Exhibition, work, leisure, key events, famous people and education. The teacher might feel that she has 'covered' the curriculum, and the children have acquired much knowledge of the period. However, such knowledge is easily forgotten if not made part of mental maps, schema or second records. Rushing children through masses of content means they do not have any time to learn anything. Along with this kind of history teaching is the tendency to ignore the skills and processes of historical enquiry in the headlong rush to 'cover' content. Study in depth means that understanding of historical concepts, themes, skills and processes may be acquired through carefully structured activities on a key problem or question. The in-depth study anchors historical knowledge and understanding in a meaningful context. Cameo 2 on housemaids in Victorian times is a good example of this.

Authentic sources

Using primary sources is essential in excellent history teaching. Children need to investigate and interpret sources for themselves and construct their own histories. If the sources used are not authentic, then their histories are fiction. They must be based on evidence. The problem with using mainly secondary sources, such as the topic books seen in every primary classroom, is that although some of the illustrations might be primary evidence, the text is not. It is someone else's interpretation of other sources. Historians question the validity, reliability and integrity of sources. This process needs to be modelled in the classroom so that children can eventually do it themselves.

Economy of sources

There is not often much money to spend on history in the primary school budget. Of course, in principle one would love to have plentiful resources for history, but one can manage very well with a few well-chosen resources. Much valuable historical enquiry may be done by focusing on one story, one picture or one set of plans. For example, the Victorian housemaids investigation used just three sources. Part of the teacher's expertise lies in selecting sources which children can investigate: in Bruner's terms, scaffolding the enquiry by taking on that important preparatory stage of searching for sources.

Accessibility

Not all forms of historical evidence are easily accessible to children. Pictures and photographs, maps and plans, building sites and music are often easier to understand and interpret than written sources. The teacher, through the teaching approaches she selects, must act as an intermediary between all sources and the children to make them accessible. The teacher plays a key role in a number of different ways. The first is working with the whole class in making sources accessible through verbal, visual and interactive methods. The second is in devising activities which will help children to 'find ways into the evidence'. An example of this might be asking children to look for where, in a picture of a Saxon village, they might hide if raiders were coming. This ensures that children look closely at the picture and properly engage with it. They will then notice details which a more cursory glance would have missed. It can mean the teacher posing a key question of a source, or using a game such as 'I-Spy' to get the children to look closely at the picture. For an investigation of street people in Victorian London, using selected evidence from Mayhew as source material, it can mean the teacher starting the lesson in role as a busker, a juggler, a costermonger or street sweeper. For an investigation of census material, the teacher would teach the concept of a census by taking a class census using the same headings as those given in the real documents (Fines and Nichol, 1997). Making documents accessible deserves some attention and is considered in more detail in Chapter 4.

Pupil communication of their understanding to an audience

The culmination of the process of historical enquiry is the presentation of a recon-structed history to an audience: the final stage in Hexter's model of 'doing history'. Presentation can take many forms: written, oral, pictorial, kinaesthetic, musical and dramatic. A historical story might be presented as a series of freeze frames, or as expressive movement. A class museum made by the children can be the culmination of work on artefacts, showing, through their written or computer-generated labels, their understanding of the objects, the people who used them and the period in which they lived. Written forms can embrace all the varied genres of writing, including, for example, poems, letters, stories, accounts, persuasive pamphlets, advertisements and explanations. These may be designed for a variety of audiences: another class, people from the past, the prime minister, readers of the tabloids and so on.

The pedagogical repertoire

In order to teach anything to anyone, one needs a broad pedagogical repertoire. The demands of history as a subject and of children's learning require that one has the widest possible range of strategies for connecting children with subject matter. Figure 2.2 presents a model of a pedagogical repertoire which serves two functions in this book. The first is of a general model of expert teaching (Turner-Bisset, 2001), which can inform one's classroom practice across the curriculum. The second is as a spine for the rest of this book, a way of structuring materials under different teaching approaches and kinds of evidence. The pedagogical repertoire consists of three aspects supporting what is to be learned: facts, concepts, skills, processes, beliefs and attitudes. The first aspect is the general one of approaches, activities, examples, analogies and illustrations for representing what is to be learned. Aspect 2 is the wide range of teaching approaches: storytelling, Socratic dialogue, drama, role-play, simulation, demonstration, modelling, problem-solving, singing, playing games, knowledge transformation, question-and-answer, instructing, explaining and giving feedback. Most of the range of teaching approaches in aspect 2 form the structure of this book.

Aspect 3 comprises those generic strategies and skills which might be termed 'acting skills'. Tauber and Mester (1995) likened teaching to acting: the two professions being

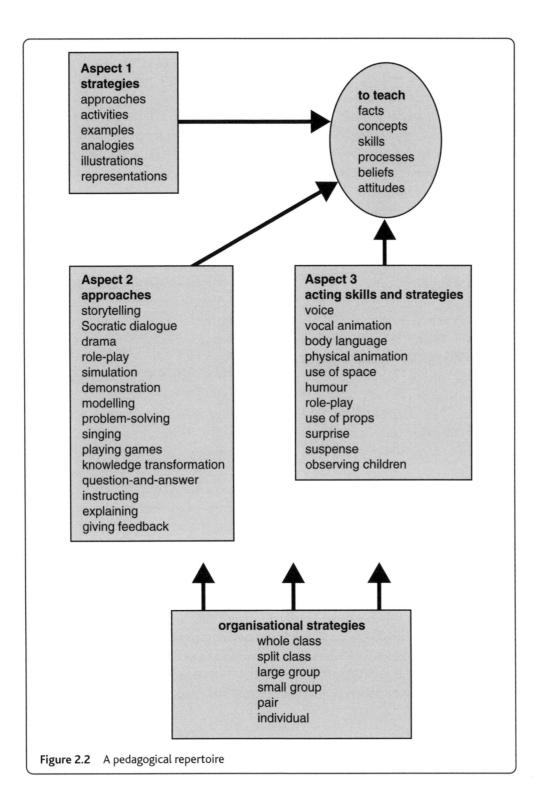

Figure 2.2 A pedagogical repertoire

strongly related in that they are both performance arts. Both teachers and actors need to hold the attention of the audience and convey conviction in what they are saying. Tauber and Mester (1995) introduced the idea of the teachers' 'toolbox', effectively an analysis of teacher enthusiasm. This comprised the top tray tools of voice or vocal animation, body language or physical animation, and effective use of classroom space. The bottom tray tools are humour, role-playing, use of props, and the elements of surprise and suspense. In the teaching approach of storytelling used in both Cameo 1 and 2 (Chapter 1), one employs the 'top tray tools' of vocal animation, physical animation in gesture and use of classroom space in moving about the room while storytelling. Stories also hold suspense: the audience can be spellbound, wanting to know what happened next. The toolbox as analysis of teacher enthusiasm is important for demystifying it, and showing its ingredients. The use of the toolbox of verbal and non-verbal channels of communication is clearly of great importance, as are teachers' engagement with the material to be taught, their deep understanding of it and their passion for the subject.

The use of suspense, surprise and humour in teaching has received less attention perhaps than it deserves. These days much is made of the advantages for learning of letting the children know what one's learning objectives are. While there is value in doing so, if every lesson starts with the class reading out the learning objectives on the board, this can lead to routine predictability. Lessons should start in different ways, in keeping with the notion of a pedagogical repertoire, providing opportunities for suspense and surprise. Humour in teaching is likewise very important, for several reasons. The role it plays in creativity should alert us to its twin functions of connecting different frames of reference and defusing tension in the release of laughter. It is in effect an opening of the mind to new possibilities, new concepts and new ways of perceiving the world. Laughter also relaxes audiences of all kinds, as public speakers and teachers both know: the seasoning of difficult material with a joke is part of the stock-in-trade of the teacher. This defusion of tension is important for learning, for opening up our minds and emotions and making us receptive. Finally, humour is important as part of the general pedagogical repertoire for managing the class, its dynamics and its complex relationships. It serves to create an ethos in which teaching and learning are enjoyable for both children and teachers alike.

The structure of this book follows for the most part aspect 2 of the pedagogical repertoire, aiming to give teachers a wide range of approaches and activities in the creative teaching of history with children. As well as teaching approaches, there are lesson plans, examples of children's work and insights into the pedagogical reasoning and creative processes underpinning the examples of teaching.

Artefacts

Introduction: The importance of objects

Objects are of central importance in teaching and may be used in myriad ways for a variety of teaching purposes across the primary curriculum. In history they are useful for teaching some of the skills and processes of historical enquiry, especially for children who may have had little or no experience of these. Most of the recent texts on teaching history in primary schools have a section on using artefacts (e.g. Pluckrose, 1991; Wright, 1992; Cooper, 1992, 1995a, 1995b, 2000; Kimber *et al.*, 1995; Wood and Holden, 1995; Fines and Nichol, 1997; Nichol and Dean, 1997; Hughes *et al.*, 2000; O'Hara and O'Hara, 2001; Wallace, 2003). Because of their appeal to all the senses, they are particularly suitable for children in the early years. If you have very little experience in teaching history, artefacts can be a good way into doing some genuine historical enquiry and experiencing some successful lessons. However, there are certain issues related to teaching aspects of history using artefacts, and it is important to be aware of these issues. This chapter gives: an overview of some of the issues involved; an insight into some of the thinking behind the activities; a range of activities which can form the basis of a teaching repertoire using artefacts; and sample lesson plans and activities.

Advantages and issues in using objects

There are many good reasons for using objects in teaching across the curriculum and in history in particular. It can generate a greater appreciation of the role of objects themselves in our lives. Objects help us in obtaining, preparing and cooking food, in providing water, heating and shelter. They are a central part of many human activities such as family life, work, religion, communication, leisure, sports, music, the arts and entertainment. If children can learn to interpret objects from their own society, they can make links between themselves and people in the past, who had the same human needs and problems. Objects can also help us to understand the lives of people from cultures which have left little or no written remains (e.g. poor people, the very young, people from cultures such as the Benin, whose historical remains are mainly artefacts and oral history). Using objects for teaching can develop knowledge, skills, concepts and attitudes among children. Durbin *et al.*, in their excellent booklet *A Teacher's Guide to Learning from Objects* (1990, pp. 5–6), list an impressive array of possible learning outcomes. These are as follows.

Developing skills

- Locating, recognising, identifying, planning;
- Handling, preserving, storing;
- Observing and examining;
- Discussing, suggesting, estimating, hypothesising, synthesising, predicting, generalising, assessing influence;
- Experimenting, deducing, comparing, concluding, evaluating;
- Relating structure to function, classifying, cataloguing;
- Recording through writing, drawing, labelling, photographing, taping, filming, computing;
- Responding, reporting, explaining, displaying, presenting, summarising, criticising.

Extending knowledge

- Different materials and what they were or are used for;
- Techniques and vocabulary of construction and decoration;
- The social, historic and economic context within which the items featured;
- The physical effects of time;
- The meaning of symbolic forms;
- The way people viewed their world;
- The existence and nature of particular museums, sites, galleries and collections;
- Symbol, pattern, colour;
- 'Appropriateness', for example, the use of rucksacks compared to handbags;
- Appreciation of cultural values.

Developing concepts

- Chronology, change, continuity and progress;
- Design as a function of use, availability of materials and appearance;
- Aesthetic quality;
- Typicality, bias, survival;
- Fashion, style and taste;
- Original, fake, copy;
- Heritage, collection, preservation, conservation.

Many of these learning outcomes are cross-curricular in nature; however, there are clearly many which apply to history in particular. In addition, there are several reasons why objects will work more powerfully for children than will pictures of objects. Some things are lost: detail, exact colouring, size, weight, mass, and the physical sensations such as smell. Tactile evidence is also lost, such as texture, temperature, shape and details of manufacture, and the three-dimensional design of the object. One also loses the feeling of age associated with the object, the concepts of original and reproduction, and most importantly, the feelings of awe and wonder which can be generated through use of an object.

Issues in using objects

There are some issues involved in using objects, and beginning teachers need to be aware of these. It is very easy for children to dismiss objects after a cursory glance and to assume they know all there is to know about them. Discussion can close down if too much emphasis is placed on questions such as: 'What is this object? How old is it?' I once worked with a reception class teacher on a Master's-level course, who was keen to do some action research on using objects with her 5-year-olds. Ultimately the work and the learning were disappointing. Despite never having been encouraged to focus on the age of objects in the taught course, her lessons with children tended to become 'stuck' on the ages of the objects she used. The 5-year-olds had only a developing understanding of time, and suggested that objects were 'millions of years old'. There is so much more that one can do with objects than concentrate on their age, and this chapter offers a whole range of suggestions and teaching ideas to use instead. Armed with a beginning repertoire of teaching approaches for objects, there is less likelihood of floundering in questions of age and time, or inappropriate activities.

Presentation of objects is very important in encouraging children to not be dismissive and to look more closely. Dean in Fines and Nichol (1997) suggests a range of ideas, including posting an object to a school wrapped in layers and layers of packaging to make it harder to get at the object, and thus rendering it more special. She also suggests putting objects in an old box or suitcase with a lock that does not work very well, so that it can take a while and a struggle to open the box. One can also keep small objects hidden in one's hand or pocket for enough time to build up excitement. One can tell a story about the object before introducing it, or during or after.

Other issues need consideration before working with objects and artefacts. It is important to work from familiar objects and experience before using old objects. In Turner-Bisset (2000b) I describe a session using artefacts with 3- and 4-year-olds. One of the objects was a bright yellow candle holder made of enamel, with a curved base to catch the wax and a handle to carry it around the house. One of the children was convinced it was a wine holder of the type he had seen adults drink from on holidays. No amount of discussion could dissuade him from this. It would have been better to use a table lamp or a torch first and then to bring out the old object. I saw this done very well by Andrew, a student-teacher in a mixed age infant class of Reception, Year 1 and Year 2 in a tiny village school. He had a modern table lamp, a candle holder similar to mine from the 1950s and an old oil lamp. With the children sitting on the carpet he used a framework of questions to promote discussion, comparison and contrast. Volunteer children sequenced the three artefacts; he then divided the children into three groups and asked them to draw one of the artefacts from the angle at which they observed it on one of three tables. As part of the term's work on light, a science-led topic, it worked well from both a scientific and historical point of view, as well as developing language.

One of the reasons for the success of this session was the careful use of a framework of questions. This is important if one is to prevent the activity from becoming just a guessing game, as Andretti (1993) warned:

> Too often such work can turn into a random guessing game. Of course some guesswork will be necessary but it should take the form of reasoned hypotheses which develop after as many facts as possible have been established.
>
> (Andretti, 1993, p. 11)

In other words, questions should be open and promote thinking and discussion, rather than closed (What is it? How old is it?). I use the framework given in Figure 3.1 with children aged 3 to 7 and use a more extensive range of questions with older children.

What does this look like?
What does this feel like?
What do you think this is made of?
Have you ever seen anything like this?
How is/was it used?
Who uses it/used to use it?
What would it be like to use it?

Figure 3.1 A framework of questions

Another issue is the way that young children in particular will flit between fact and fantasy (Wood and Holden, 1995, p. 21). Depending on one's viewpoint and the purposes of one's teaching, this can be either a difficulty or a blessing. My personal inclination would be to allow children at Key Stage 1 in particular to develop their fantasies and stories, and to use the objects as a stimulus for creative writing. After this, one could return to a drawing and labelling activity to develop other skills, knowledge and understanding. We need to engage our imaginations to make sense of some objects in any case, and I use a lot of mime, modelled initially by myself, to show how objects might have been used. The younger the children are, the more important is play with the artefacts. They need to experience through play all the possibilities of an artefact, its fantasy and real uses as a sensory way of understanding it. Older children still need some experience of mime and acting out using the objects in order to begin to understand the lives of those who used them.

Where to get objects/artefacts for use in the classroom

A common concern among beginning teachers is the problem of finding and acquiring objects for classroom use. There are a number of possibilities:

- Ask parents/older relatives to look in their cupboards and lend you objects.
- Car boot sales and charity shops are a good source of cheap objects. I find them useful for objects from the past fifty or sixty years, such as kitchen equipment which is no longer in common use.
- Some local museum services do loan collections (e.g. the Museum of London has Roman boxes for schools within the Greater London area).
- Some museums will arrange object-handling sessions run by members of their staff. These can be excellent.

Artefact activities

Once you have your objects, you will need a range of activities for teaching well, using them in different ways. As you begin to try out a few of these lesson ideas, you will adapt and change them according to your own ideas and the classes you teach.

Bag activity

This is a very good activity for introducing the skills and processes of historical enquiry to children who may have had little or no experience of them. Simply, one takes a bag or suitcase and fills it with things belonging to a real or imaginary person. The task of the children is to examine and interpret the objects (and the bag itself). Ideally one does this with a bag or suitcase prepared beforehand, but even one's handbag will do. I once forgot to put my carefully packed bag in the car before going to work in school. I improvised with my handbag, obviously removing any items of a personal nature first.

Grid activity (research)

Draw up a grid similar to the one given in Figure 3.2. Divide the class into small groups. Give each group one or two objects and ask them to fill in the grid for each object. The first column can be filled in if the children know what the object is; other than that they can leave it blank to begin with. The final column can contain sources such as reference books, topic books, the internet, people, and what they have managed to find out. If they finish their objects, they can swap with another group. The aim behind this activity is to get the children to reason using the available evidence. I always try to emphasise the lives of people behind the objects. For example, with a heavy Victorian iron, I ask children to pretend to use it (unheated of course) so they gain some idea as to how hard ironing must have been in those days.

Consequences game

This is very useful if you only have, say, eight objects on loan from the museum and a class of, say, 32 children. Divide the class into eight groups of four. Give each group

Name of object if known	What I definitely know about this object	What I think I know/can hypothesise about this object	What I need to find out/where I might look for information
Object 1			
Object 2			
Object 3			

Figure 3.2   Grid enquiry activity

an object and tell them to write (one child acting as scribe) on one piece of paper three or four questions about the object. I find it is useful to ban the question: 'How old is it? (see Figure 3.3 for an example framework of questions). When each group has their list of three or four questions, tell the children that at a given signal, they will pass on their object and the questions to the next group. Then each group has to try

---

You can draw upon these groups of questions in devising lists of questions for children to ask about objects. Older children (e.g. Year 5/Year 6) could probably tackle the whole list. For younger children it is best to select from the list and focus on three or four for Foundation Stage, five or six for Key Stage 1.

Looking at objects (2)

The main things to think about	Some further questions to ask
PHYSICAL FEATURES What does it look and feel like?	What colour is it? What does it smell like? What does it sound like? What is it made of? Is it a natural or manufactured material? Is the object complete? Has it been altered, adapted, mended? Is it worn?
CONSTRUCTION How was it made?	Is it handmade or machine made? Was it made in a mould or in pieces? How has it been fixed together?
FUNCTION	How has the object been used? Has the use changed?
DESIGN Is it well designed?	Does it do the job it was intended to do well? Were the best materials used? Is it decorated? How is it decorated? Do you like the way it looks? Would other people like it?
VALUE What is it worth?	To the people who made it? To the people who used it? To the people who keep it? To you? To a bank? To a museum?

Figure 3.3   Learning from objects

to answer the previous group's questions. For the plenary, ask one child from each group to hold up the object, another child to read out the questions, and a third and fourth child to take turns reading their answers. The whole class can then discuss the objects.

Drawing and labelling

This activity is invaluable for slowing down the pace of looking, so that children have the opportunity to really see what is there. There are several good reasons for doing this activity.

1 Drawing slows down the pace of looking. In order to draw, children have to observe detail; for example, how parts of an object are joined together, any decoration, details of manufacture. Drawing is wonderful for developing concentration and observation skills.

2 This activity is accessible for all children in a class so that those with literacy difficulties are not disadvantaged.

3 The drawing and labelling are examples of children's work, recording their understanding of an object.

4 The record of children's understanding in this form can provide material for assessment.

5 Labelling can allow children to add to their understanding of an object. More able children can be encouraged to annotate parts of an object.

Comparing old and new

If you have two objects, say an old Victorian iron and a new electric iron, you can compare them. Looking for similarities and differences is a way of working with the historical concepts of continuity (how things stay the same) and change. It is important to give structure to this task and to set a time limit for its completion. The structure of looking for five differences and five similarities gives focus to the task. It can be differentiated by asking more able children to look for more, or less able children to look for fewer, if recording their findings is an issue. Ask children to work in pairs (see Figure 3.4 for sample boxes). This is an important basic resource: one which can be adapted for comparing anything: pictures, photographs of the same street a hundred years apart, maps and so on. The two boxes may then be used as the basis for a comparative piece of writing on the objects in the report genre.

Sequencing objects

If you have more than two objects, you can sequence them in order from the oldest to the most recent. For example, if you have the two irons mentioned above and an early,

In the box below write down five things about your objects which are different:

1.
2.
3.
4.
5.

In the box below write down five things about your objects which are the same:

1.
2.
3.
4.
5.

Figure 3.4   Comparing old and new

very heavy electric iron with a two-pin plug, you can ask the children to sequence them (best done by asking volunteers to do this in front of the class) in order of age. For young children, it is advisable to stick to sequencing; older children can start to sequence using a timeline. Blank timelines are available commercially, or they can be made. You can make your own decade markers and ask the children to place the irons on the timeline within ten years of when they think the irons were made and used. Ask the children who come out to the front and place them to give reasons for their decision.

Classroom museum

This is a very good activity for pulling together and communicating what has been found out about objects/artefacts. It is also valuable for literacy, and, if computers are used to make labels for objects and signs, an appropriate use for ICT. Have ready some copies of examples of labels (enough for pairs), some which merely give information, and others which invite visitors to interact with the exhibits in some way. Give the children five minutes to sort the labels into information only/interaction and share the results. Tell the children they are going to make a classroom museum and allocate tasks: some pairs to do labels, other signs and background information depending on ability. Ask others to set up the display and invite heads, parents and governors to visit the museum. This may be done with objects on loan from a museum, or objects which children bring in themselves.

Confused card index

This is a variant on the above activity and could be practised on ordinary everyday objects before engaging in the project of making a classroom museum. One object is given to each child – they can be familiar everyday objects such as a clothes peg, a board marker, a drawing-pin, a saucepan, a fork, a button and so on. Each child writes a catalogue card for his or her object and then takes turns reading them out, omitting the name of the object. The rest of the group or class (depending on how you organise it) has to match the card with the object. This is a useful exercise for both literacy and history. It helps children to develop their own classroom museum in that they learn that they need to keep good records, in the same way that museum curators need to do so. For literacy it is a good exercise in looking carefully at objects and in writing careful descriptions of them. The catalogue card is a particular genre of non-fiction writing and this task could usefully be done in a literacy lesson.

The riddle game

This is a game I have played with many classes with much enjoyment on the part of both the children and myself. I give the class some examples of Anglo-Saxon riddles to solve (Figure 3.5). I then explain that each pair of children will be given an object

---

1.
Oft I must strive with wind and wave, Battle them both when under the sea I feel out the bottom, a foreign land. In lying still I am strong in the strife; If I fail in that they are stronger than I, And wrenching me loose, soon put me to rout. They wish to capture what I must keep. I can master them both if my grip holds out, If the rocks bring succour and lend support, Strength in the struggle. Ask me my name!

2.
A moth ate a word. To me it seemed, A marvellous thing when I learned the wonder That a worm had swallowed, in darkness stolen, The song of man, his glorious sayings, A great man's strength; and the thieving guest, Was no whit the wiser for the words it ate.

3.
In former days my father and mother, Abandoned me dead, lacking breath Or life or being. Then one began, A kinswoman kind, to care for and love me; Covered me with her clothing, wrapped me in her raiment, With the same affection she felt for her own; Until by the law of my life's shaping, Under alien bosom I quickened with breath. My foster mother fed me thereafter, Until I grew sturdy and strengthened for flight. Then of her dear ones, of daughters and sons, She had the fewer for what she did.

4.
My house is not quiet, I am not loud; But for us God fashioned our fate together. I am the swifter, at times the stronger, My house more enduring, longer to last. At times I rest; my dwelling still runs; Within it I lodge as long as I live. Should we two be severed, my death is sure.

Figure 3.5　Anglo-Saxon riddles

---

which they must look at carefully and try to keep hidden from the other children. The objects can be familiar or unfamiliar. The children then have to write down several sentences giving certain information about the object, including some or all of the following: its colour, shape, form, manufacture, function, the object being used, the place where it is usually found and the people who might use it. They then use this list of information as the basis for their riddle. They write their riddles and these are shared with the class, who have to guess from the riddles what the object is. Both the confused cards and the riddles games have as part of their purpose helping children to observe closely, write accurate descriptions, albeit in different genres, and to 'see' that there is much more to an object than its name and purpose.

The feely bag

In many ways this is a generic activity, for the feely bag may be used in many ways in the curriculum, not just in history. This is useful for a number of small artefacts, say objects which are used for writing. It might be done as part of an introduction to the history of writing, part of a sequence of activities which include comparing and contrasting, and sequencing writing tools on a timeline. Have ready a cloth bag with the objects inside. Place two chairs in the middle of your circle, or clear two spaces on the carpet in front of you. Select two children, blindfold both and let one child take an object out of the bag. He or she can use all senses other than sight and describe the object. The other child has to ask questions of the first child and guess what the object is.

Story-making

This idea comes from Bage's (2000) excellent book, *Thinking History 4–14*. The idea is that 'the story of an object is told through the actions or materials needed to produce, transport, sell, use and preserve it' (Bage, 2000, p. 116.) This is suitable for both Key Stages 1 and 2. Bage gives the example of a Greek vase. I have used a similar idea at Key Stage 1 with an old teddy. This teddy had a price tag with the original price crossed out and a lower price written beneath. With a Year 1 class, I introduced him as an item from a box of artefacts I had taken in to use with the children. They examined the price tag with some interest and began to speculate as to where he had been before he arrived at the antique shop. We had the basis of a story here and we mapped out the following stages:

- Being made in the factory
- Transported by lorry to a toyshop
- Being priced and put on display
- A child begging his parents to buy the teddy

- Christmas morning for this child with the teddy as one of his presents
- Being a special teddy, going everywhere with the child
- Getting lost one day in a friend's garden
- Friend's mother finding teddy and putting him in a shed for many years
- Shed cleared out when they moved house: teddy sent to charity shop
- Myself buying him.

These are not the only possibilities of course, but this was the story we developed, and the stages can form a plan for some extended story-writing.

Artefacts in context

As well as investigating artefacts in isolation, they can and should be investigated in context. Although objects turn up far away from their original context (they do in my house anyway!), in investigating past societies through archaeology, items are always found in a context which can give clues as to the object's nature and function. For example, at a dig of a Roman site, television's *Time Team* found fragments of pottery and metal bowls, and speculated that, as they were in what they thought was the kitchen area of a villa, these were used for cooking. While it might not seem practical to study archaeology in the classroom, there are various ways in which it can be simulated.

Archaeology: Objects in context

- Use a box with a glazed side and fill it with layers of different colours of soil, with grass on the top. Hide various objects within the layers. As a whole class activity, ask for volunteers to dig to find the objects and the whole class to map out the finds in three dimensions, thinking about what each object's position can tell us.

- Classroom archaeology for 5-year-olds: The idea behind this is that one introduces the notion of objects found in context to very young children, through the approach of using (reasonably) everyday objects and a familiar context, that of a house and garden shed. There are some important points to bear in mind here. For your task, try to choose objects that would be found in different parts of a house which children would recognise, but include one or two less familiar ones. This is actually classroom archaeology for 5-year-olds. When archaeologists conduct a dig, they painstakingly record the position in which each item was found. One of the aims of the activity is to emulate the work of archaeologists, by placing objects within the context in which they are used or found. This activity is also very valuable for the development of language and literacy. Many adjectives may be used to describe the objects, and interesting objects can generate talk. I have used a hot water bottle before now which had the children using words such as soft, furry, squishy, smelly, cuddly, cold, bumpy (it had ridges and a fleecy cover). The hand whisk was a source of much interest also, and even 5-year-old Ben immediately made the connection between this object and his mother's electric whisk.

- Museum visits: Some museums are superb at re-creating Victorian streets, Viking villages or the interior of Roman villas. Here one can see objects in a situation, often with figures of people placed so that they appear to be using the objects. The advantage of this is that the various objects are placed in context and one can see how they may have been used.

Age of children: 4–5 years. Number of children: 6

Activity: Objects: Questioning and sorting

Learning purposes/objectives/outcomes

- To experience questions being asked of modern-day artefacts (NC4).
- To learn how to ask such questions themselves (NC4).
- To explore and recognise features of objects in the made world (ELG).
- To learn about the everyday life of themselves and their families, now and in the past, through handling everyday artefacts (NC2).

Content (What will the children do?)

The children will each be given an object, which I have ready hidden in a bag. They may touch it and use all their senses to observe the object. We will talk about each object and pass them round. Each child will be given a picture/photo of their object and asked to place the object in the most likely room in the house where it might be found. Thus children will complete the display and record some of their understanding.

Where: On the carpet by the wall where my display is ready.

When: First session of the day before 'fruit' and play.

Organisation: My general assistant will be teaching and monitoring two groups; my nursery nurse will take the other small group for painting. After play I will take the next group and the children will revolve around the activities. We will repeat this later in the week. Tomorrow the children will be planning their own activities (Highscope).

Who: Green group first; then blue group after play.

Key areas of experience

- Knowledge and understanding of the world.
- Communication, language and literacy.

What I will do

I will gather the six children around me. I will show them my shopping bag and say I have brought in some things to show them. I will get out each object and hand it to a child. I will encourage the children to talk about the objects and I will ask the same few questions to model them to the children:

- What do you think this is?
- What do you think it is made of?
- What does it feel like?
- Who might use it? How?
- Where in the house might you find it?

After any talk which these questions generate, I will ask each child to place the photo of their object on the display in the room, or part of the house and shed where he or she thinks it may be found.

If the children's attention is wandering, I will move the activity on by introducing a new object. I will ensure that each child has a turn at placing the photo on the display with Blutack.

Resources

- Bag of objects: familiar and not so familiar from around the house and garden.
- Ready-made pictures or photos of objects, laminated.
- Display base: house and shed drawn on card.
- Name labels for parts of the house: kitchen, bathroom, bedroom, living room, garden shed.
- Blutack.
- Notebook to record who placed which object where and anything significant said by the children.

Assessment (What will be recorded)

- Placing of objects.
- Talk which shows some understanding of objects or how what we use has changed compared with what our parents/grandparents might have used.

Specific children

- Green Group: James, Darrell, John, Tracy, Lucille and Melissa.
- Blue Group: Lucy, Ben, Nicola, Jethro, Matthew and Sita.

Figure 3.6 Nursery/Reception lesson plan: objects in context

A final word

This chapter has been an introduction to the use of artefacts in history. The major focus has been historical enquiry and the use of imagination, but many links have been made to other subjects: science (enquiry and materials); design technology (design and function of objects); geography (objects in place as well as time); art (observation and drawing); and English (speaking and listening; using language to label and record; description and vocabulary extension; and creative writing in a range of genres). I hope you will see the links and use them creatively, for example, by using a collection of artefacts to generate and teach the concepts of questions as a literacy hour with Year 2, Term 3.

(Answers to riddles on p. 40: 1. Anchor 2. Book-moth 3. Cuckoo 4. Fish in river.)

CHAPTER 4

Using written sources

Introduction

In the course of a flight from London to Los Angeles, I generated a veritable document trail. My passport was the first item. There were a boarding pass and luggage receipt, the receipts for the coffee and croissant I consumed, the receipts for foot lotion and moisturiser, the newspaper and novel I bought to read on the flight; the airport shuttle bus ticket and the map of Los Angeles I picked up on arrival. A detective following my trail might have been able to deduce: that I had checked in one bag; where I sat in the plane; the possibility that I had not breakfasted before leaving the house; that I suffer from dry skin; my taste in books and my liking for crosswords; and that this was my first trip to Los Angeles. Most aspects of our lives are documented in some way and it is often the most trivial documents which reveal to others ordinary aspects of our lives.

Thus it can be in the past also. Recently on television I saw an example of a Roman postcard sent from one army commander's wife to another army commander's wife, inviting her to her birthday party. There was very little writing on the postcard: the main message in very neat Latin script and a little message in less neat handwriting added near the bottom of the right-hand side. It looked as if the lady had dictated the main part to a scribe (from the neat handwriting) and added her own personal message of love and friendship afterwards. I thought that this was a wonderful document. It was amazing that it had survived (the original is very fragile and in the British Museum) to be found in the remains of a fort not far from Hadrian's Wall. I found it wonderful because up until that time I had not known that the Romans celebrated their birthdays. We can glean from it that this lady was wealthy enough to employ a scribe to write her letters for her. We can also begin to imagine and to wonder: What was it like for the wife of a commander, in this cold, damp outpost of the Roman Empire, passing the time until his posting was over and they could return to their home? How did Romans celebrate their birthdays?

For the purposes of history, documents are written or printed pieces of raw source material from the past. Documents are an important source of historical evidence and it is a requirement of the *History National Curriculum* that teachers use them for enquiry with children (DfEE, 1999c). The range of possible documents is huge and one's selection of documents for classroom use depends on several factors: what you want the children to learn; the kind of historical enquiry being undertaken; and the context of the enquiry. This chapter offers suggestions for teaching activities using a range of documents, some described in detail and some outlined. One important point to bear in mind is that documents should be used in context. For example, if one were to use a replica of the Roman postcard described above, it might be in the context of an enquiry about the lives of people in the Roman army in Britain. If one planned to use a page from a school log, it might be in the context of a local study on the school and its immediate surroundings. They may be used to start an enquiry or, during the course of one, to add further evidence or to corroborate a point. Below is a list (not exhaustive) of document types which one could use with children:

- personal documents such as diaries, appointment cards, bank statements
- reports of the medical officer of health
- charters and land grants
- autobiographies
- gaol records
- diaries
- letters
- newspapers
- census records
- trade directories
- school logs and archives
- inventories and wills
- advertisements
- workhouse records
- seaside town guides

Obviously there is an important link to be made to the English curriculum, particularly in terms of the wide range of non-fiction genres represented in historical documents. Potentially there is a superb source of texts for the literacy hour, especially at Key Stage 2. However, many teachers consider documents to be far too difficult to use with children. They think that the children lack the necessary reading skills to cope with such demanding texts, yet there are ways of making such texts accessible to children. It should be remembered that often the text in children's topic books can be difficult also in terms of vocabulary, grammar and sentence structure;

yet teachers do not hesitate to use these texts with children. The teacher has an important role to play in mediating the process of reading and understanding documents, and in building children's confidence in doing so. Fines and Nichol (1997) recommend the following activities in tackling a document with children:

- whole class teaching
- constant rewards for success
- rapid scanning of the text
- repeated scanning of the text
- tasks of carefully graded difficulty

(Fines and Nichol, 1997, p. 83)

I would suggest as a generic process:

- looking at the text in its original form (often with 'old-fashioned' handwriting)
- asking children to pick out one word or phrase in the original text
- showing children a typed transcription for ease of reading
- asking children to pick out certain things (e.g. names of people and places)
- asking children to look for words which mean something in particular
- asking children what the overall document means from what they know so far
- reading whole document with the class following the text
- bags of praise at every stage

The praise is of central importance in building confidence and it is impossible to overdo it. We need to make children feel good about the tasks we set them. Reading old documents can be difficult and challenging. We need to attend to the emotional aspect of doing the task and offer rewards for each little thing children get right, even if it is only one word or phrase, or a hypothesis which may not be the most likely one but shows they are thinking.

There are other strategies one may also use:

- Make tape-recordings of the text as a support to reading. This is very important for less able children and those with reading difficulties.
- Cut up a text into short pieces, a sentence or so at most. Ask each pair of children to work on their own fragment of the text and pool the results (with lots of praise of course).

- Act out parts of the text. Stop the reading or the recording and act out, say, giving a present, or hiding under a desk during a bombing raid.
- Prompt the children to ask the questions about what is puzzling them in the text, rather than what you find of interest.

Teaching ideas using documents

In this section of the chapter, there are descriptions and brief outlines of what enquiries can be developed using some examples from the list of document types given near the start of this chapter, and the possible contexts and themes of the enquiries. Many of the documents are obtainable from local records offices; increasingly, copies of such documents are being made available online. There is one maxim of extreme importance to remember when using documents with children:

YOU NEED TO ACTIVELY TEACH THE DOCUMENT TYPE FIRST BEFORE YOU GIVE THEM AN EXAMPLE FROM THE PAST.

Personal documents such as diaries, appointment cards, bank statements

As a way into historical enquiry, I suggest creating a fictional character, using, say: a diary page; a bank statement; a couple of appointment cards; a letter; a printed e-mail; and some receipts for purchases. This paper trail, along with some descriptive details about your character, can form the 'evidence' for an enquiry about a missing person, or someone who collapses in a public place and is rushed to hospital. The children can then be set the task of finding out as much as possible about the character, including her identity, from the documents. The value of this kind of activity lies in getting children to think about how documents can tell us a great deal about a person. They can learn how to select from different kinds of evidence, and to put evidence together to reach an answer or a hypothesis. Using a computer, it is very easy to 'create' a character from imaginary personal documents such as these. Work in character-building by creating a set of documents can form the basis of character creation in story-writing.

Reports of the medical officer of health

The context for this kind of document might be an enquiry into public health in the nineteenth or early twentieth century. For example, in an examination of modern-day records of deaths, we can work out what the main causes of deaths are nowadays. The children can then be shown a table from a particular area (again the local area is good) and asked what condition the greatest number of people died from. A study of the table for York in 1909 reveals that the main killers were heart disease, tuberculosis, cancer, pneumonia, bronchitis, stroke, premature birth, developmental diseases, and old age! Children could be encouraged to ask questions about a modern and a nineteenth-century table, and about diseases of which they may not have heard. They could then compare the two tables and look at similarities and differences. The whole enquiry could be driven along by an overarching question on whether people were less healthy in that time, or why certain diseases were fatal in those times.

Charters and land grants

These can be valuable for local study or for work on the Anglo-Saxons. The enquiry might have as its focus the village where the school is located. Such a study can combine history, geography and other subjects in, for example, creating with the children a virtual fieldwork trip around the village. One part of the website could be devoted to the history of the village and there are many possible ways of presenting this. The origins of the village, the place-name and parish boundaries may often be found in old charters. I have used a copy of the grant by Offa, King of the Mercians, to St Peter's Church, Westminster, of land at Aldenham, Herts, AD 785, with Year 5 children in a small primary school within the parish. The activity I do with them is to trace the outline of the boundaries on a copy of the local map of the area and see if they can find any names or places which are boundary markers in the charter. Some of the places are easily found (e.g. the bend on Watling Street); others may only be discovered by using the modern parish boundary. Obviously this combines well with using maps as evidence (see Chapter 6) and with work on a timeline of the local area, events and changes within it.

Autobiographies or books of memories

These can be useful for adding colour and detail of past periods being studied. They have the added advantage of being written in narrative form, which is more easily accessible than some other genres and documents. An example of this is given in Cameo 2 (Chapter 1).

Using letters

This is an example of some teaching I did with a Year 4 class during a term's work on the Tudors. I typed in large print three letters from Henry VIII to Anne Boleyn. I told the children a story about Henry VIII, the reason why he wanted a son as heir to the throne and about Catherine of Aragon's inability to have any more children (she had had seventeen pregnancies altogether). I did not tell them any names, but the story put the letters into context. I then showed them the letters and said they were from this king to someone special. We focused on one in particular (shown in Figure 4.1, as annotated by a child from the class). I asked the children what the heart shape usually represented and they suggested Valentines. I said it was a clue as to what the letter was about. They instantly suggested a love letter. They were able to work out that H

*Why did Henry the VIII dervos Cathrin of Aragon?
She was getting to old to have another baby and he loved Anne Boleyn.*

Letter 3

The drawing near of that time which has for me been so long deferred so much rejoiceth me that it is as if it is already come. Nevertheless, the perfect accomplishing thereof cannot be until the two persons are together met, the which meeting is on my part the more desired than any earthly thing; for what joy in this world can be greater than to have the company of her who is the most dearly loved, knowing likewise that she by her choice holds the same, the thought of which greatly delights me.

Judge, therefore, what that very person shall do, whose absence hath so grieved my heart that neither tongue nor pen can express the hurt, which no other thing excepting that can ever cure. Praying you, my mistress, to say to my lord your father on my part that I beg of him to hasten by two days the time appointed, or that he may be at court before his former promise, or, at least, on the day already agreed. For otherwise I shall think he will not serve a lover's turn, as was his promise, nor will not allow of mine expectation.

No more at present, for lack of time, trusting soon to tell you by word of mouth the residue of the sufferings that I by your absence have sustained. Written with the hand of that secretary who wishes himself at this time private with you, and who is and ever will be,

Your loyal and most assured servant,

H. autre ne cherche R.

(H. no other seeks Rex)

Figure 4.1 Henry VIII letter

stood for Henry and AB for Anne Boleyn. I told them he wrote some letters in French, and translated his signing-off line for them. I asked them to highlight or underline all the words in the letter to do with time and love, using one colour for each. I asked them what they felt like when waiting for something exciting, such as Christmas or birthdays, and they said it was a feeling of 'I can't wait for it!' I said this was how Henry felt, longing to see Anne but having to wait. I asked for examples of time words and I read through the references to time. Next I asked for examples of words to do with love. Finally, I read the third letter aloud with them following, and asked them what the letter was about. They were able to tell me it was a love letter and that Henry was longing to see Anne. I asked them what the letter told us about Henry and Anne, and again they were able to say that he was madly in love with her. We then tried to think of as many reasons as we could why Henry had divorced Catherine of Aragon, and the children came up with the following:

1   Catherine of Aragon was too old to have any more babies.
2   She only had a girl.
3   Henry wanted a son to be a strong ruler and keep the kingdom peaceful.
4   He was madly in love with Anne Boleyn.

I asked them to write their reasons around the border of their letters and most were able to put down two or three reasons. One of my learning purposes was that they should understand that causation can be complex, and that there can be more than one reason for something happening. They had read a difficult text with help and had learned a great deal. The word 'rex' meaning 'king' stayed with them right up until the end of term and they were proud to have learned a Latin word.

Using gaol records

This is an example of teaching I did with the same Year 6 class with whom I worked on the 'Story of the Transports' (see Chapter 7). I taught them history, literacy and music for two consecutive Friday mornings. As part of the second week's work I wanted to concentrate on the citizenship aspects of the story, staying with the themes of law and order, crime and punishment and what societies do with those people who break the rules. I started by reminding the children of the story and the fact that whatever our sympathies were for Henry and Susannah, they had both stolen property from other people. I asked them to suggest ten crimes which might be committed nowadays and I would list them on the board. Soon we had a long list of crimes on the board. I then invited the children to think of the sorts of punishment which might be given for each of the crimes. They came up with largely appropriate ones: life imprisonment for the more serious crimes; shorter sentences for others; fines and cautions, or suspended sentences for the rest. We had some discussion over whether the aim of the punishment was for the convicted people to suffer or if it was meant to help them reform and commit no more crimes.

After this I showed them the gaol records from Hertford County for 1842 (Figures 4.2, 4.3 and 4.4). I wanted to use local records so that they would recognise the place-names and start to imagine the people in these familiar places in the nineteenth century. I asked the children to look at them carefully and to ask me about anything they did not understand. This was a valuable teaching approach, for it meant that the children were asking questions of the evidence. Here are some of their questions:

Who was John Holland?

What did 2/6 mean?

What was 'ag.st his beer licence'?

What was 'ag.st the Highway Act'?

Who was Charlotte?

What is vagrancy?

Is stealing peas a crime?

Is neglecting your wife a crime?

What were the Game Laws?

What was hard labour?

What did 'cal.' mean?

There are enough questions here for several enquiries. Some were easily explained, such as vagrancy and the Game Laws. We could make comparisons with today, since we have all seen homeless people in the streets. The 'old' money proved most difficult to explain. I drew comparison tables on the board, but in retrospect I would have had something already prepared, perhaps as a handout. I then showed them an extract from the gaol records of Hertford County for 1857. By now the abbreviation for calendar month ('cal.') was familiar to them. More questions tumbled out: 'What was a waist ribbon? Why would anyone want to steal manure?' 'Why were all the crimes of stealing on this page?' 'Was there more stealing going on than there had been in 1842?' 'If there was, what did this mean?' 'Were times harder in 1857 than they were in 1842?' One child pointed out that the punishments were more severe than they had been in 1842 and we discussed the possibilities. Was there a different judge for the area who liked to give hard labour rather than fines? Was hard labour seen as more of a deterrent? Was there more crime, or at least more theft in 1857 and were the courts cracking down on it? Many lines of enquiry sprang from such simple documents. The

NAME	RESIDENCE, &c.	DATE OF CONVICTION	OFFENCE	PUNISHMENT
James	Sandon	June 1 1842	Assaulting John Holland	Fine 2/6
James	Sandon	June 1 1842	Assaulting John Holland	Fine 2/6
William	Sandon	June 1 1842	Assaulting John Holland	Fine 2/6
Henry	Saint Andrew	June 4 1842	Neglecting his wife	14 days Hard Labour
John	Caddington	June 7 1842	ag.st his beer licence	Fine £2
Charles	Hemel Hempstead	June 9 1842	ag.st the Highway Act	Fine 6^s
William	Hemel Hempstead	June 13 1842	Destroying a fence	Fine 5^s
William	Royston	June 15 1842	Assaulting Charlotte	Fine 2/6
Thomas	Hemel Hempstead	July 11 1842	Vagrancy	1 cal. Month Hard Labour
John	Hemel Hempstead	July 13 1842	Stealing walnuts	Fine 5/3
William		July 19 1842	Stealing peas	Fine 1/
Henry	Kings Langley	July 27 1842	ag.st his beer licence	Fine 8/6
Benjamin	Much Haddam	July 27 1842	Stealing peas	Fine 5/
John	Albury	July 27 1842	ag.st the Game Laws	Fine £1
James	Paisley	August 2 1842	Vagrancy	14 days Hard Labour
John	Buckland	August 3 1842	ag.st the Game Laws	Fine £1
John	Standon	August 8 1842	ag.st the Game Laws	Fine £5

Figure 4.2 Hertford county gaol record: Extract from 1842: typed version

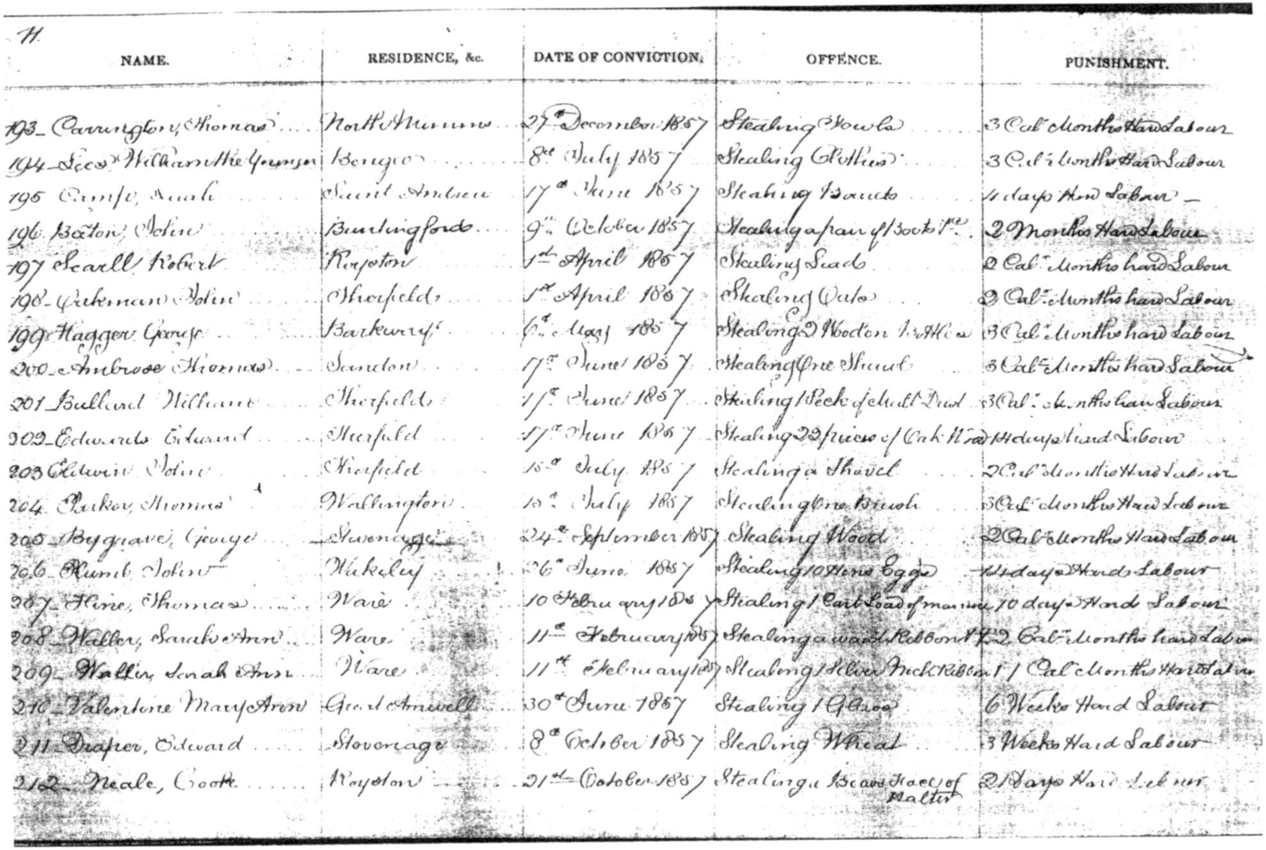

Figure 4.3 Hertford county gaol record: Extract from 1857: original version

NAME	RESIDENCE, &c.	DATE OF CONVICTION	OFFENCE	PUNISHMENT
Cavington Thomas	North Mimms	27th December 1857	Stealing fowls	3 cal. Months Hard Labour
Lees William the younger	Bengeo	8th July 1857	Stealing clothes	3 cal. Months Hard Labour
Camfu Sarah	Saint Andrew	17th June 1857	Stealing boards	4 days Hard Labour
Beeton John	Buntingford	9th October 1857	Stealing a pair of boots	2 Months Hard Labour
Seaell Robert	Royston	1st April 1857	Stealing seeds	2 cal. Months Hard Labour
Oakman John	Therfield	1st April 1857	Stealing oats	2 cal. Months Hard Labour
Ambrose Thomas	Sandon	17th June 1857	Stealing one shawl	3 cal. Months Hard Labour
Edwards Edward	Therfield	17th June 1857	Stealing 2 pieces of oak wood	14 days Hard Labour
Eldwin John	Therfield	15th July 1857	Stealing a shovel	2 cal. Months Hard Labour
Parker Thomas	Wallington	15th July 1857	Stealing one brush	3 cal. Months Hard Labour
Bygrave George	Stevenage	24th September 1857	Stealing wood	2 cal. Months Hard Labour
Plumb John	Wakeley	26th June 1857	Stealing 10 hens eggs	14 days Hard Labour
Hine Sarah Ann	Ware	10th February 1857	Stealing 1 cart load of manure	10 days Hard Labour
Wallis Sarah Ann	Ware	11th February 1857	Stealing a waist ribbon	12 cal. Months Hard Labour
	Ware	11th February 1857	Stealing 1 silver neck ribbon	11 cal. Months Hard Labour
Valentine Mary Ann	Great Amwell	30th June 1857	Stealing 1 glass	6 weeks Hard Labour
Draper Edward	Stevenage	8th October 1857	Stealing wheat	3 weeks Hard Labour

Figure 4.4 Hertford county gaol record: Extract from 1857: typed version

important point about this activity was the questioning. The questions sprang directly from the children's encounter with the primary evidence of the gaol records, and not from myself as teacher. This is not to say that the teacher should not have a steering role in initiating and following through an enquiry such as this which uses local records; only that it is important for children to generate questions as part of the process of historical enquiry.

Using diaries

An obvious example of a diary to use is that of Samuel Pepys. There is a very accessible eyewitness account of the Great Fire which can be used in a variety of ways. It is, in its original form, in too demanding language for Year 2 (the year group the Unit is aimed at) but, read with a good range of expression, recorded and played back to the children, it becomes an exciting account of a day and night of grave danger. I would actively teach the concept of 'eyewitness account' probably by using such an account, perhaps a two-minute clip from TV news or from a local paper on a fire, storm, earthquake, accident or similar shocking event. With Year 2, I would have certain sentences which contain vivid descriptions on cards: sentences such as 'Everybody endeavouring to remove their goods, and flinging into the river or bringing them into lighters that lay off; poor people staying in their houses as long as till the very fire touched them, and then running into boats, or clambering from one pair of stairs by the waterside to another.' I would then ask the children to describe (with help if need be) the picture in their minds from the description in the sentence. The whole class task would then be to create a composite drawing or painting from the evidence. Older children could analyse the whole diary extract, again working in pairs so that each pair has a sentence. Paragraphs could thus be tackled in groups, with one person from each group feeding back to the class what the paragraph is saying. One possibility is to prepare a role-play. The teacher needs to prepare five cards: Samuel Pepys; the King; Adviser 1; Adviser 2; and the Lord Mayor of London. Each card contains two or three suggestions for what the character might say. Pepys is arguing for the tearing down of houses to prevent the spread of the fire. Adviser 1 can agree and argue with him that houses should be destroyed; Adviser 2 can worry about the value of property and the loss of homes. Using the cards, choose five children to enact the scene in the King's Chamber. From this the children can write: a newspaper account, containing an eyewitness account, perhaps with key figures arguing for the destruction of houses; a play script for the scene in the chamber; or their own explanation for why the fire spread so quickly, possibly using an explanation writing frame (Wray and Lewis, 1997) to support their writing in this genre. Useful sources for documents on Pepys may be found at

http://www.pepys.info/fire.html
http://www.primaryhistory.org/fileLibrary/pdf/Pepys_and_the_Great_Fire_of_London_resource_a.pdf

The general principles of using documents have been shown to be:

- Set the document into context by using story, drama or artefact, examples of illustration to help make it meaningful for the children;
- Actively teach the document types using analogies and modern examples;
- Use the generic process on page 48 to draw children into the document;
- Give masses of praise and encouragement to the children;
- Make the document part of a larger enquiry into a historical situation;
- Bear in mind you do not always have to read the whole document;
- Employ the strategy of sometimes letting children ask the questions.

For further ideas on using documents, the English Heritage book is excellent (Davies and Webb, 1996).

CHAPTER 5

Visual images

We live in a world in which the visual image is extremely powerful and influential. Communicating through images seems to be a natural human instinct, from the cave drawings of early peoples to modern glossy magazines, in which images are used to sell goods and lifestyles. The visual image is very useful and valuable in teaching history. From an early age children are accustomed to seeing and enjoying visual images of all kinds: for example, television images, picture books, comics, magazines and internet pages. The iconic representation or visual image is one of Bruner's three ways of mentally representing the world. Visual images are immensely powerful, as all media and advertising people know, and children need to be able to 'read' and interpret a wide range of images to cope with life in general. However, images are also both an important source of evidence about the past and a marvellous teaching resource for history. Although they are obviously a different form of communication and expression from written sources, they are none the less kinds of text, which can be 'read' and interpreted. Teachers need a good understanding of how to use visual images of all kinds in teaching history; practical knowledge of obtaining and preparing pictures for use; and a broad range of teaching approaches and activities to use with pictures and photographs of all kinds. This chapter gives an introduction to all of these aspects of teachers' knowledge, understanding and skills for using the visual image in history.

Knowing the available sources

Types of image

There are many different kinds of image one can use. For those in the list below one needs to include reproductions, since obviously famous paintings are too valuable and are unavailable to take into schools. There are many good-quality reproductions one can use.

- paintings of scenes;
- portraits, single and group;

- pictures and photographs of an object or objects;
- pictures and photographs of historical scenes;
- artists' reconstructions of scenes from the past;
- engravings and reproductions of engravings;
- cartoons;
- still images from video or film.

Obtaining and preparing images for use

It has never been easier to get hold of pictures for use in classrooms. The internet is an excellent source of images of all kinds, but there are all sorts of other ways to obtain pictures. The fundamental requirement is that all pupils must be able to see the images and this has implications for resourcing.

- Large posters, say of a Greek Trireme, an Eyptian tomb or a Tudor kitchen: these may be put on display near the carpet area for use during a circle session.
- Black and white or colour overhead transparencies. These are excellent if you do not have a carpet area, or if you have the kind of class whom you like to keep firmly in their seats! These are an excellent way of focusing attention, especially the colour transparencies.
- Sets of photographs on various topics: for example, Collins do a very good 'Starting History Skills Pack' for Key Stage 1, with pictures of domestic objects, three or four for each item from 1900 to the present day, and pairs of scenes on topics such as leisure and washing from 1900 up to the present day.
- Sets of images from 'free' sources: if doing a topic on houses and homes, collect estate agents' details in hard copy or from the internet, with images of houses of different ages, for comparison and discussion activities. Print or copy the photographs and get them laminated.
- More free sources: the Argos catalogue is a useful source of pictures of familiar objects and one can use them for comparison purposes, especially with Foundation and Key Stage 1.
- Sets of pictures/photos: always aim to have one between two. I learned the hard way that one picture per group does not work. The children will need to keep turning the picture round to look at it properly and there is scope for squabbling there. Thus you need a minimum of 16 pictures/photos for a class of 30.

- Boot fairs and junk shops can be a source of photos and pictures of all kinds: I use a picture of children playing cricket in the street from the 1930s as a starting point for all sorts of things: pastimes, games, play areas, traffic, clothing and so on. A wedding photograph from the 1960s can serve as a stimulus to investigating fashion from that period.
- Images from children's topic books may be copied from the books (if need be) and laminated for use. For the ancient Greeks I use a selection of pictures of Greek pots from children's topic books, one book between two, as an introduction to all aspects of Greek life and culture.
- Images from the internet can be used. Museums often have images of objects in their collection; galleries have images of paintings they hold which may be printed and duplicated (or made into colour transparencies) for classroom use.
- Collections from the art resource cupboard can be put into dual service for both art and history. My copy of Bruegel's *Children's Games* came from just such a pack. I made 16 colour copies and had them laminated.
- If you have an interactive whiteboard and internet connection in your classroom, you can use images directly from the internet: this opens up a wealth of possibilities.

Remember: A set of pictures, laminated for durability, is often a better resource for teaching history than a commercially produced pack on a particular topic.

How to use images

Once you have obtained your image, how do you use it with children? There are many ways of using images and this chapter can only give you an introduction. Armed with this, you should be able to make a start on using pictures in the classroom. The list below comes from Fines and Nichol's excellent book *Teaching Primary History* (1997, p. 129), now, alas, out of print.

Generic stages

1 scanning;
2 observing and focusing;
3 questioning: a continuous process;
4 entering into the picture to understand what the scene might have meant to the people who were alive then;
5 using other sources to find out about the scene;

6 the recording of findings and perceptions;

7 hypothesising, speculating, interpreting, synthesising;

8 the presentation of views.

Putting all this together: teaching activities using pictures

CASE STUDY: *BABY'S BIRTHDAY*

This is a picture which I found in a Longman's pack, 'A Sense of History' for Key Stage 1. It was painted by Frederick Daniel Hardy and was first exhibited in 1867. It is a wonderful picture, incredibly rich in potential for teaching across the whole of the primary age range. The picture shows a family of mother and father and five children (or possibly one maid and four children) about to celebrate their baby's first birthday. Father is opening the door to an older couple, who, from the gift of a doll in their hands, would seem to be grandparents. It is clear from the objects in the room, the work table with sewing items and fabric, the cooking utensils by the fire and the toys, that this is where the family work, cook, eat and play. Using Fines and Nichol's generic framework, this is how I have used the picture. For Key Stage 1 it may be used to teach children about the lives of men, women and children at different levels of society from the past, from periods beyond living memory. For Key Stage 2 it may be used to teach children about lives of men, women and children at different levels of society in Victorian times. The approaches used draw upon some of the wide range of teaching approaches presented in this book.

Teaching and learning activities

1 To get the children scanning the picture and looking at the detail, I play 'I Spy'. This is done simply by dividing the class into two teams, A and B. Each child from each team takes a turn at finding an object in the picture and saying: 'I spy with my little eye, something beginning with. . . .' If no one can spot the object, the turn passes to the other team. This is good for observation skills in history, and for onset letter names and letter sounds in English.

2 By this time the children have usually been asking questions of the picture anyway, whispering to me as children take their turn ('Is that a bird in the cage up there?', 'Is that the granny and granddad?', 'What's that stuff on the plate by the fire?'). I get each child to think of a question to ask about the picture. In answering them, I sometimes call upon children in the class to answer, and sometimes explain myself.

3 Now we start to enter into the picture: I ask the children to count with me the people in the picture and then the children in the picture. By now we would

have established that someone in the room does the sewing. From the heavy military jacket lying on the table it would seem to be the father. I suggest we name all the people in the picture with suitably Victorian or old-fashioned names. Examples children have suggested are: Mr and Mrs Taylor, Elizabeth for the oldest girl, Mary for the girl with the baby on her lap, Albert for the boy, Charlotte for the girl trying to share a stool with him, and Victoria for the baby. There is usually some discussion over whether the older couple at the door are her parents or his. Once this is settled, they can either be the Taylors (senior) or another surname.

4   Getting right inside the picture: I tell the children we will make a freeze frame of the scene in the picture. The children are usually so keen to do this that I will do this twice or three times to give children a turn, 18 or 27 children out of the class instead of only nine. The children volunteer for roles and may look closely at the picture to work out their position and pose. I give them space at the front of the class or on the carpet and count them down to the freeze frame. After this we applaud and praise the children.

5   I ask the children to return to their seats and to close their eyes and imagine they are one person in the room and that it is five minutes before the grand-parents knock on the door. I then ask the children to tell me in turn one event they think will have been happening in the room at that point in time. They suggest, for example, the boy and girl fighting over the stool or the toy, or the mother fussing over the food.

6   I have ready two outline versions of the picture (these are easily made by draw-ing a rough outline of the shapes of people and large objects in the picture). I show an overhead transparency of a page from a comic and check that all the children know and understand 'speech bubbles' and 'think bubbles'. I ask the children to write speech bubbles for their character and some of the other people in the picture. With the second sheet I ask them to make and fill in think bubbles of what the characters are thinking and feeling. These activities can either stand alone, as outcomes of the work for younger children, or form the basis of imaginative pieces of writing for older children. I have had older children writing a short imaginative piece on the scene at a moment in time five minutes before that which is shown in the picture.

These ideas are just a beginning. Through the activities suggested here the children can start to tackle the overarching question: What was it like for ordinary people to live in Victorian times? The people in the picture are not the very poorest of the poor. They have work, on the evidence of the sewing items and some possessions: a toby jug, a sampler, pictures, toys, crockery (though not matching) and some furniture. They even have pets: a cat and a canary. Yet they basically live in one room, the door of which opens directly on to the street; seven people living, working and eating in the same space. They have brick floors and a rag rug: their only source of heat in the picture is the fire. The evidence in this picture paints a very clear portrait of life among the skilled artisans of the nineteenth century. From a literacy point of view, it serves as a superb stimulus to creative imaginative writing as well as a source for literacy games. In terms of themes in the picture one could explore houses and homes, birthdays in the present and in the past, clothing, and the kinds of work people did in their own homes. One could compare the interior of this cottage with the interior of a grand home, to examine the lives of people at different levels of society. This is an excellent resource which may be used economically with children across the whole primary age range.

Twenty generic activities to do with pictures

How you use pictures will depend partly on the kind of picture and partly on your purposes. The picture may be used to initiate an enquiry at the beginning of a unit of work, or as corroborating evidence as part of an enquiry, or to present a different perspective on material already examined. This list is only a beginning, and as you work with pictures more ideas will come to you.

1. With two pictures of the same object (e.g. irons) use a similar sheet to the one for comparing two artefacts (see Figure 3.4). Ask the children to find five features which are different and five features which are the same. In doing this they will be comparing and contrasting, and dealing with the overarching historical concepts of change (difference) and continuity (similarity).

2. With three pictures of the same type of object, ask the children to sequence them on a timeline. With younger children use a marker such as very old, old and new. With older children you can use date markers.

3. Compare and contrast two pictures of the same scene (say, for local history, possibly their own High Street) or two pictures of beach scenes, or old and new shops. Again, look for similarities and differences.

4. Print off an object from a museum collection (e.g. one of the Sutton Hoo treasures from the British Museum). Make it into a colour overhead transparency. Show it to the children and ask them what skills the people who made it might have to have had. Ask the children to make a list. What does this tell us about these people?

5. With a large 'busy' picture such as *Baby's Birthday* play the game of 'I Spy'. This gets children observing closely and practising initial letter sounds and names. Divide the class into two teams, A and B. B can go first. Play according to normal rules. This is a very good starting point with the right kind of picture.

6. Using all sorts of pictures, count the number of people in the picture. With a smaller number, give the people names and ages. Ask each child in the class to write a speech bubble and/or a think bubble for a chosen character. Older

children could write a paragraph imagining themselves as one of the characters and writing down their thoughts. This can produce some high-quality creative writing about the people and events in the picture.

7   Take the children back to a point five minutes before or five minutes after the scene in the picture. Using volunteers, create a freeze frame of that moment in time, or of the moment of the picture itself.

8   Show a picture of which only a fragment has survived (e.g. a mosaic, a pot or a piece of jewellery). Ask the children to complete the picture.

9   Encourage the children to ask questions about the picture. For example, I once showed a class of 8- and 9-year-olds a picture of Queen Elizabeth I being carried on a litter by some courtiers in a procession. I let the children ask questions and did my best to answer them. They were very interested in the ruffs, and I explained about their significance. This was one piece of learning which stayed with them once the term was over. The questioning session on the carpet went on for 20 minutes without any loss of attention.

10 With an artist's reconstruction of a past scene, say an Anglo-Saxon village, a Viking boat or a Roman town, set activities which invite the children into the picture. If they were an Anglo-Saxon, which would be their hut? Where would they keep their treasures? Which of the children would they be?

11 Go for a 'walk' through the picture. Invite the children to imagine they are walking through it and ask them to describe the scene using all their senses.

12 Ask what might be happening outside the frame of the picture.

13 Ask the children to provide a title and a caption for the picture.

14 Ask the children: (1) what the picture tells them; and (2) what the picture does not tell them.

15 Ask the children on what evidence the picture was based: did the artist sit and make sketches, or paint from life, or might it be an imagined scene?

16 Play a game of giving the children one minute to look at a picture. It is then covered up and the children have one minute to make a list of what they have seen.

17 Ask the children to make a list of three or five facts (depending on the kind of picture and the ability of the children) their picture tells them about life in that period.

18 Divide the children into groups. Ask each group to focus in on one part of the picture, using a magnifying glass if necessary, and to prepare a description of this one part.

19 Ask the children which character in the picture they would like to be and why.

20 Use several pictures from the same period to tell a story.

Using portraits

Portraits deserve a separate section, since they require detailed analysis coupled with an understanding of the type of evidence they present. Prior to the advent of photography, film and television, portraits were one of the main ways for ordinary people to 'see' or have an image of their king or queen. It was an important aspect of the painter's work to flatter the sitter; otherwise, in the case of people such as Tudor monarchs, the consequences could be unpleasant. At the very least the portrait would be suppressed and no copies would be allowed to be made of it for dispersal around the country. Portraits are a valuable source of evidence for investigating wealthy people, and, as long as one understands that they may not be an entirely accurate image of the sitter, they can still yield important information. Below is an account of a lesson I taught on Henry VIII (using the Holbein portrait). It is based on work on portraits in Fines and Nichol (1997). I was working with the same Year 4 class as described in Chapters 5 and 10. I pinned up a large version of this picture from a commercial pack, and asked the children who this person was. They knew it was Henry VIII despite having little knowledge of the Tudors at this stage, it being the third lesson in a term's work. I said we were going to learn how to analyse portraits using five headings:

- facial expression
- body language/pose
- dress
- props and setting
- artist's role

I modelled several facial expressions for them and they had to guess what emotion I was expressing. They were sent to tables in pairs to model, draw the facial expression, guess it and swap over after five minutes. I asked them to share some of their expressions. I then modelled several poses representing fear, confidence, tiredness and happiness, and the children had to guess what these were. Volunteers came up and demonstrated their own poses: Gavin, for example, slumped on the floor to represent tiredness. We then moved on to dress. I put on my hunger marcher's outfit of old raincoat and cloth cap (see Chapter 8): the children thought I looked like a gardener. I asked what my normal clothes showed and was horrified to learn I looked like a postwoman! Making a mental note to change my teaching wardrobe, I moved on to props and setting. For this we examined those in the portrait itself: Henry's gloves and sword, and the rich hangings and carpets in the room. Finally, we discussed what would happen if the portrait had not made Henry look good. ('The artist would have had his head chopped off, Miss!') I sent them away to work in pairs to analyse the Holbein portrait. Three weeks later when we had moved on to Queen Elizabeth I, I showed

Name: **Elizabeth I**

The face She has a small, roundish face. She is wearing bright red lipstick and her brown eyes that stand out. You can't see her ears because there hidden in her hair. She looks happy.	**Body language** Her body is thin, smart and in good condishen.
Props and setting She's sitting in her room holding a fan and glob. the Sea is out the window. Her room is pretty and her crown is beside her.	**Dress** Her dress has lots of jullrie on and is smart. It gets thiner and goes out at the waist.
The artist's role She's famos and rule's part of the world.	

Figure 5.1   Child's work: Review on the portrait of Elizabeth I

them a copy of the Armada portrait as a colour overhead, and with very little revision other than the headings, asked them to analyse this portrait (available online at: http://pavlov.psyc.queensu.ca/~psyc382/grower.html).

The children were able to do this more or less independently, which meant that my learning objectives for the series of lessons had been achieved. Figure 5.1 shows the work of one child. There is much more to be gained from the portrait in terms of symbolism, but this was due to be dealt with in a subsequent lesson on the Armada. However, it was a useful start for children tackling the portrait on their own.

English Heritage has a useful booklet on using portraits with children, and contains many more teaching ideas. The National Portrait Gallery also has packs of Tudor portraits and materials on how to use them. For teachers starting out on using portraits, the ideas in this section are a useful beginning. Pictures, photographs and portraits are kinds of texts which may be 'read' and interpreted. It is important to give children the skills to work with images of all kinds, and to be able to interpret symbolism, facial expression and so on.

CHAPTER 6

The historical environment
Maps, sites, visits and museums

We live in a country that is richer than any other in the visible remains of the past, but . . . most of us are visually illiterate.

(Hoskins, 1967, p. 32)

This country is indeed rich in visible remains from the past: hill forts, castles, great houses, churches, abbeys, cathedrals and other religious buildings, walled towns, Roman villas, Stonehenge and burial mounds are obvious forms of evidence. But while such sites are obvious, there is also history in ordinary everyday sites, such as buildings housing banks, restaurants, schools, railways stations, public houses, shops and factories. The routes of transport – roads, railways, canals, ancient tracks, packhorse routes, drove roads, bridleways – are all evidence from the past, as is the landscape itself with its record of human activity and interaction with it. The landscape is a rich historical environment, and is eminently suitable for historical enquiry with children. Although it can be very valuable to take children to grand and important sites, it is just as useful to use what is right on one's doorstep. A walk through the local area with a treasure hunt-style trail for children to follow can reveal all sorts of interesting things and provoke questions:

- A pawnshop (What was pawning? Why did people do it?)
- A post-box with GR on it and another with ER on it (Why are the letters different?)
- A horse trough with Metropolitan Police engraved on it (Why is this here?)
- A street sign: Gallows Lane (Is this where people got hung?)
- A war memorial (What was this for?)

These are all genuine examples taken from local study walks. One important learning outcome for such walks, or indeed for any local study or site visit, is to develop observation skills in children. To do so is crucial for developing visual literacy across the curriculum in general and in history in particular. This chapter is devoted to the historical environment, local study, and visits to sites and museums. Because work on maps and plans can be a part of local study, using them in history is dealt with here. There are obvious links to geography, and a local study can integrate history and geography work.

Using maps and plans

One of the compulsory study units in the Key Stage 2 History National Curriculum is No. 7, Local history study. At Key Stage 1 children need to study changes in their own lives and in the way of life of their families, those around them, or people in the more distant past. A good way into local study is through using maps. This chapter gives a brief introduction to using maps with children. A map is a 'model' of a reality, which extracts certain elements and represents them symbolically in various forms. Maps are a record of change and continuity in a landscape and can be very useful as a starting point for local history study, or study of change. The following section gives a brief selection of activities using maps and plans.

Map and plan activities

- Comparing and contrasting old and new maps: For your local area, find a modern map and an old map of the area (often available in libraries or local records offices). Select an area (it might include the local primary school) and, using the same kind of comparison and contrast sheet as in Figure 3.4 for artefacts, make a list of five changes and five things that have stayed the same. From the similarities and differences, one can examine change and continuity in a local area. For example, comparing maps from 1938 and 2001 can reveal that a village now has a bypass, the railway running through it is disused and the station has closed down. There might be other changes: the duck pond has been filled in and new housing built. Yet the basic layout of the village has stayed the same, the green is still there as are the manor house and church. This kind of task can be done with children, possibly tied in with geography work. The lists of similarities and differences can be written up, the worksheet giving the structure for the piece of writing. The important aspect of pedagogy here is that the task is finite and focused. Children may not be able to record all the differences and similarities, but they can find a limited number, and it gets them looking at the map in depth.

- Questioning: An extension of this activity is for the children to ask questions about things on the map they do not understand or know about (e.g. an ice house, a folly or a tumulus). The advantages of getting children to ask the questions have been discussed elsewhere in this book.

- The next activity could be to plan a walk around the local environment visiting places of interest or sites of changes. This can be done on a photocopy of the modern map.

- Roman place-names: For this activity you will need photocopies of a road map of England and the southern part of Scotland. It may be done in pairs, with one photocopy between each pair. Write on the board the information that 'ter' or 'ster' means 'fort' and ask the children to find as many place-names as possible on their map with this word ending. They can highlight these. The next step is to put the roads in, bearing in mind that Roman roads were straight, radiated out from London and linked up all the towns. This can then be compared with photocopies of a map of Roman Britain (easily obtainable from any Roman museum shop). If you do this with children who live near a modern yet ancient Roman road such as Watling Street, they can begin to understand that their 'main' road dates back to Roman times. The learning outcomes are: for the children to gain some understanding of the extent of Roman settlement in Britain; to use maps as a source of evidence for historical enquiry; and to develop some understanding of change and continuity in the basis of part of our modern road system.

- Anglo-Saxon place-names: Figure 6.1 lists examples of these.

  For this activity you will need A3 size two pages from a road atlas, for example one from the Hertfordshire/Cambridgeshire area and one from Cornwall. Ideally make 16 copies of each, enough for one between two, and have them laminated for long-term use. The overarching question is 'Where did the Anglo-Saxons settle in Britain?' The children look at the Hertfordshire map first and in pairs they try to find one piece of a place-name (or letter string) (e.g.

Saxon settlement names

Saxon word	Modern word	Meaning
Ham	Ham	Village
Inga(s)	Ing, in	Folk group, people belonging to
Tun	Ton	Farm
Cote	Cote, cot	Cottage
Burh	Bury	Strong place, fort
Worth	Worth	Enclosure, farm
Ford	Ford	River crossing
Leah	Ley, ly	Wood, clearing
Denu	Den	Valley
Hamstede	Hampstead	Homestead
	Hempstead	

Figure 6.1 Anglo-Saxon place-names

'denu'). There are so many place-names on this page of the road atlas that it is useful to divide up the pieces of name among the class. Give a time limit of 10 minutes, then ask how many the children have found five or more, 10 or more, 15 or more and so on. Praise the children for their efforts.

The same task may then be carried out for the map of Cornwall looking for the same letter string for five minutes. This comparison task reveals that there are very few Anglo-Saxon place-names in Cornwall and you can ask the children what this tells us about where the Anglo-Saxons settled. The learning outcomes are for the children to gain a good understanding of where the Anglo-Saxons settled in Britain, and where they did not, and some beginnings of an understanding of the word 'settlement' being related to those pieces of words meaning 'farm', 'village', 'cottage' and 'homestead'. There is also some literacy work at word level in searching for and writing down lists of those same letter strings.

- Viking place-names: A similar activity may be carried out for Viking place-names. Figure 6.2 has a list of words, word parts and meanings. For this comparison activity one would need a map of somewhere in northern England, where these place-names are common, and one of southern or western England.

- For either the Anglo-Saxon or Viking map activity, a follow-up activity might be to give the children an outline map of a locality, with physical features marked on it, and ask them to name these features using Anglo-Saxon or Viking words. The next stage is for them to choose a place to put their village, bearing in mind that it needs to be close to a water supply, fairly near woods (for building and fuel) and land for growing crops and running livestock.

- Plans: If your school is in an old building you can sometimes get hold of plans showing the site in previous years. Children could compare old and new plans

barrow – small hill	keld – cold
beck – brook, stream	kirk – church
blea – blue	knott – rocky hill
crag – rocky cliff	pike – mountain peak
dale – valley	rigg – ridge
fell – mountain, high grazing	saetr – cow pasture, high ground
garth – fenced land, garden	scale – hut, shack
gate – path, track	tarn – pond
gill – ravine	thwaite – clearing
holm – island	ton – hedge, fence
how – hill	water – lake
ing – meadow, pasture	wath – ford

Figure 6.2   Viking place-names

and come up with reasons for the changes. A set of plans of a grand house can introduce the children to the types of rooms in such a house and the family activities (e.g library, billiard room, ballroom). They can then be told they are the new landowner of the house and estate and be given the task of turning an old country farmhouse of, say, eight rooms on two levels, into a grand mansion. This type of activity comes under the heading of planning spaces as a teaching approach (see Chapter 9) and may be adapted for all sorts of historical contexts and situations: an Iron Age fort; a castle; a Roman, Greek, Tudor or Aztec marketplace; a Roman villa, fort or town; an Anglo-Saxon village; a Tudor palace; or a Greek temple. Here, the learning comes in the children thinking about how the spaces may have been used, and in engaging their historical imaginations. The subsequent visit to the Roman villa or grand house is enriched by this preparatory work. Several piles of old stones, which appear to be all that remains of an abbey dissolved by Henry VIII, take on new significance if the children can lead the teachers around, telling them these would have been the kitchens and here was the infirmary.

- Another simple, related activity is to give children pictures of a room and ask them to draw room plans. To get children used to this kind of work, they can do it with the classroom first, and then, say, have one picture for each pair of one of the rooms in Preston Manor and draw a plan of it. The pictures may be used in other ways of course (see Chapter 5), but the general principle here is of the children taking material in one genre and transforming it into another. Houses such as Preston Manor supply information, such as pictures of rooms and plans: all these may be drawn upon in preparation for a visit.

- Another kind of map activity is to get the children to plan journeys and voyages: Cortez's journey to Tenochtitlan; Drake's voyage around the world; the Transports' voyage to Australia; Boudicca's rebellion; or the Lancashire hunger marchers' long walk from Bolton to London. Some information is necessary; for example, lists of places travelled to, or for voyages, information on currents and trade winds on a world map. Maps of land will show physical features which present problems: rivers to cross or ford, mountains and swamps to negotiate.

Visits to sites and museums

What is really important about taking children on visits is that they engage with the whole business of doing history, whether that is using the skills and processes of historical enquiry, or entering imaginatively into the past. Both of these aspects of doing history are fundamental to visits. Above all, children should not be trailing round with clipboards, recording a lot of information, or finding answers to quizzes set by adults. Such activities are particularly hard on those children with literacy difficulties: struggling with spelling can take the pleasure out of the day and shift the focus away from historical learning. Often the sites and museums are so rich that we want our children to experience everything. Our own excitement at seeing wonderful places and marvellous remains in museums can sometimes result in overkill as we try to ensure children do not miss anything important. As a result we do too many of the wrong activities with them. The list below highlights some bad activities to do with children at museums.

- Tell the children what to notice: 'Look!'
- Try to look at everything and 'see nothing'.
- Try to show the children too much.
- Hire the sort of guide who gives a lecture, often in language way above the children's heads.
- Give the children a worksheet and a clipboard.

There are several advantages for children in going on visits to sites and museums. It gives children an opportunity to enquire at first hand, with a multi-sensory experience in three dimensions. In fact these visits bring children face-to-face with a reality totally different from that experienced in their classroom. John Fines (Fines and Nichol, 1997) commented on how too often there are glass barriers between children and the relics of the past, but there are ways around the barriers. Some museums run object-handling sessions where children can have the opportunity to handle precious and rare objects from the past. In some cases, children can experience being a person from the past, becoming involved with storytelling, dance, music, drama and role-play. This section of the chapter suggests a number of activities which may be done at museums, galleries, sites and in the environment. It is best to prepare for the visit by engaging children intellectually and imaginatively with the site or museum. Examples are given for one site: St Albans Abbey, which is a rich treasure of a resource to visit with children. These examples may be drawn upon for a whole range of other sites. In the descriptions of activities which follow, the preparation activity often leads into the tasks to be done on site.

Activities

- A planning spaces activity. Abbeys were complex sites: one way of generating understanding of such sites is to use a mapping activity. Prepare a timetable of a monk's day, including activities he might be involved in, such as work of various kinds and prayer (see Figure 6.3 for an example). Read through this

2.00 a.m.	Rise for Matins and Lauds (Prayers)
4.30 a.m.	In bed
5.00 a.m.	Breakfast
6.00 a.m.	Prime (Prayers)
7.00 a.m.	Reading in cloister and mixtum
8.00 a.m.	Tierce (Prayers)
9.00 a.m.	Chapter meeting
10.00 a.m.	Reading or work
12.30 a.m.	Sext and none (Prayers)
2.00 p.m.	Dinner
3.00 p.m.	Reading or work
5.00 p.m.	Vespers (Prayers)
5.45 p.m.	Supper
6.00 p.m.	Compline (Prayers)
7.00 p.m.	In bed

Figure 6.3   A monk's day

timetable with the children and allow them to ask any questions they may have. Give the children some large A3 size blank sheets and, on small pieces of paper, outline map drawings of the various buildings and spaces which go to make up a monastery: the church, the chapter house, the cloisters, the gatehouse, the monks' dormitories, the refectory, the library, the kitchens, the infirmary, the gardens and so on (see Figure 6.4). The children, working in pairs, are given the information that they have been nominated as the new Abbot of a monastery to be built on a grant of land from King Offa. The task is to move the pieces of paper representing the different buildings and spaces around on their blank sheet until they have a sensible plan. For example, have they got the kitchens near the refectory and gardens for ease of picking fresh vegetables? Would the monks' dormitories need to be near the church to be handy for getting up to pray in the middle of the night? It is important that children understand something of the monks' lives before attempting to plan the spaces. Once the children are satisfied with their plan, they can glue the pieces of paper in position on the A3 sheet and label the different parts of the building. Geographical refinements can be added in. Which way would the church have to be aligned? Should the kitchen gardens be south-facing? This preparation work gets the children's imaginations going on a fantasy monastery, and gives them something with which to compare the reality when they do go on the visit. It also gives the children some status as experts: instead of the guide telling them that this is where the monks would have slept, they can be the ones telling the

Abbey church
Great gateway
Almonry
Stables
Water-gate
Long house
Guest's house
Great courtyard
Well
Refectory
Cloisters
Abbot's parlour and chapel
Chapter house
Dormitories
Infirmary
Library
Vineyard
Monks' cemetery
Orchard
Almoner's gate
Kitchen gardens
Fishpond
Sacristy
Prior's house
Chamberlain's house
Abbey meadows

You will need to do a little research into what all these buildings were and their likely shape, but you may know a great deal already from your own second record (for example, that cloisters consisted of a kind of covered colonnaded walkway forming the four sides of a square, with a garden or lawn in the centre).

Figure 6.4 Key to Abbey plan showing types of building

teacher. This kind of approach may be used with villas, ancient settlements, towns, castles, Roman forts, marketplaces and even complex sites such as the Tower of London.

● One useful approach is to create a picture trail for the children to follow. You can take a number of pictures of key items and places you want the children to see, give them the pictures and ask them to find the real thing or place; for example, the mosaic floor in a Roman bath house, or the kitchen area in a monastery. To return to the St Albans Abbey context, the children could be given pictures of key places in the Abbey, such as St Albans tomb and the Watching Chamber, and be encouraged to ask questions about what features in their pictures. When they visit the Abbey, they can look for the pictured sites and prepare two or three sentences to present to the group in the plenary, which takes the form of a tour around the Abbey conducted by the children. This again places them in role as experts. With a site as rich as this abbey, pairs or groups of children could have different pictures, and in the plenary the knowledge becomes shared with the whole group. This approach may be adapted for all kinds of sites, museums and gallery visits.

- In a gallery (such as one in a grand house), ask the children what they can tell you about the person who collected the art or objects displayed.

- Divide up the subject (e.g. with a ship, making one group the experts in brass, another in wood, another in iron, another in ropes and so on). This is another example of putting the children in role as experts and gives them status and responsibility.

- Look at small parts of one site; for example, on a trip to the Tower of London, focus on the Medieval Palace, and stage some storytelling or role-play there (see below).

- Ask the children to look round them, then gather them together and ask what spoke to them. What object or picture, which room, captured their interest and imagination, and why?

- Following this, ask each pair or small group to go back to this special area and prepare to introduce it to the rest of the class – putting them in the role of experts on one small part of the site or museum. The children thus become guides and show adults around. Follow-up work could be to produce a children's trail around the site or museum.

- Ask the children to draw their favourite item or room, so that they really look at it.

- Use a camera but ration the shots, asking them to record only what is most important: this can lead to debate and discussion.

- There are several books which deal with the organisation and practicalities of taking children on trips; this is not the main focus here, but it is worthwhile briefing parents and helpers as to what to expect with regard to learning purposes and activities, and what they can do to help.

- Ask the children to try to answer key questions about a place (see Figure 6.5). The questions could be divided up between groups of children, so that, say, one group focuses entirely on how this place is connected to other places. This

Present	Past	Influence of the past on the present
What is this place like?	What was this place like?	What elements of the past can we seen in this place?
Why is this place as it is; how and why does it differ from or resemble other places?	Why was this place as it was; how and why did it differ from or resemble other places?	What influences have these elements had on this place, and how does this influence differ from or resemble what has happened at other places?
In what way is this place connected with other places?	In what ways was this place connected with other places?	In what ways have past connections influenced how this place is now connected with other places?
How is this place changing, and why?	How did this place change, and why?	How did this place change; and why and how are those changes reflected in the present?
What would it feel like to be in this place?	What would it have felt like to be in this place?	How does the past influence what it feels like to be in this place?

Source: From Copeland (1993)

Figure 6.5   Key questions about a place

gives the children a clear focus at a site. These generic questions can generate other questions about aspects such as siting, fitting into the physical land-scape, the number of buildings, their structure and function, and how many people lived there. The children have some time to look around and find answers to the questions through observation and recording, the results of which may be presented as a guidebook entry for a local tourist guide on the history of that particular place.

Storytelling, drama and role-play at historic sites

Many sites and museums have excellent education services and it is quite possible to buy into these: for example, at St Albans Abbey there are a whole range of trails and workshops aimed at different Key Stages, including one on the dissolution of the monasteries. Such trails involve an element of storytelling and multi-sensory ex-perience. At Preston Manor in Sussex, the children can be given roles of the different servants and spend the day in role, acting out the tasks which that particular servant would have had to do. Some teachers prefer to use the knowledge and expertise of site staff and, while this is a good idea, it is also good to join in with role-plays to learn more about how to create and run them.

I will always have two or three stories prepared to tell at historic sites. The dramatic setting can greatly enhance the atmosphere and help to engage the children's imagination. In the box below is the skeleton of a story: its essentials. These can be fleshed out by using your own imagination to tell the story. Here is the outline of a story suitable for telling at a castle, or castle remains:

In the kitchen of a castle, a servant boy, Eric, is helping to prepare for a great feast. He doesn't mind turning the handle of the spit but it is hot work, and he wishes he was working with horses, his long-held ambition.

Eric slips away from the kitchen to watch the visitors arrive, a noble lord, Earl Huntley, and his knights from the next manor.

In the stable, watching the squires remove the saddles and rub down the horses, Eric overhears one of them talking about a surprise attack on his own lord, Sir Geoffrey, and his men, that very night.

The visiting lord wants this castle and land for himself and intends to take the castle by surprise when everyone is relaxed at the feast.

Back in the kitchen the cook tells Eric off for wandering and asks him to take wine to his lord and the visitors. Eric tells the cook what he has overheard. The cook decides they have to warn Sir Geoffrey and take some action.

Eric goes up to the lord's chambers and sees the lord is alone for a few moments. Boldly, he asks to speak to him and Sir Geoffrey, since he is in a good mood, listens to him.

The cook prepares two casks of wine: one is the normal one; the other is for the guests and to which a sleeping potion has been added.

At the feast, Earl Huntley rises to give the signal to his men to attack, and suddenly feels very sleepy . . . as do his men.

Sir Geoffrey is amazed, but the cook and Eric show him the weapons concealed beneath the cloaks of the visitors. They strip the sleeping bodies of the weapons and the servants carry them outside the castle walls and dump them on the ground, without horses, weapons or armour.

When Huntley and his men awake they slink off back to their manor. They will think twice before attempting such a trick again.

Sir Geoffrey offers to reward Eric for his part in foiling the treacherous attack by making him a squire to serve a knight and work with the horses.

Against the background of the castle, one could easily imagine such events occurring. To flesh out the story, one might start by setting the scene:

> Sir Geoffrey de Ward is holding a feast to celebrate his safe return from the Crusades. He has invited his neighbour, Earl Huntley, whom he had fought alongside in the Holy Land. A great feast is being prepared in the castle kitchen. There is a huge stack of freshly baked loaves on the long tables. There are cauldrons big enough to feed hordes of people. At the chopping block the cook trims pieces of meat and stuffs several geese. Hanging from the beams are sacks of wheat, joints of meat and several pheasants. Servants check the meat roasting in the great ovens. At the spit where a whole ox is being roasted stands a young servant boy, Eric. He is hot and tired from the steam and heat in the kitchen. He longs to steal outside and away from the intense damp heat into the cool fresh air. . . .

A useful activity for teachers is to continue and prepare the rest of the story. Chapter 7 contains arguments for the value of storytelling, whether in the classroom or at historic sites; examples of stories and how to use them; and material on how to prepare stories for telling.

- A story about people connected to that site. The obvious story from St Albans Abbey is that of St Alban himself, but there are others. Instead, use a story such as that of Athelstan to teach the children about life in medieval times and how the Church would tax local people to pay for its building and upkeep (see Chapter 1, Cameo 1, and opposite). Through the story, the children gain some understanding of the power of the Church in people's everyday lives and some of the issues of funding such a major complex of buildings and monastic life. Again, if the children re-create the medieval marketplace, they can compare that experience with that of the modern market.

- A drama activity acting out some of the events which happened at that place. One obvious choice is the dissolution of the monasteries during the reign of Henry VIII. This can be done after the planning spaces activity. The children will have read the monks' timetable and gained some understanding of a monk's life. Give each child a role-card with a different monk's name, age, role and character on it (see Figure 6.6 for examples). Allow them to ask you questions about their roles and what they would do. Then tell them they have had a letter from the King's commissioners telling them that their abbey is to be dissolved. The Abbot has to call a meeting of the monks to discuss what they should do. Should they write back and protest that they do not live in sinful ways and do not deserve this treatment? Should they get ready to barricade the Abbey and fight the King's men? Or should they allow the commissioners to come in and value everything, get ready to move out, and accept the King's pension?

Many years ago on a green hillside overlooking an abbey there lived a medieval peasant and farmer called Athelstan. He had a wife, Alison, several daughters and one son, Nicholas, who was old enough now to work on the land and help his father with the animals and the crops. Athelstan liked his plots of land overlooking the great Abbey. It was only a short way into town next to the Abbey to walk his animals to market. Of an evening he and Alison would often sit outside their house and look down on the winding stream, the fish pool where the monks caught their fish, the Abbey gardens and the Abbey itself. Nicholas was not with them in the evenings for he had met a pretty girl, Mary, the daughter of a farmer over the other side of the hill, and he was out courting her.

One day, Nicholas came to Athelstan and said that he wanted to be married. Athelstan was pleased, for it was time Nicholas was off his hands. The girls were growing up and he needed the space for them. Heaven knew how he was going to get all those girls married off! So he and Alison gave Nicholas their blessing. But there was a problem. Before he could get married, the custom was that he had to have a house. Athelstan had some money saved up: a bag of gold coins he kept hidden in his mattress. He sighed, for it was a lot of work, but said that if Nicholas helped him with the building, he would build him a house and he could get married.

All through that long hot summer the building proceeded. Both men got extremely muddy making wattle and daub for the walls, dusty cutting timber, and splattered with droplets from the crude plaster. But the house went up. Mary and Alison helped out by doing some of the work in the fields, and by bringing the men food and drink. At last the walls were done, and from selling his chickens, sheep and goats in the market, not to mention the delicious butter and cheese that Alison made, he had just about got enough money to finish the roof. Then the house would be finished and the young couple could get married.

One evening towards the end of the summer, Nicholas was surprised to see a monk from the Abbey plodding up the hill towards his house. He and Alison looked at each other worriedly. What could this be? He had paid his tithe that year, hadn't he? While his wife went to fetch ale for the visitor, Athelstan waited, chewing his lower lip in anxiety and anticipation of trouble. For trouble it certainly was. Brother Mark kept the treasury for the Abbey and handled all the money. He said: 'Good evening, my friend, I hope you are well, and your wife and children also?'

Athelstan replied that he was and Alison handed the monk a wooden cup with ale in it. Brother Mark sipped his ale and then said: 'You will have noticed that we are rebuilding the west wall of the Abbey church?'

Athelstan muttered yes, but to tell the truth, he had been so busy and was so tired from his own building he had not noticed it. He peered down at the Abbey. Yes, there was scaffolding up: something was happening.

Brother Mark cleared his throat. He said: 'The matter is that we need extra funds to pay for this work. It must be done. The old wall was collapsing. We need money to pay for materials and workmen. We know you are a good faithful Christian and will not hesitate to give generously.'

Athelstan, who went to the little church over the other side of the hill every week, couldn't argue with that. But if he gave Brother Mark his money, the roof would not be finished and Nicholas could not move out and get married.

Playing for time, he said: 'I don't have that much right now. I have been building for my son. I can try to get some together, but I will need to go to market first. When do you need the money and how much?'

Brother Mark replied: 'I can see that you need a little time. But our need is very urgent. I will come again next week at the same time and take a tithe [one-tenth] of what you have made.'

When the monk had finished his ale and gone, Athelstan and Alison breathed a sigh of relief. He took a few coins out of the little bag and set them aside for the Abbey. Then he put the bag with the rest of the coins, all big gold ones, up the chimney as far as it would go.

The following week when Brother Mark came, the good weather had gone. The evening was chilly and they were both indoors with the girls asleep on their straw mattresses. Alison lit a fire in the hearth and they waited nervously for the knock on the door. When it came, Alison rose to let the visitor in and give him refreshment.

He sipped his ale as before and then said: 'Now, Athelstan, where is the money for the Abbey?'

Silently Athelstan handed him the few silver coins. 'Is that it?' asked Brother Mark in disbelief.

'It's been a bad week. When I took my stock to market, I could not get a stall, there were so many farmers there with all their stuff to sell. I hardly made a thing and had to walk the animals home again!'

Brother Mark looked at Athelstan as if he did not believe a word. 'But you must have more than this!'

Athelstan put his hand in his pocket and pulled out more silver coins. Brother Mark shook his head and said: 'You must have more than this – you have one of the finest holdings on the Abbey's land!'

Athelstan and Alison quaked with fear. If the monk did not believe them he had the power to turn them off their land. 'Mind if I look around?' said Brother Mark.

'Not at all,' replied Athelstan.

Alison spoke for the first time and asked the monk not to disturb the children.

The monk wandered around, looking into pots, peering into the cauldron and inspecting everything. Then he stood gazing at the roaring fire and knew he was defeated.

He said: 'I will take my tithe and go, Athelstan, but mind you try a bit harder next time!'

When he had slammed the door shut, they breathed a sigh of relief. Shortly after, Nicholas arrived home and they told him what had happened. They worked every hour of daylight that week to finish the roof. A few weeks later the young couple were married and settled in their house. But Athelstan said to himself: 'That was a close one!'

The monks in a monastery or abbey did lots of different jobs such as bee keeping, wine-making, brewing, milling, looking after animals, growing fruit and vegetables, harvesting, fishing, building, carpentry, stonemasonry and copying manuscripts. They also spent much of the day praying. Some monks had specific duties and they were given special names:

- Abbot – the monk in charge
- Prior – the Abbot's helper
- Sub-Prior – the Prior's helper
- Cellarer – the monk in charge of stores and supplies
- Cook – the monk in charge of cooking meals
- Sacrist – the monk in charge of the abbey's treasures
- Chamberlain – the monk in charge of clothes and bedding
- Guest Master – the monk who looked after abbey guests
- Almoner – the monk who gave food and clothes to the poor
- Infirmarer – the doctor monk
- Librarian – the monk who looked after the books and manuscripts
- Herbalist – the monk who made medicines
- Cantor or Precentor – the monk in charge of singing
- Illuminators – monks who paint pretty pictures in manuscripts
- Choir or cloister monks – ordinary monks
- Novices – boy monks
- Master of the Novices – the teacher monk
- Lay brothers – non-monks who worked at the abbey
- Lay servants – hired help

Example of role-card

Name:	John
Age:	51
Role:	Librarian

Character: He has spent his whole life in the Abbey since he was a boy and now looks after the collection of books and manuscripts. He loves the Abbey. It is his home and he does not want to leave it.

Figure 6.6 Monks' jobs and role-card

This chapter has been an introduction to using maps and plans and to doing history in the environment. It has only skimmed the surface of what is possible, but it has introduced some valuable ideas. These ideas may be summed up in the following key principles, involving historical enquiry, the exercise of the historical imagination, and children in role as decision-makers acting in the historical context:

- Engage the children in activities which involve historical enquiry and all related processes and skills such as questioning, observation, interpretation, recording and communication;
- Engage the children in exercising their historical imagination through story-telling, drama and role-play;
- Engage the children in role as decision-makers, planning spaces, making decisions (how many Roman soldiers to place on guard at the Roman fort, how many to do the cooking and other chores);
- Engage the children in role as experts, leading the teachers and helpers around, sharing their newly acquired knowledge with others to engage with it actively.

Above all, do not lecture to children or give them clipboard questionnaires or quizzes!

CHAPTER 7

Storytelling
'Putting the book down'

There are three powerful arguments for storytelling in history. One springs from the discipline of history itself, one from cognitive psychology and one from pedagogy. History is the imaginative reconstruction of the past using what evidence we can find. Historical evidence is often fragmentary or incomplete. Historians use their imagination in constructing or reconstructing their understanding of past peoples, events and cultures. Much history is concerned with creating narratives of past events from evidence. There is inevitably selection and ordering of events to make a coherent whole and an interpretation of events. Narrative is a fundamental part of history, most apparent in the final products of historical processes, the written accounts of past periods, events and people. However, there is more than this to narrative within history. There is a wealth of theory on narrative, far too much to detail here (for a brief summary, see Rosen, 1988). One of the central tenets of this book is that history is an umbrella discipline (Cooper, 1992, 1995a, 1995b, 2000). Stories, like songs, dance and music, are part of every culture, past and present. Anthropologists understand the importance of stories in a culture; as part of their discipline, they have to know the stories of a culture, who tells them, when and how (Rosen, 1988).

Bruner set out to show that history is one of two possibilities in the way that we order experience. These two modes are the 'narrative' mode, and the 'paradigmatic' or 'logico-scientific' mode. He stated that the paradigmatic mode works through 'categorisation or conceptualisation and the operations by which categories are established, instantiated, idealised and related to one another to form a system' (Bruner, 1986, p. 12). His view of the narrative mode was that it worked by constructing two landscapes simultaneously:

> the landscape of action, where the constituents are the arguments of action: agent, intention or goal and situation, instrument, something corresponding to a 'story grammar'... and the landscape of consciousness; what those involved in the action know, think and feel, or do not know, think and feel.
>
> (Bruner, 1986, p. 14)

The beauty of history is that it is simultaneously concerned with both modes of thought. In historical enquiry, by asking questions, investigating evidence, ordering information from evidence and reaching a conclusion or new hypotheses we are employing the logico-scientific mode of thought. In interpreting evidence, we are using 'the second record' (Hexter, 1972) of all our experience to date, which is both logico-scientific and narrative in nature. For example, we may have a series of linked ideas on the Second World War, with concepts such as evacuation, rationing, the Blitz, the Battle of Britain, the blackout and doodlebugs helping us to order our understanding of what the war meant to people at home. In addition, we will have heard stories perhaps from older family members, eyewitness accounts, read books, watched films and documentaries which have become part of our second record and help us to interpret evidence (a ration book, a picture of bombed buildings or a letter from an evacuee). Finally in presenting history, we often use the narrative mode 'to tell the story' of past events whether orally through storytelling and drama, or in written form as history books.

The third argument for using storytelling in history comes from pedagogy and from pedagogical content knowledge (Turner-Bisset, 1999a, 2001). Storytelling is a very ancient and potent form of teaching, an approach known and recognised by religious leaders. Stories seem to be fundamental to human nature. We all enjoy stories, whether in the form of written narratives such as novels, or television programmes, films and plays. There seems to be a human need or desire to know 'what happens next', a need exploited to the full by the makers of soap operas, and in earlier times by writers such as Dickens and Hardy, in writing novels in serial form. Narrated stories have a particular magic which is hard to unpack. Magic is not too strong a word in this context. I have seen audiences literally 'spellbound' after a telling. Both teller and listeners are caught up in an imaginative re-creation of past events and people, which functions simultaneously as a shared, collective group experience, and as multiple individual experiences as each listener interprets the story according to his or her second record.

To read a story off the printed page and to tell the same story orally are two totally different experiences, both for teller and listener. To understand why, we need to explore the differences between the two. In reading a story, the teacher's attention is focused on the words in front of her or him. Although teachers can and do employ expression to good purpose in story reading, there is a tangible difference when the story is told. In telling, one's eyes are on the audience. Making eye contact is one of the most valuable aspects of storytelling, for one can draw in the listener, and the very act of eye contact builds a bridge between teller and listener. 'Eyes convey meaning powerfully; we communicate emotions in this way' (Turner-Bisset, 2000b, p. 176). Putting the book down makes this eye contact possible. It also makes other things possible, such as gesture, movement and inviting the listeners into the story. These aspects of storytelling exploit the all-important non-verbal channels of communication which are such an important part of good teaching (Turner-Bisset, 2001). With no book to hold, one can mime actions in a story; for example, hiding a bag of gold up a chimney, calming a horse in the blacksmith's, or polishing a silver spoon. One can, in the words of John Fines, 'take the story for a walk' if it involves travel from one place to another, or the usage of different settings, by moving around the classroom and 'creating' those places in the minds of your listeners. Finally you can 'invite' your listeners into the story by moving towards them and addressing them as if they were characters in a story. They do not have to make any response, but the mere act of this invitation serves to draw them in and heighten the imaginative processes. This is partly to do with one of the 'bottom-tray tools' of non-verbal communication, the 'teacher's toolbox' (Tauber and Mester, 1995), which is surprise. A storytelling and all it involves holds the constant possibility of surprise which a skilful teacher and/or storyteller can exploit to the hilt. Storytelling gives the teacher the opportunity to use the non-verbal channels of communication very effectively.

From the point of view of pedagogy, this is powerful stuff. Alexander (1995) reminded us that 'it is essentially in the discourse between teacher and pupil that education is done, or fails to be done' (Edwards and Mercer, 1987, quoted in Alexander, 1995, p. 159). Storytelling is a particularly potent, intense form of discourse. Some people might think that for pupils it is a passive activity, just sitting still and listening. I would argue that despite surface appearances, it is on the contrary a particularly active form of engagement with the teacher, in terms of what is happening in the minds of pupils. My hypothesis is that storytelling functions simultaneously as enactive representation, in the dramatic lived experience of the story, as iconic representation, in the creation of pictures in the minds of teller and listener, and as symbolic representation, through the symbol system of spoken language.

As regards pedagogy, it is extraordinarily efficient and effective. A storytelling may occupy 5, 10 or 15 minutes (perhaps longer in the hands of very gifted or experienced storytellers such as John Fines or Betty Rosen), but a great deal of learning can be achieved during such a telling. To learn about how people lived in Tudor times, a class might research from the internet or a range of topic books on different aspects of life in that period, but an oral telling of Elizabeth I and the Tides letter can furnish similar information far more economically and lastingly. The ordering of experience through the sequencing of events in a spoken narrative seems to have a much more lasting impact on the human mind than does a collection of facts and concepts, or even an organised web of linked ideas. Teachers might set a comprehension test based on a passage read from a historical topic book: the likelihood is that a week or even a day later, much of what has been written about has vanished from children's minds and made no impact on one's memory, or schema or second record. The same information from such a text, conveyed by means of a told story, would appear, on the contrary, to remain in memory and become accommodated into schema in terms of children's learning, or part of the second record in terms of doing history. Some proof of this is given in the example story and children's work which this story generated. Narrative, as a fundamental means of ordering experience, seems to act as a catalyst to learning.

Yet there is more. Stories are an excellent way of communicating facts, concepts, ideas, technical language, values and attitudes to children. For example, through the telling of the story of Boudicca's rebellion, one can teach such concepts as rebellion, invasion, loan, tribe and humiliation. The explanation and visual representations of ideas conveyed by the story serve to underline meaning through the repetition of key-words and concepts. The story seems to make meaning transparent. Quite difficult abstract ideas can be taught through storytelling (and history is packed with abstract ideas and concepts, such as kingship, democracy, loyalty, authority, community, power, duty and slavery, as well as concepts peculiar to history which often serve as shorthand ways of communicating complex systems, events or cycles of change, such as the feudal system, the Black Death or the Renaissance). I have written elsewhere of telling a story about 'The King's Feather' to a group of 5- and 6-year-olds who were able to understand 'falconer' and 'falconry' after one telling, despite the concepts being new to them (Turner-Bisset, 2000b). Children who have never seen an Egyptian royal seal or a sarcophagus may none the less have a very accurate concept of these things from a telling of Howard Carter's discovery of the tomb of Tutankhamun. Furthermore, the rich example of this particular tomb serves to communicate both the concept of the 'afterlife' and the central importance it held in the religious beliefs of Ancient Egyptians.

Mention of the discovery of the tomb of Tutankhamun brings me to an additional advantage to storytelling: it is an excellent means of communicating or inspiring awe and wonder in children. There are in circulation at the time of writing some training materials on teaching for those involved in Ofsted inspections. One such video features a brave young student-teacher attempting to teach a class about Tutankhamun through a selection of passages from a written version of the story stuck on the board. The children's task is to put the passages into the correct order. Now while there might be a place for this kind of sequencing activity in both English and history, it is likely that, shortly after the lesson, much will have been forgotten about the topic. How much more potent to tell the story and arrive at that moment when Howard Carter, after his long years of lack of success in finding a royal tomb, peers through the just-opened threshold and sees, by the light of a flickering match, 'everywhere the glint of gold!' Through the telling of the story of the discovery, children can enter imaginatively into what it felt like to be Howard Carter at that moment. They can also experience awe at the collection of 'wonderful things' and wonder at this great treasure sealed away underground for the benefit of the long-departed pharaoh. I have as yet no store of research evidence, but it is my hypothesis that the engagement of emotions during storytelling makes possible children's learning of difficult ideas, and the understanding of words, ideas and concepts in history. As a means of teaching about historical situations or sense of period, it is one of the most important tools in the history teacher's pedagogical repertoire.

These then are the three arguments supporting the use of storytelling in history: the nature of the subject discipline; the understandings from cognitive psychology, and the insights from pedagogy and pedagogical content knowledge (Shulman, 1986a, 1986b, 1987). In the following section, I give an example of a story which I have used many times with teachers, student-teachers and children. It is a story of particular power and appeal, parts of which will be analysed in this chapter. It also lends itself to a range of follow-up activities, not just in history but across the curriculum.

THE STORY OF THE TRANSPORTS

The story I am about to tell to you is completely true in every detail, apart from one little thing. Everything in this story really happened. It began many years ago in the county of Norfolk, where a young man named Henry Cabell was working in the fields on a bitterly cold day. His hands were red and raw from hoeing along the rows of turnips, for this story happened before the days of farm machinery and many jobs had to be done by hand. It was very hard work, yet cold in the biting east wind. The wind whistled through his trousers and made him shiver despite his physical labour. Before long he saw his dad, Henry Senior, coming towards him with another man from the village, a bit of a bad character called Abe Carman. His dad greeted him and they chatted, Henry resting his arms on his hoe handle. His father did most of the talking. He said: 'You know that big house on the hill? Well, Abe's got a little job for us both. The grand folks are away in London and it's empty: not a soul there. We can get in tonight and get some food and stuff. What do you say?'

Henry said, 'But that's stealing! I can't do that!'

His dad said, 'Look at you, Henry, in your thin clothes and battered boots! When did you last feel warm? When did you last have a good meal?' For their wages as farm labourers were very low, and they often went hungry and ill-clothed.

'I know,' said Henry unhappily, 'but I don't really want to do this.'

Abe spoke up then. He said, 'The owners are away and we can go when the watch is at the other end of the village. We need you. There's a little window you can get in. Come on! This will be easy. It's only the once!' For Henry Senior had 'helped' Abe before on his 'little jobs', but they all knew this would be Henry's first time.

Late that night under cover of darkness, they moved silently towards the house. All was in shadow, and the little scullery window, as predicted by Abe, was unfastened. Wiry Henry slid himself in and unlocked the door. They crept through the house, filling their sacks with food and with materials to make into warm clothing or to sell. They were so hungry they took the pickled meat from the casks in the cellar, and so cold that they took the bed hangings off the four-poster beds. They left the house as quietly as they had come, but then disaster struck! The watch was early, and they were arrested and taken before the judge to be sentenced for robbery and housebreaking.

The judge was fed up. Every day there were more and more criminals for him to deal with, low common people who stole property from the likes of him. The prisons were full to overflowing and yet still they appeared before him every day. The judge believed in setting an example. In ringing tones, he announced that the three were to be taken from this court into a place of public execution and hanged by the neck until they were dead. Someone spoke up on behalf of the boy, for he was only 19 and it was his first offence.

The judge sighed and agreed to be lenient in this case. Abe Carman and Henry Senior were hanged, and Henry was taken away to Norwich Gaol to await transportation to the colonies for 14 years.

Meanwhile, one afternoon in another part of Norfolk, a young maidservant, also aged 19, Susannah Holmes, was cleaning the family silver. She yawned as she polished, for she had been up since 6 a.m., cleaning the fireplaces, lighting the fires, carrying up hot water for washing, cooking breakfast, and cleaning the rooms. The afternoon was her 'easy' time, but she always had jobs to do. This was all she had known since she was 12 years old. She gazed at the spoon she held and thought that if she were to sell it, she would not have to work for a whole year! She could not help herself and slipped the spoon into her apron pocket. Just then her mistress came in and caught her in the act.

'Susannah! What are you doing?'

'Nothing, miss! I mean, just cleaning the spoons!' she stuttered.

Her mistress seized her apron and felt the hard outline of the spoon.

'You disgraceful girl! After all my kindness to you! You ungrateful child!'

Susannah's mistress called the watch. Susannah was taken away and the judge sentenced her to 14 years' transportation to the colonies on account of her extreme youth.

So Susannah was taken to Norwich Gaol, a great big dungeon of a place beneath the castle. There in one big cell, amidst the filth and squalor, the rats and mice and cockroaches, she and Henry met and fell in love. Just over a year later, Susannah gave birth to a baby, a fine strong boy whom they named Henry. And still they waited for news of transportation since Henry was first sentenced three years before.

Why was it taking so long? The answer was: there was nowhere to send them! Prior to this time, the government had sent criminals to the American colonies as convicts to work. But since the Americans had won the War of Independence, they had refused to accept the dregs of this country – and who can blame them! It was years before it was decided to send the convicts to this vast new country which had been discovered on the other side of the world: Australia.

Prisoners were sent for from all over England, from Devon and Derby, Wiltshire and Wales, from Newark and Frome. And so it was that one day, John Simpson, a kindly senior turnkey (for that was what we called prison officers then), came to Norwich Gaol with a list of prisoners for transportation to Australia as part of the First Fleet. He called out the names of the prisoners. Susannah was on the list, but not her baby of course (for who knew of him?) or Henry Cabell. Susannah sobbed her heart out. She was devastated at the thought of leaving them both behind. John Simpson took pity on her for he was a kind man, and suggested that she bring the baby; they might let it on board, but Henry would have to wait. He would see what he could do to allow them to travel together.

John Simpson, the other turnkey and the women prisoners set off on their long and arduous journey across England by stage-coach from Norwich to Plymouth docks. As it neared nightfall each day, they stopped at an inn. John asked the first innkeeper: 'Do you have a room for the night for myself, and perhaps a barn or stable for the women prisoners?'

And the innkeeper would say: 'Yes I have a fine room for you with a good fire and good food and ale. There is a barn round the back of the inn where the women can sleep.'

The next day they travelled onwards and in the evening John asked the second innkeeper: 'Do you have a room for the night for myself, and perhaps a barn or stable for the women prisoners?'

And the innkeeper would say: 'Yes I have a fine room for you with a good fire and good food and ale. There is a barn round the back of the inn where the women can sleep.'

The next day they travelled onwards and towards dark, John asked the third innkeeper: 'Do you have a room for the night for myself, and perhaps a barn or stable for the women prisoners?'

And the innkeeper would say: 'Yes I have a fine room for you with a good fire and good food and ale. There is a barn round the back of the inn where the women can sleep.'

And so it went on until they reached Plymouth docks. They alighted from the stage-coach and headed up the gangplank The captain of their ship, a nasty piece of work, was shouting at the prisoners as they came on board. He stopped Susannah and said: 'You can't bring a baby on this ship. My papers say nothing about a baby! Get rid of it! Throw it overboard: it'll never survive the voyage anyway! More than my job's worth to carry a baby!'

Susannah broke into more weeping, and as she sobbed, kindly John Simpson came to the rescue again. 'Susannah, you have to get on board now! But give me the baby and I will ride to London and try to get permission for the three of you to travel together!'

Still weeping, Susannah kissed her baby and handed him to John, wondering if she would ever see her little boy again. John got the fastest horse he could and rode back to London, somehow managing to get the baby fed on the way. As he neared London he found the same inn again and asked the innkeeper if he knew of a good woman who had recently lost her own child who could look after the baby for a few days. The innkeeper did know of such a woman and John handed over the baby. He then rode on to the Home Secretary's grand house in central London, the home of Lord Sydney himself. He knocked on the door and the maid answered.

'Have you got an appointment? Lord Sydney is very busy.'

' No,' panted John. 'But please let me in! This is a matter of great urgency!'

He pushed past her into the hall. There a male secretary was writing at a desk. He turned to John in surprise, wondering what this strange travel-stained man was doing in the house. He was about to order him to leave when Lord Sydney, with his hat and silver-tipped cane, came down the grand staircase on his way to the club to dine. John turned to him and said: 'Please, my lord, I have to talk to you urgently about a case of great sorrow! Please listen to me!' And he told his tale of Henry and Susannah.

To his credit, Lord Sydney listened to every word. He mused aloud on the strength the young couple had shown so far, and how useful such a couple would be in the colonies, in the new empire that Britain was building across the world. He ordered his secretary to make three copies of papers authorising John to collect Henry from Norwich Gaol, and for the three to travel together to Australia. He ordered the maid to ask the head groom to prepare his fastest horse. He signed and sealed the documents and gave them to John, saying: 'Ride, man, as if your life depended on it! The First Fleet sails at the end of next week. You have just enough time to collect Henry and the baby and ride to Plymouth. Good luck, man!'

With that, he was off to his club, swinging his cane. John climbed on to the horse and it galloped swiftly as the wind. The governor of Norwich Gaol was surprised, but, on reading the document, let Henry go. The horse coped well with the two of them, but once back in London, John found another fast horse while Henry was reunited with his son. Then with John on one horse and Henry and the baby on the other, they rode hard for several days until they reached Plymouth docks. The captain could not believe his eyes when he saw the official letter, but he let Henry and the baby on board. Great was the rejoicing when the three of them were together again. Susannah cried for joy this time.

There is more to the story: the nine long months of difficult voyage to Botany Bay; the landing at this bleak and barren place; the legend of Henry carrying the Captain of the First Fleet, Captain Arthur Phillips, ashore, thus making himself the first white convict settler to set foot in Australia (this is the only bit that might not be true); the sailing on to Sydney Cove; the founding of the convict settlement; the four long hard years on half rations; Henry and Susannah's eventual freedom and respectability; his developing business interests of hotels and stage-coaches; their ten further children; their deaths in their eighties only a few months apart, to their eventual burial in the family vault. In 1968 on the 180th anniversary of the landing of the First Fleet, the first reunion was held in Australia which celebrated convict ancestry, with over 100 descendants of the Kabells (for that was how they spelled their name now) coming together in celebration.

Source: Adapted from Bellamy (1977)

Using this story in teaching

This is a tremendous story, full of possibilities for history and across the curriculum. The fact that it started in 1783 and hence does not obviously fit into an area of study at Key Stage 2 should not discourage anyone from using the story. Throughout the early part of the Victorian period, convicts were being transported to Australia for much the same kinds of crime as those committed by Henry and Susannah. Their case can serve as a particular instance of widespread events which are historical facts. The themes arising from this story are those of law and order, crime and punishment, how societies treat those who do not abide by their rules, and migration, enforced or otherwise, to far-distant countries. This, as well as being exciting history, is the very stuff of citizenship. The story can stimulate wide-ranging discussion in the immediate context on rules in the classroom or school and in the national context in considering how our society deals with those who break the rules. There is room for moral reflection too on whether it was right for Henry and Susannah to steal the things they did, and what drove them to steal. Finally, with its undertones of the Christmas story, of the convicts having only barns and stables to sleep in, and Susannah making that difficult journey with the baby, the story has enormous appeal. It taps into some of our deepest emotional feelings about love between adults, parental love and potential loss of both. Who cannot empathise with the plight of Henry and Susannah, thinking they will lose each other and their child? The story also generates astonishment at the severity of the legal justice system in the eighteenth and nineteenth centuries, as well as discussion as to why punishments were so harsh. What follows is a selection of activities which have been trialled on children, with examples of children's work, and an example session plan for the initial stimulus session.

A Year 6 class in a middle-class suburb

This class had been doing the Victorians, using mainly topic books and the internet to research information. They were highly motivated and enthusiastic, and well used to class discussion which their teacher handled with consummate skill. As soon as I saw this class on a school visit I was desperate to work with them. They were of mixed ability, with most at Level 4 in literacy and numeracy, but with a handful of very able pupils at Level 5 and above, as well as about eight pupils working either at or towards Level 3. I had two consecutive Friday mornings to work with them.

I started by telling them the story up to the point where John Simpson goes to Lord Sydney's house to ask for help. I stopped and told them they would find out how the story ended later that morning, but for now I wanted them to discuss in pairs or threes for one minute how they thought Lord Sydney would react to John's tale. As is usual, they came up with a variety of responses: that he would send John away without listening to the whole story; that he would listen kindly and allow all three, Henry, Susannah and the baby, to travel together; that he would send the convicts off together but adopt the baby who would grow up to be someone famous; that the good woman would keep the baby; and so forth. The children fed back their ideas to the whole class orally.

Next I explained that we were going to act out the story. There was much enthusiasm and many hands went up to try to claim leading roles. I told them everyone would have a part, that some involved many lines, some only a few lines, and some no lines at all. They could volunteer for what they wanted. I did not know the class, this being my first encounter with them. Thus the key roles went to a range of children, not just the most able. I had a number of small laminated role-cards ready to give out, one to each child. I revised the different scenes. I asked them to work in pairs at their tables for ten minutes to write down in draft some lines of dialogue they thought they might use as their characters. This was very interesting. For example, if one of the less able children had difficulty thinking of lines for themselves, and there were more able children at the same table who had roles as convicts without any speech, I found that after a few minutes, these children were working together to create dialogue: genuine co-operative group work. This preparation time was essential to the success of the drama.

We had the luxury of an empty classroom next door. I seated the children in a circle on the carpet. I explained where the different scenes would be: Norwich Gaol; London with the first inn and Lord Sydney's house; Salisbury with the second inn; Exeter with the third inn; and Plymouth docks where the First Fleet was waiting at anchor. All other scenes would be played out in the central area and children not involved in a scene would wait on the carpet until the right moment. I asked the children to move into position, the three innkeepers at their posts around the room, the captain at the docks, and the convicts (those children without speaking parts) in 'Norwich Gaol'. The teacher had a convict role-card so he settled down in the 'Gaol' with the children.

I explained further that this was not polished drama for the Christmas play, but drama for learning. We would act it out without stopping. If someone forgot their lines or what to do next, we could all help out. I would act as narrator if necessary. I gave a signal and we began. The children threw themselves into their roles and it went smoothly: some children consulting their jotters for their lines; others acting more confidently without their books. I came in as Lord Sydney (for only I knew the ending to the story) and acted his musing aloud, and then decided, for the sake of empire-building, that the three should travel together. The children cheered when they heard what 'Lord Sydney' had to say. It was very moving. The silence of the children at the end was testimony to the impact the story and drama had had on them. Then one girl broke the silence and turned to me: 'That was wonderful, Miss,' she said, 'Can we do it again?'

After this we returned to the children's classroom next door and I set the task of writing the story of the transports in their own words. This was to be completed for homework. I offered a written version of the story from my sources, and a page of extracts from a newspaper in the Norwich City Library Archives, on which the story was based. A few children asked if they could use the sources to help them, but most were immediately engaged in the writing task. An example of their stories is given in Figure 7.1. Betty Rosen has written extensively on the value of getting children to rewrite told stories, and readers are directed to her excellent books (Rosen, 1988, 1993). In writing a narrated story, children re-engage imaginatively with the story and add significant detail of their own, which shows both their understanding and interpretation of the story. It gives material for assessment of historical understanding. From the point of view of literacy, rewriting a narrated story releases children from having to deal simultaneously with the compositional and the secretarial aspects of writing. The story is already there in their minds and they can concentrate on getting it down on paper. The quality of the writing produced by these children was superb. A subsidiary purpose to the teaching had been to generate high-quality pieces of extended writing in Key Stage 2, an area of concern in literacy teaching identified by Ofsted (2000). I collected the stories into a book to share with the class.

Below is a list of all the follow-up work I did in those two mornings. Some items which involve music or documents are dealt with in more depth in other chapters (e.g. Chapters 4 and 10).

The Story of Henry and Susannah

This is a true story about two people called Henry and Susannah who fell in love.

Henry was a nineteen-year-old young man. He was very poor and worked all day as a farmer. One day as he was working his father and a man asked him if he wanted more food and clothes. Of course Henry said yes but he wasn't too sure when his father said they had to steal. His father somehow persuaded him that it will be worth it when they had luxurious food and clothes.

When Henry and his father and the man crept into the old dark building, they stole as many things that their hands could carry. Hangings from the four-poster bed. Pickled meat and lots of silk. They did not notice that there was a watchman watching them. . . . They were sent to the judge because of stealing and the judge said Henrys father and the man should be hanged, but Henry should be sent to a jail for 14 years.

Susannah was a nineteen-year-old maid. She had been working as a maid from the age of 14 and everyday she would cook dinner, clean cups and, mugs and spoons and knives and lots more cutlery. One day as she was polishing a spoon she thought of how much money she would make if she sold it. She decided to steal it and just as she was putting it in her pocket her mistress walked in Her Mistress was so ashamed of her because she trusted her. Susannah was sent to the judge and she too was sent to a jail for 14 years.

For the first few years, Henry and Susannah knew that they were both in love. They secretly got married and had a baby called Henry junior!

However, one day John Simpson came to the jail with a list of names. The names of those people were allowed to go Plymouth docks where they could go home. Susannah was on the list but Henry and the baby were not. Susannah begged to John Simpson that he could let her husband and baby come, but John said only the people on the list can come but the baby can come but I will try and get you all together.

It took Susannah and the baby many days to reach Plymouth docks and when they finally had there the chief of the boat refused to let the baby come on board. Susannah sobbed but Johns Simpson reassured her that he would look after her baby. Susannah finally got on the boat and John Simpson went back on his horse carrying the baby in one hand and the reigns in the other.

John Simpson went to London and hired a woman to look after the baby. Then, he went to Lord Sydney's office. Lord Sydney was a rich man and John thought that maybe if the judge listened to lord Sydney about the problem about Henry and Susannah then maybe the judge will let Henry free.

Anyway, John asked the secretary if he could speak to lord Sydney but he was going to a party and refused to listen. Simpson begged and finally lord Sydney gave in. Simpson told Lord Sydney everything, and right away Lord Sydney made his secretary write a letter to the judge saying Henry should be free. . . . The judge let Henry go.

Henry, Susannah, and Henry junior were all finally together and they were all so strong that they lived all through what had happened. They had 10 more children and Henry and his family were not poor anymore because Henry had a very highly paid job and when he died at the age of 82 Henry junior took his place!

The End

Figure 7.1 Children's work: The Story of Henry and Susannah

Follow-up work to the transports

- Playing dance and song tunes on melodeon and concertina, both Victorian inventions, treating them both as artefacts and as a means of experiencing and enjoying some of the music which the convicts took with them from England to Australia.

- Discussion on crime and punishment in Victorian times and in the present. Generating a list of crimes today and likely punishments: links to citizenship.

- Examining and interrogating gaol records for the local area for 1842 and 1857. Here I simply gave the children facsimiles of the original records with typed copies on the reverse and the children asked me questions about them ('Was neglecting your wife a crime in those days, Miss?' . . . It was and still is!). We were able to determine that in this area at least, punishments became more harsh between 1842 and 1857 by comparing crimes and punishments from both years.

- Examining individual prison records and creating such records for Henry and Susannah, with date and time arrested, crime, possessions and clothing.

- Singing and studying ballads of transportation such as 'Australia' (see Chapter 10). These were used as a means of corroborating evidence for the story of Henry and Susannah and as a model for writing in ballad form. After drawing their attention to the kinds of simple forms of four-line stanzas and second- and fourth-line rhyming, I set the task of writing the same story in ballad form. This was completed as homework, and the resulting ballads of Henry and Susannah were collected into a book as before. An example of their ballads is given in Figure 7.2.

- Using the picture *The Last of England* (Ford Madox Brown, 1855) as a focus for discussion on the voyage and its difficulties. This was an unplanned piece of teaching. A very able girl was typing up her story which ran to several pages, and her mother asked her what it was about. On hearing the story, the mother produced a colour copy of the picture to take in. We examined the evidence in the picture including items such as the cabbages hanging in nets around the side of the ship as a precaution against scurvy. The picture generated further interest and discussion, and was used on the front cover of the book of ballads written by the class.

- I gave the children internet references for the First Fleet, on which they could look up the names of those who sailed and the ships they sailed in. One of the sites lists Susannah but not Henry. I asked the children why this might be the case and they replied that Henry was not officially in that sailing. There is a wealth of information and evidence on the internet about the First Fleet (see e.g. www.wikipedia.org/wiki/First_Fleet http://www.pcug.org.au/~pdownes /dps/1stflt.htm . . . www.angelfire.com/country/AustralianHistory/firstfleet.htm).

Henry and Susannah

Henry is nineteen in age
And susannah the same
Both gonna do steeling
Both stupid and lame.

Thay're in the same torture
Thay've both been caught bradly
By sneaky knight watchman
His father Hung sadly.

They met in the prison
And soon fell in love
The baby came down
As is from above.

Susannah to go
And Henry to stay
But thats an unfortunate
Price to pay.

John simpson he said
He would come to their aid
So he rode back to London
And a promise was made.

They could all go together
So as they all set
A new life in Austrailia
Away from the lot.

And They All Lived Happily Ever After

Figure 7.2   Children's work: Henry and Susannah

How to tell stories in the primary classroom

This section includes information on: how to go about telling stories to primary-aged children; how to prepare stories for telling; ideas for activities after the telling; and adapting ideas for different age ranges.

For the telling of stories it is good to have the children grouped around you, facing you, and able to make eye contact with you. As we have seen, eye contact is an extremely important ingredient in storytelling. With younger children it is a simple matter to have them gathered on the carpet for storytelling. Older, larger children can present more problems. The choices are to have them at their desks, in which case you need to demand that they turn their chairs and face you, the teller, not their friends across the table. I often get children to move furniture and create a circle: this works very well. One can seat older, bigger children on the carpet, but the snag is that there is often not enough room. Furthermore the teller can be hemmed in by a sea of arms and legs, and be unable to move. Movement is not always essential to a good telling, but it can be an important ingredient. Gesture is vital and you need at least the space to do that without poking a child in the eye. It goes without saying that you need to ensure you have everyone's attention before starting. However, once you have begun the story, it is likely that you will hold their undivided attention. Even a difficult class can become spellbound and, if there are fidgets, eye contact comes in useful as a means of holding order and attention: a look is enough to stop unwanted activity.

With this particular story I mime: Henry hoeing in the fields in the bitter cold at the beginning; the burglary; Susannah polishing the silver and putting the spoon in her pocket; the judge taking his seat on the bench to pronounce sentence; Susannah holding her new baby; John Simpson reading from a list of female convicts; the journey, by going to three different children in different parts of the room and asking them for a room as if they were the innkeepers; the captain of the ship with his whip; John's desperate ride with the baby, and so on. I use movement and gesture liberally to help create the pictures in my listeners' minds. Storytelling in this way blends into drama and is truly an enactive representation of an historical situation.

Learning stories to tell is not a matter of learning them by heart. It does not work like that. The best explanation I have found is from Betty Rosen, who suggests that when we tell stories, it is like running a film in our heads. As tellers, we visualise the people and events of the story; as listeners, the audience do the same. The sequence of images unfolds like a film, a visual representation of the words of the story. Part of the magic lies in this re-creation of people and events. Thus in preparing for story-telling, one needs to have a sequence of events enriched by significant detail. I learned how to prepare stories for telling from Rosen's (1988) *And None of it was Nonsense* (Chapter 5, 'Selecting and preparing material for story telling'). She states a 'basic foursome' for preparation (see below). This is of course related to telling any kind of story, not just an historical one, but the foursome may be adapted for history.

Story preparation

1 Find a story you like massively: a story your imagination will relish, cherish and nourish.

2 Get all the facts and details together, even those you will later reject: there is a lot of lesson preparation involved, although, with luck, your pupils will never guess!

3 Decide what you are going to include, note it down in sequence and, in the process, consider particularly carefully how you are going to begin.

4 Visualise the start precisely; by this I mean allow the opening to occupy – take over – your imagination. This will go a long way towards ensuring that you will speak with your own voice a story that has become your own.

(Rosen, 1988, p. 54)

There is much that is useful here. Certainly when you start telling historical stories it helps to choose ones you like a great deal. It helps you to make them your own and assists the process of selecting events and details, and sequencing them for a telling. 'The Transports' was only the third story I ever told, and it helped that I had encountered the story as the basis for a folk opera while living in East Anglia in the 1970s. The first story was 'Demeter and Persephone', partly because it is a Greek myth likely to be used during a history study unit on the Ancient Greeks, and partly because I have always loved the story. The second was a self-devised story about a medieval peasant and the Abbey tax collector, told as part of fieldwork around St Albans Abbey (see Chapter 6, Figure 6.6). In all these cases I went through the process described by Rosen of selecting and rejecting material and sequencing it for a telling. I then select about eight points or scenes in the story and attach to them significant detail. There is an example of the skeleton of a story in Chapter 6 (p. 79).

Finally I work on the opening scene, and again there is an example of this in Chapter 6. When I first began telling stories I wrote them out in longhand, to have as an *aide-mémoire* when telling, but I soon realised that once launched into the story I did not need to consult the written versions. Now I find it enough to have the list of points and significant detail to hand, and to read it through before telling. Beginnings are so important that they need to be practised aloud. After several tellings, the tale becomes your own, and it is rare for you to need to keep referring to notes prior to telling the story. It will be different each time you tell it and that is no bad thing, for it means that the story is a living, organic entity, re-created each time it is told.

This sounds like a great deal of work, and in a sense it is. However, it is very valuable preparation for several reasons. In the process of selecting material for a story, you can read several different versions of historical events. This enhances your background knowledge of the period and gives you an understanding of the different interpretations of events. It also enables you to develop your own interpretation, your own telling of the story and your own historical understanding. From the point of view of developing in-depth subject knowledge, the process is invaluable. The next group of reasons are to do with the realities of preparation in the busy work of being a teacher. It is worth indulging in this kind of detailed preparation for storytelling as a kind of 'capital investment' for future teaching. Once prepared and told, a story stays with you and may be used over and over again on different groups of children. Thus what seems like a huge amount of work in the short term is in fact preparation for a lifetime's work of teaching. One need not have a story for every period of history told: in fact it is good practice to use the whole range of teaching approaches. However, a good story as part of a medium-term plan can serve as the inspiration and stimulus to good historical learning and teaching as well as learning in other parts of the curriculum.

There are many things one can do before, during or after a telling. Here is a selection:

- Before a telling, ask the children to fold a piece of A4 paper into eight by folding it in half lengthways and then crossways. They then unfold it and, as you tell the story, they draw a picture of a scene from the story in each of the eight squares. This gives the children a transference from the oral form into the visual or iconic form of representation (Bruner, 1970). Such a task can considerably aid subsequent written work.

- After a telling, children in Foundation Stage or Key Stage 1 can draw a sequence of pictures telling the story and write a caption for each one.

- Depending on age and ability, children in Key Stage 2 could draw either a comic strip of a story in cartoon form using speech and think bubbles, or a complete written narrative, as I did with 'The Transports'.

- Ask the children to write a version of the story from the point of view of one of the characters in it.

- Stop the story at a key point and ask the children to discuss in pairs what might have happened next: they then feed back their ideas to the whole group. This is very useful for engagement with the story and for getting the children's responses to it. This can lead into drama work.

- Tell the story and then introduce a piece of evidence which gives a different interpretation of events in the story (e.g. the story of Guy Fawkes first without and then with the Mounteagle letter).

- Tell the story and ask groups of children to prepare freeze frames of significant points in the story (see Chapter 8, 'Drama techniques'). These freeze frames may be performed one after another, making an enactive representation and interpretation of the story. This is also a form of expressive movement.

- Use the story simply as a springboard into discussion, whether of historical issues and concepts such as cause and consequence, change and continuity, or of moral, cultural and social issues.

- Once the story is secure in the children's minds, ask them to write it in poetic form.
- Ask the children to write letters or cards from one character in the story to another (rather after the fashion of the Ahlbergs' wonderful Jolly Postman books).

This is just a beginning. Once you have started telling stories as part of your history-teaching repertoire, you will have your own ideas about where to take them for the particular learners in your teaching context.

CHAPTER 8

Drama and role-play

Drama is the art form of social encounters and it offers a rich experience for learners. It also offers an opportunity to construct imaginary worlds from different times and cultures. It enables speculation, modification and transformation of our understanding through examining different people's perspectives, alternative possibilities and the consequences of our actions. Through drama one creates a situation with a set of human problems to be resolved in some way: thus it is invaluable as a way of teaching understanding of historical situations. Drama is a medium *par excellence* for teaching history. History is fundamentally about people: in examining evidence (e.g. artefacts and documents from the past), we are trying to get at the lives behind the evidence. Drama can help us to do this in three ways. First, it can act as a means for exploring material presented in stories, documents, artefacts and other forms of evidence through enactive representations of past events, lives and situations. Faced with the decisions which people had to make in the past (e.g. whether to flee the rebels marching on London to depose you as monarch, or to gather an army of loyal soldiers and face the rebels in battle), we can begin to understand the historical situation from the inside. The second value of drama lies in its engagement of the emotions. Through acting out a scene of Mary I consulting her advisers on whether to stand her ground or to flee, the participants in the drama as well as the observers experience or are privy to the emotions which might be felt by someone in such a crisis: fear, anger, anxiety, pride in oneself, a sense of duty to the country and inner strength in facing up to the danger. Finally, drama has very strong links with play. In enjoying imaginative play, children re-enact situations, both familiar ones such as school, and unfamiliar ones such as invasion by aliens from another planet, or knights guarding a castle. They will invent situations, allocate roles, create 'pretend' spaces for action (e.g. the forest, the spaceship), and suggest events and actions, literally making it up as they go along. In teaching through drama, teachers will be drawing on some of these processes and harnessing children's natural way of learning.

Beginning teachers quite often shy away from teaching approaches such as drama. There are good reasons for this. First of all, a beginning teacher has not always learned yet of the need to act, to perform, as an essential part of teaching. The main issue is behaviour management. It seems much easier and less risky as a beginning teacher to settle the class with a worksheet, keep them in their places, and avoid a potential riot. These are understandable fears and, with certain classes, one has to go through this kind of work, getting them to stay on task, to accept the boundaries of your behaviour management and learn to respect you. However I would make a plea to all beginning teachers to know something about drama as a teaching tool, and be ready to use it when they feel sufficiently confident to do so. The potential rewards in terms of enhancing the quality of teaching and learning are great. The good news for beginning teachers is that one does not need to attempt a whole class drama straight away. There are many varieties of drama-teaching techniques which one can use primarily for their own value in learning, but also as a means of experimenting with drama and building confidence as a teacher.

Drama techniques

- *Conversation*: Addressing a child as part of a storytelling as if that child is a character in the story. This has already been described in Chapter 7. The child does not have to respond, but through the act of addressing the child and making eye contact, it can draw children into the story through the immediacy of dialogue. This acts as a change of viewpoint in the story, which I prefer to liken to what happens in a ballad which may start off in the third person, but break into dialogue as emotion builds and the characters in the ballad express themselves verbally (see Chapter 10 for further ideas on using songs and ballads in teaching history).

- *Teacher in role*: The teacher takes on the point of view of someone else from the past, and performs a monologue (rather like Alan Bennett's *Talking Heads*). This can really serve as a means of bringing the past to life, taking children right into the heart of a historical situation as experienced by that one character. John Fines argues that the power of the teacher in role lies in 'being able to feed pupils information about the historical situation under consideration; helping the class gain confidence in taking on a role themselves' (Fines and Nichol, 1997, p. 196).

- *Hot-seating*: This is an extension of role-play in which the teacher stays in role as a character from history and invites the children to ask questions directly of that character. The children thus question or interview the historical character. This should be done before attempting to have the children prepare and take on such roles, as a kind of modelling of what is involved. The important point to note here is that it takes substantial preparation for the teacher to do this well, and the same holds true of children taking on historical roles.

- *Making maps or plans*: This is an approach described by John Fines (Fines and Nichol, 1997). It is a collective activity in which the class make decisions about a place or a building in which the drama will take place. As such it has something of the nature of play: that part of imaginative play in which children allocate roles and set out where the various scenes are going to be enacted. Like other approaches it can be adapted for a range of historical situations (e.g. re-creating an Anglo-Saxon village). From this it is an easy next stage to move children into role.

- *Still image/freeze frame*: This is a very useful approach which may be adapted to a range of teaching resources and historical situations. Pupils use their own bodies to 'freeze' a moment in time or a particular theme. It may be done with a whole class or with a small group of children. For example, as part of a sequence of activities designed to engage children with the painting *Children's Games* (Bruegel the elder, 1560), a class of Year 2 children were asked to study the picture and choose one of the games to represent as a freeze frame. A few minutes' preparation time were given to get into position. Then, at a pre-arranged signal, the children 'froze' in their poses and held them for a few moments to make a living re-creation of the picture (internet reference: http://www.artchive.com/artchive/B/bruegel/bruegel_childrens_games.jpg.html).

- *Active image*: Children use their own bodies to bring to life historical situations by reproducing the actions of the characters. For example, Year 3 children were shown a video of Vikings rowing up the Thames as part of their term's work on invaders and settlers. Their teacher drew an outline of the ship on the playground and the children got into position as Vikings rowing the ship. They rowed steadily, then 'rammed' the ship into 'London Bridge' in an attempt to destroy it, just as the Vikings had on the video.

- *Small group*: Fines termed this 'Forum theatre', a technique in which a small group of children act out part of a historical situation while the rest of the class act as observers and/or commentators. This can be useful for highlighting key moments in history, or just generally exploring a historical situation based on evidence or story. For example, with the Guy Fawkes story, a small group of children could act out the bringing of the Mounteagle letter to James I's secret agents and re-create the conversation at that point in time.

- *Overheard conversations*: These are conversations which add more information, but which we should not have been able to overhear; for example, Henry VIII meeting with spies to ask them to collect any information which would be useful to him in getting rid of Anne Boleyn. Cartoon pictures of the sort that feature in the Terry Deary books can be useful here, with the content of the speech bubbles blanked out for the children to suggest what the characters might be saying. From this starting point they can begin a dialogue or conversation which pairs or small groups can then act out.

- *Meetings*: This is a very useful approach in which the drama is rather formally set up as a meeting, as, for example, discussed in Chapter 13, where the children re-create the meeting held by the Iceni tribe to decide what to do when the Romans recalled the loan from Seneca. The comparative formality of the situation can lend structure to a drama. Giving a range of roles from those characters who will need to say a great deal, to those who may speak only once, or elect not to speak at all, provides scope for participation at a variety of levels and the possibility for the shyer, more inhibited children to take a lesser role. The teacher is also in role and can initiate the drama, but needs to allow the children to make suggestions and decisions.

- *Full drama enactment of a historical situation*: This is a very powerful teaching approach and, like all these approaches, can have a considerable impact on children's understanding of historical situations. An example is given in Chapter 7 of the re-enactment of the story of the transports to Australia. Rather like the meeting, but less formal in structure, the children are given role-cards and again the possibility of taking on greater or lesser roles. In this form of drama, some preparation time is needed to prepare lines and actions. The teacher should also be ready to take on a part, and it may be useful to choose a key role, especially if that character is privy to important and significant information on which the narrative of the drama hangs.

All of these techniques and approaches have their place in teaching history, depending on one's purposes for the lesson or sequence of work. In the next part of the chapter, a detailed example is given of one of these drama techniques to show the reader how to go about preparing and using it. Role-play has been selected because of its great value as a learning approach for understanding a character from the past.

Role-play and hot-seating

- Role-play is a particularly valuable teaching approach for history in the primary classroom.

- Although it features in several books about teaching history in the primary school, there is very little insight given into how to go about creating and performing a role-play.

- This chapter will give some examples of how a role-play was created from historical evidence, and its performance and follow-up work.

There is a thin dividing line between story and drama. In fact I like to think of story and drama as being part of a continuum of an extremely powerful form of representation: symbolic representation in the spoken language used in both; iconic representation in the images they create in the mind; and enactive representation through the medium of doing in drama, and personal re-creation in the mind of the narrator and listener in storytelling. Perhaps one of the reasons for their power and effectiveness in teaching is that they involve all three forms of representation simultaneously.

In performing a role-play, the teacher steps into the shoes of a character from the past and becomes that character. Like all the presentation of historical enquiry, it is only ever an interpretation of that person's feelings, thoughts, behaviour and motives. However, it can also present the flavour of a period, as well as the individual character, and to an extent the culture of that period. In role as a wealthy Roman lady, one can include material on the day-to-day problems of running a Roman household, or, as a Tudor sailor, one can introduce children to the realities of life on board a ship on a long voyage. One speaks to camera as it were, like one of Bennett's *Talking Heads*, Frankie Howerd in *Up Pompeii*, or Pauline Collins in *Shirley Valentine*. In doing so, one gives a kind of commentary on the times from that individual's viewpoint. This can be immensely useful in helping children to understand the reasons for events, the personal as well as the political beliefs, personalities and motivations which, for example, caused the split with Rome in Tudor times.

For a role-play it is essential to create a script, even though, as in storytelling, one does not learn it by heart or repeat it from memory. This is because creating and performing a role-play is something of a test of subject knowledge. I would always recommend that the children 'hot-seat' the character afterwards, for the following reasons:

- It prolongs the special (sometimes magical) atmosphere of the role-play.
- It allows children to probe the character's thoughts, feelings, beliefs and motivations.
- It makes possible 'interaction' between the children and the character from history.
- It can extend and deepen the content knowledge given in the role-play.
- It allows children to engage in historical enquiry, by asking their own questions of the character.

Role-play and hot-seating thus make particular demands on the teacher. It is quite possible to be asked questions to which one does not know the answer. Thorough preparation is essential. Not all the material researched will be used in the role-play script. On some occasions depending on the nature of the questioning, one draws on the additional information during the hot-seating. The value of this for the teacher is enormous. One gains from the research and preparation in depth a quality of subject knowledge of a period or problem which is not easily achieved by skimming a range of topics in juvenile books or from internet sites. In the preparation the teacher extends her or his second record (Hexter, 1972) through the interpretation of the material, transformation into the form of the script, and performance in the actual role-play. This second record is then made available to the children through the teacher's performance and the period of questioning.

For beginning teachers, the question is: How do I go about creating a role-play script? What follows is an example of a role-play which I created in response to the need to teach children about the hunger marchers of the 1930s in Britain. In most juvenile books this receives cursory treatment: a double-page spread with usually a photograph of the Jarrow marchers and an account of that march in 1936. To be fair to the producers of most of these books, their remit is to give a flavour of most aspects of a historical period or a past society. Thus each aspect of a culture tends to get a double-page spread. The problem with this kind of historical knowledge is that children (and teachers for that matter) are likely to emerge from the reading of it only with the fact that in 1936 some of the workers of Jarrow marched to London to protest at the loss of jobs and wages and the resultant hardship. The detail of what it was like to live in those times, and the understanding of the historical situation, the causes of the unemployment and the effect it had on working people's lives, are missing from the learning. It is hard to assimilate detail from these factual children's topic books; it is not easy to know about the detail of a past period or situation from a factual account. Turn it into a performed narrative, however, and the detail stays with us for much longer.

These follows the script of Thomas Unsworth, a Lancashire hunger marcher, which I researched, created and performed in 1998.

THOMAS UNSWORTH: A LANCASHIRE HUNGER MARCHER

Hullo, everyone. I'm just going to come in here and take me boots off, 'cos they don't half hurt. I hope you don't mind. I've been marching a long way and my feet really hurt. Why was I marching? Well, listen to this and I'll tell you.

My name is Thomas Unsworth and I come from Bolton in Lancashire. I work in the mill, or I used to. I'm a weaver by trade. I started on the power looms, but my masters saw I was a good worker and put me on the hand looms. I did well at first, met Annie, that's my wife, and we've got three little ones, Eva, Frank and Elsie. Everything seemed to be going so well. We'd got a little house to rent on Canal Street, and the children were growing up fine and strong. But then the hard times came. The boss came to me one day and said he was putting me on a short week, cutting my wages like. Well, that were bad enough, but then they said there was no work at all, and I had to tramp the streets, looking for work – me – a skilled craftsman. I couldn't get benefit to start with; there were some rules about waiting five weeks; so we managed somehow. Annie went out cleaning in them big houses by the park, but they paid her hardly anything, and I took the kids coal-picking on the slag heaps to get enough coal to keep us warm.

It wasn't just me and my family, you understand. There were thousands of us, all looking for work, walking the streets, going coal-picking. And it went on for months and months. The benefit wasn't enough, nowhere near enough. The government used to bring out these leaflets on how you could keep your family on so much a week, but we weren't getting even that. There were all sorts of rules, and there would be a gap like, when you got nowt at all. Folks were pretty desperate. Some blokes used to go out and dig the coal-dust from between sleepers of the old railway line that ran between the pit and the mills. If they were caught doing it, they were arrested and there was a fine of 10 shillings, which was a disaster to folk like us, as you can imagine. Blokes who'd got children who were suffering perhaps from flu or pneumonia, or old people suffering from TB, they would go scraping to get a little bit of coal. But they wouldn't beg. The greatest sufferers were the womenfolk, because they deprived themselves. I reckon that some of them went to an early grave because of the fact that they starved to death, because they'd give to us men, and the children, and starve themselves, and that's a fact.

Then we heard about this movement, the National Unemployed Workers' Committee or something. We just called it the movement. They was organising marches on London, not just from Bolton, but Manchester and Barrow, Newcastle, Scotland, Wales and Plymouth. We was going to march and lobby the government for full maintenance. On the morning of 31 October 1922 70 of us gathered in Victoria Square. There was lots of speeches and cheering. I said goodbye to Annie and the kids; it was going to be a while before we saw them again. We set off in good spirits and at Manchester, we met with the 200 men from Salford and Openshaw. They were not so well kitted out as us. It was cold and wet: the wind and rain soaked their poor underfed, poorly clothed bodies. We shared what we had with them, for the Right to Work Council of Bolton had raised funds to help us.

We knew it was going to be hard. We'd have to go to the workhouse in each town and ask the board of guardians for food and a bed for the night. Well, I say a bed; more often it was a heap of straw. And all we had to eat at first was bread and cheese. We had it for dinner at Stockport, supper at Macclesfield, and dinner again the next day. At Leek we actually had butter and jam to go with it – don't know who fixed that. But there was nowhere to sleep there and we had to bed down, there were three hundred and fifty of us by then, in the market square. At Ashbourne, things were grim. We had a desperate search for enough food, and so it went on. The worst place we came through was St Albans, they're a load of toffs there. They didn't support us and some of the younger men, the hotheads, got into fights and had to be arrested. But not me: I keep out of trouble. And that's what happened, that's why I was marching. All we ever wanted was either a proper job or enough money to keep ourselves and our families. We never wanted no trouble. I'll stop a while now – do you want to ask me any questions about it all?

Research, preparation and creation

I had browsed through a number of juvenile books on Britain since the 1930s and become interested in the hunger marchers. Here was a topic likely to appeal to children, for the themes of unemployment, hunger, deprivation and peaceful protest are, it would seem, universal in human life, as much with us across the world as in

Britain, in the twenty-first century. I did a library search and came up with six books (this in a university library). Five were about the Jarrow march and the sixth seemed more general: *The Hunger Marchers in Britain 1920–1940* (Kingston, 1982). This immediately intrigued me: did this mean that people were marching on London for *20 years*? None of the juvenile books had given any indication of such a thing. They had hinted at the fact that there had been other marches, but all attention was focused on the Jarrow march. What had been happening in 1920 to make people start marching then? And had it gone on until 1940? Twenty years is a long time for people to be protesting. From my own second record of family life, I knew that my mother had endured considerable hardship and unemployment in the years after she left the mill where she had worked as a weaver since leaving school. I ordered all six books and skim-read them as a preparatory task for the selection of material.

My original idea was to prepare a role-play as one of the Jarrow marchers. This was, after all, in the National Curriculum for history, though only as a suggestion. Then I realised that by choosing a different march on which to focus, I would also be teaching the fact that the marches went on for many years. Here the Preface to Kingston's book had some impact:

> The purpose of this book is to restore to the hunger marchers the place which they occupied during the interwar years and their proper place in the history of those times. The myth that Jarrow alone can represent the protest against unemployment needs to be dispelled. Whereas two hundred men marched from Jarrow on one occasion, the hunger marchers trudged to London from every corner of the land, from Devon as well as from Scotland, from Kent as well as from Wales, from Norfolk as well as from Lancashire, six times, and in their thousands. Behind those thousands were more thousands willing to march and many more thousands who aided the marchers' departure from their homes and their progress along the roads of Britain. The persistent protest, against all odds, of those ill-fed, ill-clad, ill-housed heroes – and heroines – of depression offers a sharp contrast with those shabby decades.
>
> (Kingston, 1982, p. 7)

I was hooked. I read the book from cover to cover, and if there had been time I would have tried to get hold of Wal Hannington's book, *Unemployed Struggles 1919–1936* (Hannington, 1977) to read further on this subject by someone who had taken part in a number of the marches. However, as all teachers know, time for preparation is finite, even though an infinite amount of preparation could go on. I began to consider which march I would choose. I was interested in the Devon march, as I had lived in Devon for a number of years and knew places mentioned on the march. I was also attracted to the women's march, as it is not generally known that women marched as well. In the end I selected the south Lancashire march of 1922, as I knew I could do the accent well, having been born there. The first paragraph introducing the character is invention: Unsworth was a common family name in my local village and Thomas was my grandfather's name. The other names were common first names of the period. The part about becoming a skilled hand loom weaver and going on short weeks is based on my mother's own experience in the cotton mills of Lancashire in the early part of this century. The rest is drawn from eyewitness accounts of the march in the Kingston book, by those either on the march or involved in its planning and support. Altogether it took about three days to do the reading, thinking and writing, but the end result was a role-play and hot-seating activity which has been used on numerous occasions with a range of audiences and ages. All have been drawn into the world of the 1920s and the 1930s, into the depression years and the hardships. The detail of people digging out coal-dust from between the railway sleepers, risking a fine to do so, is extremely poignant and very moving. The reality of this historical situation stays with the listener for a long time.

Follow-up work

After the role-play, the character can be hot-seated in role, and further information and understanding about the period and historical situation communicated. After this, there are a number of possibilities:

- Simply ask the children to write their story of Thomas Unsworth in their own words, either as prose for older children, or as captioned pictures for younger children.
- Create a series of freeze frames of different points in the story. Brainstorm with the children as to what these should be and select children to prepare each one. Perform them as a sequence.
- Offer small pieces of primary evidence from books of the period: eyewitness accounts, diaries and journals, newspaper articles about the marches. Ask the children to look for sentences which confirm Thomas Unsworth's story.
- Show the children some examples of ballad forms and ask them to write the story as a song or poem.
- Ask the children to prepare the speech which the leader of Thomas' march would have made to the prime minister when they arrived in London to hand in their petition.
- Ask the children what is worth marching for in their lives. What wrongs would they like to see righted? What is a good basic standard of living for everyone?
- Show the children a map of England with the physical features and place-names of those towns through which the marchers passed. Ask them to plan the marchers' journey. Which places might they avoid on the return journey and where might they stay instead?

Such a story lends itself to citizenship activities as well as to history, drama, music and English. It may seem like a great deal of work, but the rewards in terms of children's learning and the establishment of such a story in one's teaching repertoire are great. This chapter has presented a very brief introduction to drama in history. Readers are encouraged to try out some of the ideas and indeed use the example of this role-play to make a start on using drama in their teaching. This chapter should help to demystify some of the processes of developing drama for learning with children.

CHAPTER 9

Simulations and games

Enquiry is a major part of the fundamental syntactic structures of history, but since so much historical evidence is incomplete, humans tend to 'fill in the gaps' by re-creating past events and periods through imaginative reconstructions of the past. This can be a powerful teaching tool as well as a genuine aspect of history. This chapter deals with simulations and games as particular forms of imaginative reconstruction. They are examples of enactive representations of historical situations, and as such are immensely valuable in making even quite complex situations accessible to children of differing educational needs and attainment. Through simulations and games, as in drama and role-play, children can understand historical situations 'from the inside'. They have something in common with drama and play, to which they are closely related. In both simulation and drama children can take on the roles of characters from the past and face the same problems, struggle with making the same kinds of decisions, and deal with the consequences of their actions. Like drama, simulation can engage the emotions and stimulate the imagination. It is, however, more controlled than drama. In a simulation the teacher preparing the material adheres much more closely to the historical situation, whereas in drama there is more freedom for the children to take the story or situation where they want it to go. For beginning teachers, simulations are probably easier than drama to handle. They can be done often with children safely in their seats, although in a simulation involving message sending, there may be some movement around the classroom, but this can be easily controlled. This chapter presents: an example of a simulation; ideas for devising your own and accessing those already written; examples of how to use games in history; and historical computer games in children's learning.

Example of a simulation

Cortez and the conquest of the Aztec Empire

Teaching and class management
In this kind of simulation, there are a number of rounds. An example round is shown in Figure 9.1 and further rounds from this simulation in the Appendix. The idea is that new

Spanish: Round 1

You are Cortez, leader of the Spanish expedition sent by Velasquez, Governor of Cuba, to explore, trade and search for Christian captives in Yucatan and the Gulf of Mexico. You hear rumours that Velasquez thinks you are too ambitious and plans to have you removed from the expedition.

Do you:

1   Carry on getting your ships ready and not worry about Velasquez?

2   Cut short your preparations and sail for Yucatan?

Aztecs: Round 1

You are Montezuma, ruler of the great Aztec Empire, which comprises several different tribes. You hear stories of many signs and omens that the god Quetzelcoatl is returning to take back the Empire from you. A mountain has been seen moving on the waters of the Gulf: a Spanish ship. You believe that the white men are signs that the god Quetzelcoatl has come back.

Do you:

3   Send supplies of food and presents to the Spanish?

4   Send a small army to deal with the Spanish invaders?

Consequences sheet: Round 1
Spanish Aztec

1	3	*Cortez*: You have to deal with a group of soldiers who come to remove you from the ships. This delays you and you lose some men, but you set off. *Montezuma*: Because you do not attack the Spanish, you weaken your position for the future. Spanish lose 10 men; Aztecs lose 5000.
1	4	*Cortez*: You have to deal with a group of soldiers who come to remove you from the ships. This delays you and you lose some men, but you set off. *Montezuma*: Your army attacks the Spanish port of Veracruz and kills some of the Spanish force. Spanish lose 25 men; Aztecs lose 5.
2	3	*Cortez*: you sail away early with your 11 ships and avoid Velasquez' men. *Montezuma*: Because you do not attack the Spanish, you weaken your position for the future. Spanish lose 0 men; Aztecs lose 5000.
2	4	*Cortez*: you sail away early with your 11 ships and avoid Velasquez' men. *Montezuma*: Your army attacks the Spanish port of Veracruz and kills some of the Spanish force. Spanish lose 2 men; Aztecs lose 5.

Figure 9.1   Cortez and the conquest of the Aztecs

Blank outline:

Spanish Round 1 decision

We chose: (Number of decision)

Decision in full

The Aztecs chose: (Number of decision)

Decision in full

The consequence was:

Filled in example:

Spanish Round 1 decision

We chose: 2

2 Decision in full: Cut short your preparations and sail for Yucatan.

The Aztecs chose: 3

Decision in full: Send supplies of food and presents to the Spanish.

The consequence was:

2 3 *Cortez*: you sail away early with your 11 ships and avoid Velasquez' men.
Montezuma: Because you do not attack the Spanish, you weaken your position for the future.

Spanish lose 0 men; Aztecs lose 5000

Figure 9.2   Example of a simulation decision sheet

information is given to the children in each round, and they have to make a decision as to what to do next. The children then get a consequence sheet to show the outcome of their decision. Divide your children into groups of four. At each table have one pair who represent the Spanish and one pair who represent the Aztecs. Tell the children there will be five rounds. In each round they will receive certain information about the historical situation and they have to make a decision about what to do. It is a good idea to read through each round sheet and each consequence sheet with the whole class and to write the difficult names and who they are (leaders, gods, tribes, places) on the board before-hand. They write down their decision on a decision sheet, an example of which is given in Figure 9.2 (you can have enough made up for the class headed up as either the Spanish or the Aztecs, with spaces for the children to write down the consequence and the number of men lost). They then have to keep their decision secret from the other pair until they receive the consequence sheet for that round. After each round the children receive a consequence sheet which tells them what has happened as a result of their decisions. The two decisions, Spanish and Aztec, have to be taken together. The consequence sheets also give the numbers of Spanish soldiers lost and the number of Aztec soldiers lost. At the end of the simulation the children can add up the points and see which teams have lost the fewest or the most soldiers. They also have in their decision sheets a record of what decisions they took and the consequences of those decisions.

At the start of this simulation the Spanish have 500 men and the Aztecs have 100,000. It looks impossible for the Spanish to conquer the Aztec Empire but they have some points in their favour. The empire is composed of several tribes, some of whom would quite like Montezuma to be toppled from his position as emperor. Thus some of the 100,000 Aztecs at times swing over to the Spanish side and support them.

This is very useful as a teaching tool. The children become very engaged in the simulation, waiting eagerly to find out what the outcome of their decision will be. At the same time, they are being introduced to the information, based on evidence, as to the events of the conquest, and, through engaging with the material in the decision-making process, gain a deeper understanding of the events than they would have from reading the words on the page or watching a video reconstruction. The material also reveals the sheer difficulty of the task facing Cortez and the amazing turn of events as two very different cultures came into contact for the first time. In reading about the conquest, one skims over months and years of time in a few moments. However, in doing the simulation, some effect of the passage of time takes place, even though it is a scaled-down representation of the actual time frame of these events. One begins to understand that like many invasions and conquests, it didn't all happen overnight. The simulation is a good representation of the time, the difficulty, the decision-making and the consequence of one's actions.

Ideas for devising your own simulation and accessing those already written

It is perhaps helpful to explain how I went about creating the Aztec simulation. I had previously used other simulations devised by Nichol and the Nuffield Primary History Team (Fines and Nichol, 1997; Nichol and Dean, 1997), in particular the Spanish Armada simulation available from the Nuffield Primary History website. I had the pattern of the sequence of rounds and outcomes to use as a framework for this simulation. I then looked for sources of the evidence to use for the information in each round. At the Aztecs exhibition at the Royal Academy in 2002, I bought just two books. One was the exhibition catalogue, full of colour reproductions of Aztec remains, including artefacts of all sorts, codexes, pictures and background information on each item in the exhibition. The other, a book, was *The Aztecs: Rise and Fall of an Empire* (Gruzinski, 1992), which contained a mixture of primary and secondary sources. The primary sources included pictures and many documents: poems translated from native Aztec languages; myths and legends; letters written by Hernando Cortez himself; and other documents. These are the only two sources I use in teaching the Aztecs, in keeping with the Nuffield principle of economy of sources. The catalogue provides colour pictures for a variety of purposes, and the documents are useful as evidence for the simulation and for other purposes. Using the evidence from this book, I created the simulation by selecting five key points in the story at which each leader would have to make a decision. The Armada simulation by Nichol has three decisions per round: I restricted this to two to make it simpler. In including the information I tried as far as possible to use materials from the primary evidence, thus maintaining closeness to the historical situation. As a final stage I went through the simulation and made a numerical tally of how many men each side lost in each round and established that there would still be some Spanish left over at the end of five rounds. This was more of an acute problem for the Spanish, as they had only 500 men to start with (though they did gain several thousand allies from the natives). The Aztecs probably had several million, but I kept it down to 100,000 to offer a contrast in the numbers on each side and to give an idea of how heavily the Spanish were outnumbered. The tally is important, for one does not want to be in the middle of a simulation and have children complain they have run out of soldiers on their side!

This is just one kind of simulation and there are others. The Armada has already been mentioned and there is another excellent one in Fines and Nichol (1997) of an Anglo-Saxon village's farming year. This is based on a country life simulation and on the idea of having a number of families in a village. Each family has two chance cards for each season of spring and autumn, with two major changes which each family has to face. Each pair or group of children in the class becomes a family. The cards always have a problem happening to them such as loss of crops, illness or injury, and a good thing, such as a glut of crops or animals. The children have to send messages or negotiate orally with the other families to solve their problems. In doing this simulation with children, it has become apparent to me that the game also deals with issues of citizenship and community, for it is very clear that each family in the village is dependent on the other families. Without mutual dependence and support, some families would starve. Yet another kind of simulation is a planning spaces type of simulation, an example of which is given in Chapter 6, whereby the children plan out an abbey or a new grand mansion. This type of simulation, of planning spaces, may be used in a variety of ways (e.g. mapping out houses, churches, castles, palaces, marketplaces, temples, railways, villages, towns, or a labyrinth for the Minotaur).

Whatever type of simulation one uses, whether it is planning spaces, sequences of events, or one involving chance cards, the principles are always the same. Simulations have three elements: 'the historical situation; the roles of the characters involved, and the problem they have to face and have to resolve' (Fines and Nichol, 1997, p. 203). The historical situation is both the context and the material to be understood: a detailed description of the situation, the people, the place, the problems and possible solutions. Some situations or places have common elements, for example, Roman towns or castles. Teachers and children can use their knowledge of these elements to plan out a particular example. Simulations require that children take on roles, as in the examples given in this chapter. Each role needs to be described in sufficient detail for the player to take realistic decisions, and this can be done by different means: laminated role-cards with sufficient information (an example is given in Chapter 6); the kinds of decision information sheets used in the Aztec simulation in this chapter; or planning the roles in the case of creating a village with a number of different families. There must always be a problem or a series of problems to be solved.

In fact the key to historical simulations is putting the children in role as decision-makers. Instead of children being passive recipients of information, they have to work with the information given in the simulation to make it their own. In terms of schema theory, they are actively engaging with the material to be learned, assimilating it and, through the decision-making process, accommodating it to their schema, or mental maps of the world. They re-enact or re-create past moments in time, such as Cortez's decision to sink his ships so that the Spanish had nowhere to go except onwards to Tenochtitlan, and Montezuma's decision, heavily influenced by his religion and particular worldview, to greet the invading Spanish as gods rather than men. Through taking the decision themselves, they come to understand the consequence of that decision. This is a powerful way of teaching about cause and consequence. The strength of this teaching approach lies in its handing over to the children the power to make decisions. An analogy may be drawn here with the idea of Seymour Papert, who, in writing about children using Logo (a particular kind of computer language), stated that it handed the control in learning back to the children (Papert, 1980). Instead of children responding to what the computer does, they are the ones making the decisions and giving the commands. This is true of both historical simulations and certain types of computer games, between which close links can be made.

Using games in teaching history

There are two ways in which one can use games in teaching history. The first is through playing historical games devised by the teacher, or produced commercially, as a means to learning particular factual information, concepts, skills, processes, values and attitudes. The difference with games as opposed to simulations is that the children have slightly less control. For example, if the moves in the game are controlled by dice, spinners or the toss of a coin, then some element of decision-making is removed and much more is dependent upon chance, which also plays a role in historical causation and consequence. The second is getting the children to devise their own games, as in the example given in Cameo 3 in Chapter 1. Both are valuable.

Teachers and commercial games

Again, a major architect of playing games with children is Jon Nichol. I have used his Anglo-Saxon invasion game in both its guises, the simple, shorter version and the ten-round version, with both intending teachers and children, and it works extremely well. Jon's creation does not appear in this book, but the principles can be summarised (and see Nichol, 1979). The children are shown a map of the eastern part of England from Kent up to Lincolnshire, stretching as far as Hampshire in the southern centre of the country. It is marked out in small squares and on one of each of five squares is the name of an Anglo-Saxon tribe: East Saxons, South Saxons, Anglos, Friesians and Jutes. The children play it in groups of five, each child taking on the role of one tribe. Depending on the toss of a coin, they can settle on a number of squares according to an information sheet which gives a kind of chronicle of events over 250 years of Anglo-Saxon settlement. The information sheet also sets out the rules of the game as to which squares can be taken, working rather like the game of dots and lines I used to play as a child. At the end of each round, each child writes down what happened in that round, a positive event which allows them to settle many squares, or a negative event such as a lost battle or illness, which means they settle few or no squares. The writing down of the event, good or bad, creates for each child a kind of Anglo-Saxon chronicle. Thus the activity is useful for literacy, in the reading of the instructions and working in the instruction genre, and in the making of the chronicle. For history it is immensely valuable, since it teaches concepts of invasion and settlement through an enactive representation. It also teaches that the processes of invasion and settlement by the Anglo-Saxons were gradual and occurred over hundreds of years. Sometimes they gained much ground; at other times settlement was constrained by circumstances. Again the game is a good representation of the notion of gradual settlement. Children learn too that it wasn't just one tribe, but five different tribes who settled in Britain from different parts of northern Europe. Even those children with literacy difficulties can join in with tossing a coin and marking captured squares, though they may need help in writing their chronicle.

The contrast between this game for teaching concepts of invasion and settlement and those recommended in the QCA's Schemes of Work could not be more obvious. Figure 9.3 shows what Unit 6B has to offer (and Units 6A and 6C on the Romans and the Vikings in Britain start with the same two identical lessons).

The first suggested teaching activity is quite a good idea, namely to relate concepts of moving for various reasons by ourselves and our families to concepts about whole groups of people migrating in earlier times. But as the author of the unit points out, this would have to be handled with sensitivity and care, especially if there are any refugee children in the class. This is not to argue that one should not do this kind of work with children, only that there are alternatives. Instead, storytelling about a character from Roman, Anglo-Saxon or Viking times could introduce children to the key concepts of settlement, emigration, immigration, refugees, invasion and conquest. The activities suggest that teachers take opportunities to use and explain these terms. Explanations without representations of any kind are far less likely to be either understood or assimilated into children's schema.

Lesson 1

Objectives

Children should learn:
- to relate their own experience to the concept of settlement
- to recognise that people have been moving between different areas for a long time, and that some reasons for moving were the same as those of people alive today

Possible teaching activities

Discuss the children's and their families' experiences of moving home to live either in a different part of the country or in a different country. Use a map to establish where they moved to and from. Encourage the children to suggest why they or their families moved, and list the reasons given. Help them to sort the reasons into those where families chose to move and where they had to move.

Take opportunities to use and explain words such as *settlement, emigration, immigration, refugee*, and how these are different from words such as *invasion, conquest*.

Lesson 2

Children should learn:
- to use the terms 'invade' and 'settle'
- to place the Anglo-Saxon period in a chronological framework
- to recognise characteristics that place Anglo-Saxons as having lived a long time ago in the past
- that Anglo-Saxons invaded Britain and that the period of invasion was followed by a period of settlement

Possible teaching activities

Ask the children to find the dictionary definitions of the words 'invade' and 'settle'. Ask them to write their definitions in a two-column grid. Lead a discussion to develop the children's understanding of these terms.

Give the children cards with words and phrases that could be connected to either invasion or settlement (*e.g. stay, arrive, conquer, land, visit, remain*). Ask the children to place the cards in the correct columns on their grids. Ask them for feedback as to where they placed each word and why.

Establish that groups of people have been visiting, invading and settling in Britain for a very long time. Ask the children to look at the class timeline and pick out the people and events they have already learned about (*e.g. the Great Fire, Florence Nightingale*). Discuss with the children whether these people or events happened a long time ago, and which occurred the longest time ago.

Give the children pictures of Anglo-Saxon people. Encourage them to suggest clues which indicate that these people lived a long time ago. Help the children to place the pictures at the appropriate place on the timeline.

Give the children pictures showing a variety of Anglo-Saxon images (*e.g. in armour, in battle, town life, country life, home life*). Ask the children to sort them into invasion and settlement groupings. *Source*: QCA/DfEE (1998)

Figure 9.3   Extract from QCA scheme of work for the Anglo-Saxons (6B)

The second teaching activity is frankly dull, and has much more to do with literacy out of context than it does with history and literacy in a meaningful context. The initial activity has children looking for dictionary definitions of the words 'invade' and 'settle'. The teacher then has to 'lead a discussion to develop children's understanding of these terms'. The next activity is a sorting activity of words and phrases, placing the cards with key words on them in one of two columns, 'invade' and 'settle'. This activity seems to me to have very little to do with history, being a word-sorting task. The whole of this part of the lesson seems to be based on an understanding of teaching as telling and explaining, without a single representation in sight. The next part veers off into chronological work, trying to place the period of Anglo-Saxon settlement on to the class timeline. The difficulties of teaching time are explored in Chapter 12, and I would suggest that the method in the QCA scheme may not be very helpful. It might be better to concentrate on the 250 years or so of Anglo-Saxon settlement. In addition, this is too much for one lesson. It is better to teach a few concepts well, rather than try to include too much. Despite this, there is more: pictures of Anglo-Saxon people (with no indication that these artists' images of people from the past are based on any kind of evidence) for children to look for clues that these people lived a long time ago; and to place on the timeline images of Anglo-Saxons previously sorted into 'invade' and 'settle' groupings; and a final 'discussion' with the children on the relationship between 'invasion' and 'settlement'. Apart from the dullness of all this and its heavy literacy focus, it is doubtful whether all children in the class would benefit from such activities. In contrast, the Anglo-Saxon settlement game teaches concepts of 'invasion' and 'settlement' much more powerfully through an enactive representation: the children themselves become the invading and settling tribes.

The idea behind this kind of game may be adapted for other invasions and settlement periods in British history, and for parts of other study units. In fact, other games which have invasion as part of the intrinsic nature of the game, such as chess or chequers, may also be adapted. It is also possible to create games based on 'trail' games, whereby players follow a trail, using a dice to establish moves. These games can be a representation of time, of various concepts and of factual information. They might incorporate 'chance cards' such as those one finds in 'Monopoly', treasure cards (status symbols as in the 'Game of Life'), and decision-making (again, the 'Game of Life', in which, at the outset, one has to decide whether or not to go to university). The whole point about games, as with simulations, is that children have to play the role of someone else (in a historical game, a character from history), and to enter fully into the historical situation. The game itself supplies the problems to be faced.

Commercial games which are widely available are also useful for teaching some historical knowledge, skills and processes. There are too many to list here but mention of a few should indicate the possibilities. Games such as 'Guess Who' introduce processes of reasoning, deduction and elimination to children. 'Cluedo' and other murder games can operate in the same way. Journey games such as 'Journey Through Britain' involve travelling to a number of locations in the British Isles, and answering,

'Trivial Pursuit' style, one of several questions, many of which are historical. This kind of game can teach outline or background knowledge, which can be dismissed as trivia, but none the less some outline knowledge can be useful as a context against which to place a study in depth. Both are required in the History National Curriculum. There are also traditional ancient games, such as 'Tabla', a reproduction of a Roman game available commercially, which children can play to gain an understanding of one way of occupying leisure time for Roman peoples.

An investigation of types of board games and ways of playing can prepare the ground for children designing and making their own games, as in Cameo 3 (Chapter 1), which involved the children making their own board game of Drake's voyage around the world. This may be adapted for other events and other periods, for example, Cortez's conquest of the Aztecs, Odysseus' travels, Boudicca's rebellion and so on. All of these game-designing activities require that children engage actively with the historical situation, and with the problems faced by characters in the past. Through the act of knowledge transfer from one genre such as a story or a timeline, into another, that of the board game, children engage with the material to be learned. When I have done the Drake board game activity with children, the enthusiastic response of the children has been remarkable. Such enthusiasm and enjoyment can be harnessed to learning what such activities have to offer. Once made, the games can become class resources, or may be used by other classes. I would also suggest that a selection of board games, for developing historical knowledge, skills and processes, be kept in the classroom as an essential teaching resource, as well as valuable activities for children to do once other work is completed.

Historical computer games

Properly speaking, it should be my children writing this section rather than myself, since they have field-tested several useful games. The kind of games I am thinking of are commercial ones such as 'Settlers', Pharaoh' and 'Cultures', rather than some of the software produced especially for the schools market. Some of the schools games are rather dull and pedestrian, and can unwittingly shift the focus from historical learning to navigation of the screens because of the design of the game. Neither do I mean the sort of game in which one merely has to collect information. In contrast, some of the commercial games replicate the best features of simulation and board games. They usually involve the player in role, having to face problems within the historical situation, and making decisions. For example, 'Cultures' is set in AD 1050 and features a group of Vikings settling in America, trading and fighting with other Viking tribes and three races, the Mayans, Indians and Eskimos. They have a range of landscapes in which to operate in the wider context of the game, thirty different occupational groups and all the elements of resource management, trading, military operations, diplomacy and discovery. There is a detailed booklet setting out how to play, and there are many different scenarios and problems. One's success as a player depends upon one's ability to balance the wider strategic demands of the game with the needs and wants of the individual members of one's clan. This is a simulation on a huge scale. 'Settlers' is similar, with the possibility of settling different peoples in history, such as the Romans, Anglo-Saxons and Vikings. 'Pharaoh' does something very much the same, only in Ancient Egyptian times. If I had any doubts about children playing these games, they were dispelled by overhearing a conversation as one child sat at the keyboard:

Eleanor:	I don't know what's the matter here. I can't get my crops to grow!
Harriet [peering at the screen]:	Oh, I see what it is. Your Nile didn't flood properly! Your crops won't grow if the Nile doesn't flood.

It seems to me that the game was teaching, among other things, the fundamental importance of the Nile to Egyptian agriculture, the economy, the well-being of the people and ultimately the culture of Ancient Egypt itself. This is one use of ICT which I think is entirely appropriate to history. Much more complex simulations may be done with computer games than those prepared by teachers, though both are valuable. In teacher-made simulations and games, one involves the whole class with all the advantages of social learning this brings. The snag with computer games is that they are typically for one or two players, although some have scope for multi-player operation. I would still argue that having a selection of such games in the classroom, and having children playing them as extension activities, with reporting back to the whole class, is a valuable approach in enhancing children's learning.

CHAPTER 10

Music and dance

Introduction: why music?

Music is a fundamental aspect of every human culture. It does not matter where one goes in the world, there will always be music, song and dance. To understand fully a past society or culture, one needs to know something of that culture's music, song and dance. Music is so important that people take their music with them to wherever they are transported, as slaves or prisoners; or as emigrants seeking a better life or fleeing from religious or racial persecution. One obvious example is that of the black African slaves shipped to the Americas, bringing with them their African rhythms, song and dance traditions. These in turn became synthesised into country and urban blues using the guitar, an instrument which was introduced to parts of America from Spain through that country's exploration, conquering and dominance over the native indigenous cultures. From this rich melting-pot sprang rhythm and blues, rock and roll, Elvis Presley (the first white singer with a 'black voice'), rock music, reggae, and ultimately much Western popular music of the twentieth and twenty-first centuries, far removed though it may seem in some of its more sugary or formulaic manifestations. Music fulfils a basic human need for self-expression through sound and rhythm. It can also act as a vehicle for communication when other forms are banned or frowned upon, serving a political and social purpose, as in the case of the black South African miners, who, forbidden to drum in the traditional way by their white mine-owner bosses, devised a form of drumming on their gumboots which they wore in the mines. Thus the gumboot dance was born, a highly intricate form of dance in which the miners beat out traditional rhythms in patterns of movement. Their bosses could not punish them for this, since they were not using drums! These same miners also sing in the kind of four-part harmony – soprano, alto, tenor and bass – learned from white Christian missionaries in their schools and churches, an aspect of white high (and low) art culture transported to Africa during the eighteenth and nineteenth centuries. Wherever people go, in time and place, they take their music with them.

This chapter deals with how to use music, song and dance in teaching history. It is not so much concerned with the performance aspect of these forms of expression, as with their use and value in the primary curriculum. This is not to say that performance is of no importance; only that in history teaching one is much more interested in songs, music and dance as historical evidence, as artefacts made by people for a variety of purposes: to express a mood or feeling; to communicate emotion; in celebration of customs or rituals which are central features of a culture (e.g. carols in European societies, or circumcision party songs in Madagascar); to act as social commentary on the times; to give a personal response to wars and disasters of all sorts; and a host of other purposes. Thus this chapter presents: arguments for using the value of music in the teaching of history; links to storytelling, drama and expressive movement; examples of suitable songs, music and dance for the primary age range; a case study example of using music with children as historical evidence; planning and class management of such lessons; follow-up work; and sources. Most books which aim to guide beginning teachers in teaching history give some general suggestions for the use of music in teaching. However, there is very little guidance given in how to use such music with children. This chapter is different. It gives detailed guidance on how to use a range of songs, music and dance with children, even if one is not a music specialist.

The value of music in history

There are several arguments for using music in history. The first and most important one is given in the introduction to this chapter, namely the central part played by music in all cultures across time and place. If one regards history as an umbrella discipline (Cooper, 1992, 2000), embracing all aspects of a culture including science, technology, art and craft, language and literature, religious beliefs, customs and practices, social and political aspects and music, then music is as deserving of our attention as any other aspect. Of course there is the role of historical significance to consider in the selection of historical content and processes to be taught, but music has a part to play in helping us and children to understand what life was like in the past. Music, dance and song are evidence from the past: a sea-shanty to help sailors with the labour of raising sail or anchor; a waulking song from the Hebrides used by weavers making Harris tweed; a love-song lamenting a loved one going off to war; or a courtly dance. Music in all its forms can tell us something about a past society, ways of thinking, and the kinds of instruments and musical forms used. Through the re-enactment of the song tune or dance, children can gain access to the minds and emotions of people from the past. They can enter imaginatively into what it might have been like to be a sailor, a soldier or a maidservant. Finally, children can present their understanding of the past through music: a song, a dance or a composition.

The next set of reasons are to do with children's learning. Theories of children's learning are dealt with in greater depth in Chapter 2, but some brief mention is required here. Children learn in different ways: their learning is individual and idiosyncratic, related to personality and cognitive development. Two of the most important theories in this context are Bruner's theory of mental representation (Bruner, 1970), and Gardner's theory of multiple intelligences (Gardner, 1983, 1993a). The notion of there being three ways of representing the world mentally – enactive, iconic and symbolic representation – was explored in Chapter 2. Gardner introduced the notion of there being eight intelligences: linguistic; musical; logical-mathematical; spatial; bodily-kinaesthetic; interpersonal; intrapersonal; and naturalist. In terms of Gardner's multiple intelligences, it follows that some children in each class will have a predisposition towards musical intelligence in their individual combination of intelligences; therefore one needs to provide for children who learn primarily through this channel. Music is a powerful form of enactive and symbolic representation with the additional advantage that it engages people simultaneously through the intellect and through emotions. One only has to think of how the makers of, for example, romantic movies employ this knowledge to their advantage, to heighten emotion at key points in a story. In short, music can be seen to reach parts of children other parts of the curriculum do not reach. In terms of teaching for diversity and for inclusion we omit music at our peril, since we ignore its huge potential for enhancing learning among a wide range of learners.

The final reason is in some ways the least important, though its statutory force would seem to render it the most important reason for the inclusion of music, both as a teaching approach and a form of evidence. The History National Curriculum (HNC) (DES, 1991; DES/QCA, 1995; DfEE, 1999c) requires it. Since the inception of the HNC, it has always been a requirement, one of a range of forms of historical evidence considered appropriate for historical enquiry by primary age children.

Links to storytelling, drama and expressive movement

One of the main forms of music considered in this chapter for use in the primary curriculum is British traditional folk-song. There are good reasons for this. Folk-song was composed by ordinary people for an audience of ordinary people. British traditional folk-song encompasses a wide range of songs: ballads, shorter lyrical songs, work songs, songs of political commentary, love-songs, songs which tell of how political events in the wider world impinged upon the lives of ordinary people, broadside ballads giving news of the latest horrible murder (thus fulfilling the role of the tabloids in relaying atrocities, disasters, murders and salacious stories), and songs of ritual and ceremony. They are an incredibly rich resource, a kind of underground music of the British Isles and deserving of everyone's attention.

There are strong links between storytelling and folk-songs. Narrative is an important part of folk-song. Many songs tell a story: all ballads do. To tell a story in the form of song heightens the emotion generated by the song. One of the distinguishing features of folk-song in general and ballads in particular is the shift in narrative voice, from the third person to one of the characters in the song speaking in the first person, moving the story forward through dialogue. Ballads have an economy of words: there is often no introductory 'he said'; rather the listener is left to infer from the meaning who is speaking and to whom. The move from narrative into dialogue is another device which intensifies drama and emotion. Given these properties of folk-songs, they are eminently suitable as a basis for drama, for a re-enactment of past events. Such drama may be mimed, spoken or executed through expressive movement. A song or ballad may be divided into a number of scenes. Each group of children in a class can take one scene and devise a freeze frame to communicate that point in the narrative, and the whole sequence of scenes or freeze frames performed as expressive movement. Through this kind of learning activity, all children, including those with literacy difficulties, can access the meaning of the song and its historical content. These are enactive, kinaesthetic representations or forms of experience: through their very nature a wide range of learners can gain access to the curriculum. To experience historical content through one genre and express it in another genre involves the active engagement of learners with the material to be learned. From the point of view of schema theory the children are working on the material, and making it part of their map of the world.

Examples of songs for use with children

'My young man'

This is a well-known children's song, eminently suitable for use in the early years. It has a number of advantages, not least a very memorable catchy tune. I sang it one year to a group of postgraduate student-teachers: they were still singing it in the pub three days later. It is a lively, strong dance tune in a major key. It bounces along with joy, an emotion totally in keeping with the sentiments of the song. It may be sung unaccompanied or with some simple accompaniment on guitar. It needs at the most only three chords (D, G and A major) although you can get away with using just two: D and A major. I cannot recommend too highly the use of the guitar in primary classrooms. It is relatively easy to learn to a good enough standard to use in school; one can strum chords on it; and very importantly for beginning teachers, one can maintain eye contact with the children while playing. For those still learning class and behaviour management, this is extremely important. I use a melodeon myself to accompany this song, because given the bouncy nature of the instrument, it goes well with the song. However, beginning teachers may not have time to learn the melodeon; the guitar is much easier to learn in a short space of time.

The advantages and possibilities for the song are as follows:

- In terms of history, the song contains evidence of how women used to dress at the time of the song, probably in Victorian times. This could be corroborated by the children through examining pictures of women in Victorian times and comparing the clothes in the pictures to the clothes in the song. One possibility for pictures is to use Beatrice Potter books, as she dressed her animal characters in Victorian clothes. There are many other sources however, including internet images and pictures in class topic books. The overarching historical question might be: 'What did women wear in Victorian times?' This could generate an enquiry into clothes of that period and comparison work with clothes we wear today. Resourceful teachers will recognise the possibilities for collecting some Victorian-style items to go with the dressing-up clothes, and the play which might be generated from this song, as well as creating pictures of people in Victorian dress. By treating the song as evidence, even relatively young children can begin to address the question: 'How do we know what people wore in Victorian times?'

- The song contains some archaic vocabulary, (e.g. bonnet, kirtle, shawl, petticoat) (National Literacy Strategy Year 4 Term 2 (DfEE, 1998)). This presents opportunities for work at word level. The word 'kirtle' is relatively easily explained through a simple examination of its root word 'kirt', the removal of the ending 'le' and the addition of 's' at the front. It becomes the modern 'skirt', and indeed a kirtle was an old term for either a dress or a skirt.

- For very young children, the song introduces colours: blue, green, brown and white. One possibility for extension work, having done some enquiry using pictures into what else Victorian women wore, is to generate additional verses using other colours. This activity links into the next set of possibilities for the song, which are its further uses in terms of literacy.

- This is a very good song for children learning to read. It uses a very simple structure with a great deal of repetition. Children are quickly able to predict the structure of each verse, even if not all the class are actually reading the words on the page, the flip-chart or the overhead projector. Only the last verse differs, in that the young lady is going to the church rather than to the fair. Other than that, each verse is the same other than the item of clothing, the colour and the following line. Thus, to create additional verses, children need only provide part of a verse. To date I have no research evidence on this, but I suspect that the combination of music and words acts on the memory in a deeper, more lasting way than do words alone, fixing in memory the letters of each word, or its graphic shape. There is a research project to be done on this aspect of using songs in the classroom!

- The tune is in fact a dance tune following the common format of a 32-bar tune played AABB, where A is the first eight bars of the tune, played twice, and B is the second eight bars, also played twice. This format is used in British folk dance and in much morris music. Thus there are possibilities for using it for a folk dance. However, I would simply play it as a dance tune either live or one of the recordings available of it and invite the children to move to the music as the tune suggests, using their imaginations. Some children will leap about indiscriminately, but there will be those who begin to exploit the inherent rhythm, and they will find themselves doing a traditional English hop-step – the tune is crying out for this. The ability to perform this step will come in useful in dance sessions.

I have a bonnet trimmed with blue
Do you wear it? Yes, I do.
When do you wear it? When I can,
Going to the fair with my young man.

Chorus:
My young man, my young man
Going to the fair with my young man.   (*twice*)

I have a kirtle trimmed with green
The finest one that ever you've seen,
When do you wear it? When I can,
Going to the fair with my young man.

Chorus

I have a big shawl trimmed with brown
The finest one in all the town,
When do you wear it? When I can,
Going to the fair with my young man.

Chorus

I have a petticoat trimmed with white
Do you wear it? Yes, I might.
When do you wear it? When I can,
Going to the church with my young man.

Chorus: (*last time only*)
My young man, my young man
Going to the church with my young man.   (*twice*)

Figure 10.1   Song: 'My Young Man'

All in all, this song is a marvellous resource for the primary age range, with possibilities for historical enquiry, interpretation of evidence, range and depth of historical under-standing, literacy work (the song can be a text for the literacy hour), and cross-curricular links to the study of pictures, creative work, song-writing, music and dance. I have yet to meet a child (or adult for that matter) who did not respond to this simple, infectious song. It is an excellent resource for the whole primary age range from 3 to 11 years, but of particular value in the early years when one cannot have too many songs.

'Greensleeves'

Alas, my love, you do me wrong
To cast me off discourteously
For I have loved you well and long
Delighting in your company.

Greensleeves was all my joy
Greensleeves was my delight
Greensleeves was my heart of gold
And who but my lady greensleeves.

Your vows you've broken, like my heart
Oh, why did you so enrapture me?
Now I remain in a world apart
But my heart remains in captivity.

I have been ready at your hand
To grant whatever you would crave
I have both wagered life and land
Your love and good-will for to have.

If you intend thus to disdain
It does the more enrapture me
And even so, I still remain
A love in captivity.

My men were clothed all in green
And they did ever wait on thee
All this was gallant to be seen
And yet thou wouldst not love me.

Thou couldst desire no earthly thing
But still thou hadst it readily.
Thy music still to play and sing
And yet thou wouldst not love me.

Well, I will pray to God on high
That thou my constancy mayst see
And that yet once before I die
Thou wilt vouchsafe to love me.

Ah, Greensleeves, now farewell, adieu
To God I pray to prosper thee
For I am still thy lover true
Come once again and love me.

Figure 10.2   Song: 'Greensleeves'

This is a beautiful song and one to which I have found children respond very readily. It was supposedly composed by Henry VIII, but there is no certainty about the composer. In introducing the song, teachers are best to say: 'I think . . .' or 'It is possible that the song was composed by Henry VIII'. Variants of 'Greensleeves' may be found throughout the English folk tradition, both as song airs and dance tunes. For this song I present an account of how I used it with a Year 4 class of 28 children. The context for this work was this class, 17 of whom had reading ages below their chronological age, in an urban school serving a housing estate on the edge of London. Five of the children had specific language difficulties, two of whom were in the process of being statemented. Altogether in terms of literacy the class was skewed towards the lower end of the ability range. They were a delightful if challenging class to teach. I taught them history, literacy and music every Wednesday afternoon for a term. The medium-term plan was developed in response to their interests during the early introductory outline work on the Tudors. They were particularly interested in Henry VIII and Elizabeth I; thus the plan I developed reflected their interest. I introduced the tune of 'Greensleeves' in the first week by playing it on the concertina as an example of a Tudor song. Purists might object to this anachronism, for the concertina is a Victorian instrument rather than a Tudor one, but it is what I play; so I used that. It is played just as easily on the recorder, which is much more an instrument of the period and readily available in schools for children and teachers alike. The children enjoyed the tune and hummed along to it, some swaying in time to the music.

I then placed an overhead transparency of the first verse on the projector, and we sang the verse, first unaccompanied, and then accompanied by the concertina. The children learned the words easily, despite not understanding all of them. At the end of the first verse, I asked them if there was anything which they did not understand, and they asked about the words 'to cast me off discourteously'. I explained what these meant and we sang the verse again twice. This formed part of a 25-minute music session at the end of the afternoon during which I played a number of Tudor, eighteenth-century and Victorian dance tunes. The following week, when we settled on the carpet for the music part of the lesson, several children came to me and said, 'We have learned the verse and chorus from last week. Can we have some more please?' I had not asked the children to learn it; they had done so out of a desire to repeat the pleasurable experience which they had had in the lesson. I taught them another verse that week and we sang the two verses. At the start of the third week's whole afternoon session, one boy came to me and told me he had learned the tune on the recorder. Again, I had not asked him to do this: he had been motivated by the beauty of the tune and that desire to repeat the enjoyable experience. Over five weeks we learned the whole song by heart and accompanied with concertina and recorder: several children were playing the tune on the recorder by this time.

In terms of the history curriculum, I was working almost entirely within Key Element 2: Range and Depth of Historical Understanding as far as the song on its own was concerned. The children were learning about the lives of men, women and children in Tudor times by experiencing music which would have been commonplace at that time. The song and tune are evidence from that period. They exercised their historical imagination through the re-creation of the song and their choice of recorder for accompaniment. During the weeks in which we were learning this song, the children were studying Henry VIII, through portraits (see Chapter 5), written evidence (see Chapter 4) and storytelling (see Chapter 7). Some of the written evidence used comprised pieces written describing Henry VIII by, for example, the Venetian Ambassador to the Court of Henry. The evidence gave accounts of his many skills in sport, dance and music as well as physical descriptions. Another set of evidence comprised parts of three love letters written by Henry VIII to Anne Boleyn, during the period when she was away from Court and he was desperate to see and love her. The children did some work on these letters (see Chapter 4), challenging though these texts were. Gradually the song began to take on new meaning for the children. They asked me: 'Did Henry VIII really compose this song?' 'If he did, was it to Anne Boleyn?' (who at that stage did indeed 'cast him off discourteously'). Set into context with the other pieces of evidence, the possibilities for interpretation of the song increased. We did not answer the questions definitely: I let the children express their own opinions. It was enough that they were engaging in the skills and processes of historical enquiry and 'asking and answering questions about the past' (Key Element 4: Historical Enquiry, DES/QCA, 1995).

'The Horse's Bransle' (pronounced 'brawl')

During these same weeks I was playing this tune to the children. It had a remarkable impact on them. It was one of a selection of tunes which I assembled to play to the children, and it became one of the most requested. For some of the lessons a research assistant was observing my teaching and she recorded the response of the children to the music. For the earlier part of each afternoon's lesson I worked the children hard. I will be honest about the fact that I used the promise of music to encourage some of the children to tackle and complete the tasks I set ('If you don't finish we won't have time for music!'). But bribery is, if we are honest, an acceptable weapon in the teacher's armoury. The moment I started playing tunes, the researcher noted a palpable change in the atmosphere in the classroom of almost visible relaxation in the children's posture and body language, particularly noticeable when I played this tune. We asked ourselves 'What were the children learning?' It was not easy to answer this question, but it was clear that *something* was happening. (There is another research project in there.) The tune is very appealing. It is a 48-bar tune with the structure AABBCC. The first two parts are in a major key; the third part shifts into a minor or modal key depending on which version is played. It should be noted here that many traditional tunes do not keep to the 'rules' of the conventional harmony of Western music, perhaps because much of it was played on homemade instruments such

Figure 10.3 Tune: 'The Horse's Bransle' (Thoinot Arbeau, 1588)

as pipes, whistles and bagpipes. The availability of notes on the instruments would have affected the tunes played, which is one explanation for the many variants of traditional tunes and airs which abound. The strangeness of the shift from one key to another fascinated the children (similar shifts occur in 'Greensleeves') and they listened absolutely rapt. We worked on the rhythm which is a straightforward 4/4 with four beats to a bar, by clapping out the rhythm while sitting on the carpet. This took place most weeks as part of the music session until the last week of the term, when I took them into the hall and taught them a simple dance to go with the music. The music is open to interpretation, and indeed several different dances can be performed to it, but this I what I did.

PREPARATION: MOVING TO THE MUSIC

- Children find a space in the hall and stand still.

- To the A music, they move for eight steps round the hall, and stand still and clap for eight steps. Repeat several times, using the B and then the C music. Count out the eight beats with the children. This is to get them used to listening and counting the beats/steps.

- Teacher demonstrate the side-step, galloping movement for eight steps.

- Form the children into one long line down the length of the hall and get them to gallop across the hall for eight steps in time to the C music.

- Demonstrate (with an assistant or child): a back to back; a right-hand turn: a left-hand turn.

- Organise the children into pairs and get them to do these movements to the B music.

- Form the pairs of children into two long lines facing each other across the hall.

THE DANCE

A1   Lines of children holding hands taking four steps forward and four steps back. Lines of children take eight steps forward, one line make arches and the other goes through the arches; turn to face again.

A2   Repeat A1.

B1   Let go hands. Back-to-back right shoulder, repeat left shoulder (16 steps).

B2   Right-hand turn partner (eight steps); left-hand turn partner (eight steps).

C1/C2   Top two couples gallop down to bottom of set; the rest clap in time to the music.

This may be repeated as many times as wished. I have not stipulated that boys and girls should pair up: whether or not they do depends on their age and the school ethos. Sometimes boys prefer to dance with boys and girls with girls! This is a simple dance which teaches some of the basics of folk dancing and doesn't involve swinging, which is a move that I have observed children (and adults, for that matter) can have some difficulty with. In performing this dance the children are engaging in the simple sort of dance which would have been done by the upper and lower classes alike in Tudor times. They are engaged in imaginative reinterpretation of the past as well as in enjoyable physical exercise. They are learning to enact moves in a sequence: sequencing being a skill which cuts across the curriculum (maths, English, PE, history, dance, music). In working together as a whole group, they are involved in co-operative group work.

CASE STUDY: 'AUSTRALIA', A SHORT BALLAD FROM SUFFOLK

Come all you young fellows,
Whereso'er you may be
Come listen a while to my story.
When I was a young man,
Me age seventeen,
I ought to been serving Victoria, our Queen.
But those hard-hearted judges,
Oh, how cruel they be
To send us poor lads to Australia.

I fell in with a damsel,
She was handsome and gay,
I neglected me work,
More and more, every day.
And to keep her like a lady
I went on the highway,
And for that I was sent to Australia.

Now the judges, they stand
With their whips in their hands,
They drive us, like horses,
To plough up the land.
You should see us poor young fellows
Working in that jail yard;
How hard is our fate in Australia.

Australia, Australia,
I would ne'er see no more,
I'm worn out with fever,
Cast down to Death's door.
But should I live to see,
Say, seven years more,
I would then bid adieu to Australia.

Figure 10.4   Song: 'Australia'

This case study refers to material already presented in Chapter 7 on storytelling, namely the 'Story of the Transports'. My learning objectives for the song were as follows:

● To corroborate the 'Story of the Transports' and the nature of crime and punishment in the eighteenth and nineteenth centuries by investigating the words of a popular song of the time (history).

- To use the text as a model for learning about and writing in the ballad form (literacy).

- To transfer knowledge of folk tunes played the previous week to composing a tune for this song.

I found the song in a collection but had no tune for it in my memory. I had heard the source of the song – Bob Hart, an old country singer, performed the song in a pub in Suffolk in 1973 – but I had no recording and no recall of the tune. However, I did not view this as a problem, rather as an opportunity. Singers in the past may not always have had a tune to go with a song (the words of which they might have purchased from a street vendor, a broadside ballad seller of the type described in Mayhew (1851)). This would not have deterred anyone. The singer would have drawn upon an existing tune in his or her memory, or composed a new one.

The previous week, I had played to the children, a Year 6 class (for background and context see Chapter 7), tunes such as 'Click go the Shears' and 'Waltzing Matilda'. I played these for enjoyment and to illustrate the point that music travels around the world, people taking their own music with them to far distant places, in this case, the transports to Australia. Both tunes started life in England with different sets of words. Both tunes surface in Australia with new words, one about sheep shearing, while the other has been turned into a sort of unofficial national anthem. You cannot keep a good tune down!

I played the tunes again and reminded the children of how the words had been replaced by new sets of words. I showed them the words to 'Australia' and asked the children if they would work out the 'story' of events in the song. This they found easy to do. (Readers: take a few minutes to do the same and consider the emotions felt by the person narrating the events of the song.) I then asked the children to look at the rhyme scheme of the song and we commented on the pattern of rhyme. I explained that this was one of many ballad forms. The four-line stanza with the end of the second and fourth lines rhyming is a very common pattern found in ballads, though it is not the only one. I set the task of taking the 'Story of the Transports' which they had heard, worked on, acted out and rewritten in their own words the previous week, and turning that story into 'The Ballad of Henry and Susannah' (see Chapter 7, Figure 7.2).

There is some sound theory behind the setting of this task. I was concerned here with the children learning in a way which would stay with them – in other words, deeply – about the transports to Australia. Through this task they would be transferring their existing knowledge and understanding to a new genre: from prose to poetry; from straight narration to the ballad form. In so doing, they would be revisiting their knowledge of the story. Some children would also learn the new concept of the ballad form: a poem or song which tells a story. Some might already know this and be revising this knowledge. In terms of writing, the demands were not too severe. The plot and sequence of events was already familiar. Thus the children only had to work at shaping the material into the new genre (Rosen, 1988, 1993). They did not have to deal simultaneously with both compositional and secretarial aspects of the writing task, because the compositional demands had already been dealt with in the previous week's work. Certainly the children wrote poems of high quality, of which the example shown, from one of the least able boys, is only one example.

For homework I set the tasks of completing the ballad and composing a new tune for the song. I explained that the old tune had become lost and, like singers of old, we would need to supply a tune for 'Australia'. I asked them to think about the emotions in the song (sorrow, sadness, regret, loneliness, hatred of judges, longing to see England again).

Planning and class management

Planning and preparation

By far the most important aspect of preparation for using music in teaching history, or indeed in any subject, is to listen to the music a great deal and make it part of one's daily life. Two separate pieces of wisdom, both from different sources, come to mind here. The first is from a fellow teacher educator, a classically and jazz-trained musician, who maintained that one of the biggest influences over what music we grow to like is what we actually hear most frequently. Popular music is dominated by what gets played over the airwaves; thus people come to like what they hear frequently, and to buy it. We grow to love what we are accustomed to hearing. Often, people do not get to hear any genuine traditional music either of their own or any other culture, and dismiss it without due consideration, or they hear watered-down, bowdlerised or popularised versions and assume that is all folk music is. There is a wealth of music available, and one of the aims of this chapter is to point the reader towards some of the best of what is out there. In any case, folk music is worth listening to, part of the rich cultural heritage of any society, and valuable for the Anglocentric history curriculum of the English primary school. The second piece of wisdom is an old Irish saying that: 'It takes 21 years to become a piper: 7 years' listening; 7 years' practising; and 7 years' playing.' No one is expecting hard-pressed primary teachers to become expert musicians, but the listening is important. Play tapes of the music while driving to work or doing the ironing, until you find yourself humming the tunes and remembering fragments of the verses. Whether or not one learns the songs and tunes oneself, it is important that children get to hear the music frequently too. The plan should involve a clear method for learning the song (children will very quickly do this by heart), and have objectives related to appropriate aspects of the primary curriculum. The examples in this chapter have shown four different songs or tunes being used in different ways for a variety of learning objectives (and Chapter 1 contains a cameo of a song being used as a source of evidence about housemaids' lives). In each case the song or tune is part of a selection of evidence, investigated and experienced in conjunction with other forms of evidence.

Follow-up work

Most of the songs and tunes given here incorporate some ideas for follow-up work. I am using this term in an all-embracing sense of work which 'fits' on either side of the musical work. Below are some generic suggestions, and some specific ones for other activities/sources of evidence which may be used with music.

Generic suggestions

- Choose songs around a theme to which the historical content is related (e.g. mine work, weaving, sea songs) so that the song becomes another source of evidence to use alongside others.

- Ask the children to emphasise particular kinds of words or references to events using highlighters, to aid the process of extracting information from the songs as texts.

- Ask the children to set information from different sources side by side in columns to aid comparison of what the different source types are saying.

- Sing songs or play tunes several times purely for enjoyment.

- Ask the children who might have sung the song, and for what purposes; and who might have composed the song.

- Using the existing verse pattern, ask the children to generate additional verses.

- After performing a dance, ask the children what the dance tells us about people who lived at that time and performed such dances. From doing simple dances with children as described with 'The Horse's Bransle', they gave me answers such as: people were very fit then; they must have been quite intelligent because they made up these dances; they were very social (*sic*) because they liked to dance with other people; and they enjoyed dancing to beautiful tunes.

CHAPTER 11

Classroom discourse and generic teaching approaches

Introduction

Classroom discourse is of immense importance in teaching, regardless of subject matter. It can take many forms: whole class chanting; ritual (as in taking the register); recitation; teacher and pupil questioning; question-and-answer sessions to monitor understanding of previous work; reading round the class; story reading; storytelling; explanation and exposition; drama; role-play; formal debate; whole class discussion; and small group discussion. Some of these forms are easier to execute than others: for example, the last two forms of discussion are not seen as often as some of the others. The inherent difficulties of managing class talk: of allotting turns fairly; of drawing in reluctant speakers; and of steering the discussion without dominating it, all mean that the phrase 'class discussion' which appears on many a lesson plan may mean or turn out to be something very different, more like a recitation or question-and-answer session for recall of previous learning, than genuine discussion. None the less, it is important for teachers to have explicit understandings of the varieties of classroom discourse, and to work towards mastery of all its forms. Talk is so important in classrooms that it cannot be left to chance and good intentions. Used well, talk is a fundamental aspect of learning. As Alexander (2000, p. 430) puts it:

> The talk that takes place between teacher and pupil – and less commonly amongst pupils themselves – is not merely the vehicle for the exchange of information. It is a vital tool of learning.

What does all this mean in terms of teaching history in the primary classroom? It follows that we must offer our children as many opportunities as possible for fruitful interaction both with the teacher and with other children. There is a wealth of ideas for generating a range of speaking and listening activities in this book, but two aspects deserve closer consideration. These aspects are explored in this chapter which presents two sections on key aspects of classroom discourse in teaching history: questioning and Socratic dialogue.

Forms of classroom discourse

Questioning

Questioning is important in the teaching of history, for two reasons. First of all it is a generic teaching skill. It is of vital importance to master it. There is not the space for a whole treatise on questioning here, but some brief points may be made. It is important for teachers to be aware of the types of questions they ask and the highly skilled nature of this particular aspect of teaching. Phillips (2002) asks whether questioning is 'a clever art' or 'a competence to be learned?' Certainly one can become competent at questioning, but I would argue that from early struggles with questioning, through a basic level of competence, one can achieve a kind of mastery, in which it becomes almost an art form. One only has to watch experienced teachers perform: their questions seem to flow; children respond appropriately; genuine discussion develops; and children are evidently learning. 'Effective questioning involves an extraordinarily complex array of characteristic features, traits and skills' (Phillips, 2002, p. 66; Brown and Edmondson, 1984; Dillon, 1988). To these I would add deep subject knowledge as an essential component. It is important to examine the types of questions one asks and to develop some metacognition of the processes and features of effective questioning.

Second, questioning is an essential part of the process of historical enquiry: 'History is thus a discipline which has at its core the framing of questions, the questioning of sources within the context of the situation at the time' (Dean, 1995, p. 2). Too often, children are asked to 'find out' about an aspect of a past society with no more specific direction, using children's topic books or juvenile literature, or these days the internet. Such finding out is not genuine historical enquiry for it is not driven by questions and therefore there is no attempt to follow the processes of historical enquiry. These are as summed up by Fines and Nichol (1997) quoting Hexter (1972) presented in Chapter 2. The problem with 'finding out' is that the children have no means of assessing which information they find is relevant or valid. Faced with the wealth of information there tends to be available nowadays, the temptation is to copy indiscriminately. This is neither good history nor good learning. Fortunately, questions now have a higher profile in exemplary material for teachers. In the QCA Schemes of Work each example unit has a 'Key Question' aiming, like Counsell's 'Big Question', to drive along historical enquiry and to generate further questions (Counsell, 1997).

Generating good historical questions is an important skill in both teacher and children alike. Nichol (1984, pp. 46–7) devised an extremely useful list of question types in history teaching. Teachers can use these questions to promote certain responses and ways of thinking, to analyse the kinds of questions they ask, and to develop metacognition or at least awareness of the question types they use most frequently.

1 A data-recall question (e.g. 'When was the battle of X?') requires the pupil to remember facts without putting them to any use.

2 A 'naming' question (e.g. 'What is the name of Y?') asks the pupil simply to name something without showing how it relates to any particular situation.

3 An 'observation' question (e.g. 'What is happening in the picture?') requires pupils to describe something without relating it to their knowledge of the situation.

4 A 'reasoning' question (e.g. 'What does X tell us about Y?') expects pupils to explain something.

5 A 'speculative' question (e.g. 'How do you think X came about?') requires pupils to speculate about historical situations.

6 An 'empathetic' question (e.g. 'How did X feel about that?') asks pupils to empathise with people in historical situations.

7 A 'hypothesis-generating' question (e.g. 'Why did X occur at that time?') requires pupils to speculate in a more advanced way, using historical knowledge.

8 A 'problem-solving' question (e.g. 'What evidence is there that X happened to Y?') expects pupils to weigh up evidence.

9 An 'evidence-questioning' question (e.g. 'How reliable is X to tell us about Y?') asks pupils to interrogate the evidence.

10 A 'synthesising' question (e.g. 'From what you have found out, write an account of . . .') pulls all the information together and encourages the pupil to resolve the problem.

(Nichol, 1984, pp. 46–7)

The challenge for the beginning teacher of history is to be able to employ all of Nichol's question types, moving from the information (or 'closed') questions to the understanding, imagination, reasoning and reflection (or 'open') questions. We have to ask ourselves what kinds of thinking we wish to promote in our children.

As well as teaching asking questions, it is of central importance that children ask questions also. Too often in classrooms it is teachers who ask the questions and children who answer them. Apart from being a statutory requirement in the History National Curriculum (DfEE, 1999c), it is vital that children get to ask their own questions for several reasons. When we present them with historical evidence, they often have their own questions which they don't get to ask in the classroom setting. These questions can be of good quality for generating a historical enquiry, or they can be trivial questions. The 'enquiry questions' may be used to generate an enquiry within several weeks' worth of a medium-term plan.

Questioning is a skill which needs to be taught explicitly, and I have found the following exercise to be useful and valuable when starting an enquiry with children. In a Year 5 class I gave all the children a piece of coloured card and asked them to write down one question about the topic. Here is a list of child-generated questions about the topic of the Victorians.

The children's questions

- When did Queen Victoria rule?
- Did children go to school in Victorian times?
- Where did Victorians live?
- Who were the Victorians?
- What date did Queen Victoria die?
- What did people eat in Victorian times?
- Did Queen Victoria get married and who to?
- Did she have any children and what were their names?
- Did Victorians have trains?
- Did Queen Victoria have any pets?
- What were Queen Victoria's hobbies?
- Where did Victorian children go to school?
- What toys did Victorian children have?
- What was Queen Victoria's middle name?
- What did her husband do?
- When did Queen Victoria die?
- What was her favourite food?
- How old was Queen Victoria when she got married?
- Why did Victoria become Queen?

I suggested to the children that we could be detectives and find out the answers to some of these questions. I said that some questions could be called trivial, in that you could just look up the information in a book or on the internet and find out the answer in a few minutes. Others I called enquiry questions: ones which could take a great deal of investigation to find out about, and which could have complicated answers: for example, 'Did all Victorian children go to school?' might lead us to think about whether only rich children go or whether there was a change during the Victorian period. I asked for three volunteers to read each question in turn: the class had to advise them which pile to put them in. For this sorting activity there would be three piles: trivial questions; enquiry questions; and those which were 'in between', which might lead to a small enquiry.

The purposes of this activity were these: to consider what sort of questions the children were asking, and to engage with the concepts of trivial and enquiry questions. There was no suggestion that there were 'good' or 'bad' questions, only that there were different types of question. This exercise raises awareness of different types of questions and their uses. Another approach with older children would be to share Nichol's framework of question types shown earlier in this chapter and to ask them to sort the questions according to this framework.

Socratic dialogue

Questions also play a role in the next form of classroom discourse to be considered: Socratic dialogue. This may seem a far cry from primary classrooms, but it is a very ancient form of teaching and learning in European culture. It is attributed to Socrates (Russell, 1961), though it may have been practised by Ancient Greek philosophers before Socrates. He taught by engaging in a particular kind of dialogue with his students. He would pretend ignorance on some matter or topic, and ask his students to set out their ideas or beliefs on that subject. He would then demonstrate through a series of questions that the student did not know as much as he thought he did, or that there were logical inconsistencies in his thinking (Fox, 1995, p. 134).

These ancient dialogues seem a world away from present-day classrooms, but they capture some key ideas about learning and teaching, and a mode of discourse which we can still use today. The first key point is that the teacher and pupils are collaborators or partners in an investigation about a topic from which they can both learn. This is in contrast to a mode of discourse in which the teacher is the authority on the topic and the pupils are the ignorant ones, there to learn from the teacher. The next key idea is that in discussion we can test out ideas critically, examining them for weaknesses and inconsistencies. Socrates saw himself as a 'midwife of truth' (Russell, 1961; Fox, 1995), using his own form of questioning to help the student to discover errors in thinking and bring to the surface of his mind a new understanding of a topic or problem. It is this kind of dialogue which is used in various forms in this book, not question-and-answer sessions for factual recall or naming questions, but questions which require children to draw upon their existing knowledge and to apply it to historical situations. In Socratic dialogue we enact teaching as conversation. We engage children in enquiry and struggle and do it by asking questions which encourage application of previous knowledge and which result in conversation. In Chapter 13, two examples are given of creating ancient ships in the playground with children, one Roman, one Viking. Both of these lessons used Socratic dialogue to encourage children to draw upon what they already knew of ships powered by oars, and their knowledge of measurement, to move the children towards the imaginative reconstruction of being a slave or soldier aboard a fighting ship.

CHAPTER 12

Ticking the boxes

This chapter is a controversial one in many ways. It deals with aspects of teaching history which need to be considered, but which are not as straightforward as some textbooks would suggest. These aspects are:

- chronology and teaching about time;
- outline and background knowledge;
- the use of QCA schemes of work and commercial schemes;
- the use of ICT in all its forms;
- assessment.

The title of this chapter makes reference to the fact that these are all important aspects to some degree. Ofsted inspectors may well be looking for them as some of the criteria by which they will judge the quality of history teaching in schools. The reference in the title, 'Ticking the boxes', is to a kind of assessment which, though it might inform teachers to some extent about children's attainment and progress in history, may not be as useful or valuable as other forms of assessment. The topics of this chapter are interrelated and there will be some cross-referencing between topics as appropriate. Thus, to employ the current educational jargon somewhat ironically, this chapter attempts to hit several targets by dealing with a number of important issues. Possible teaching approaches and strategies will be given at the end of sections of this chapter where appropriate.

Chronology and the teaching of time

Chronology as one of the key elements is clearly important, but I would like to argue that too great an emphasis can be given to chronology in the teaching of primary history, given the small amount of time available for teaching this subject. There are of course good reasons for teaching about time. Any understanding of time is underpinned by understanding about sequencing of events and the skill of sequencing, about numerical methods of showing periods of time, understanding of scale, knowledge of the language of time and time vocabulary. In order to understand historical situations, it is often necessary to sequence events in chronological order. An understanding of the correct or probable sequence of events (depending on the evidence of the sources we consult) can lead to an understanding of cause and effect, two other major related historical concepts.

As well as an understanding of sequencing and the ability to do it, children also need an understanding of numerical methods of representing time. This is more necessary and appropriate in Key Stage 2 than in Key Stage 1, where the emphasis needs to be on sequencing, with simple timelines using, for example, a child's age in creating a personal timeline. From this early stage one then needs to move on to the use of dates, decades, centuries and the whole system of AD/BC reckoning. This has to be linked to the concept of scale, since the divisions on a timeline, say of decades in the Roman occupation of Britain, use scale as an intrinsic organising concept. Ten metres on a timeline running around a classroom wall might represent a decade or a century, depending on the scale chosen. It is important that the scale divisions are accurate, so that we can give children some understanding of the time vocabulary used, the passage of time, and ultimately an understanding of long passages of time. The word 'ultimately' is used here to reaffirm the difficulty children (and some adults) have in comprehending huge stretches of time: such understanding does not happen overnight. A timeline which extends from a classroom down a corridor and out into the hall can be very useful as a visual representation of the vastness of time.

The language of time and time vocabulary need to be taught to give children some way of communicating their understanding and negotiating the common ways of expressing time, which they might encounter in children's history texts, in video programmes, and on the internet. These are often taken for granted by adults, but can take anything from months to in some cases years for children to master. Consider, for example, the common confusion over 'yesterday' and 'tomorrow' among 4- and 5-year-olds. It takes a while to establish the correct use of these terms, perhaps through 'news' and journal-keeping activities in the early years. Stowe and Haydn (2000) point to a wide range of ways of expressing time reference points: in fact a rich and varied vocabulary of time language. Time is thus a complex construct with mathematical, linguistic, conceptual and psychological aspects. The existing research evidence suggests that learning about time is difficult and occurs at different rates in different learners (see e.g. Stowe and Haydn, 2000). Stowe and Haydn argue strongly for the centrality of time both to the substantive nature of history and to children's understanding of cause and effect, continuity and change. They recommend more teaching about chronology rather than less. Yet despite the strengths of their arguments, I would still maintain that it is more crucial at primary level to teach about historical enquiry and interpretation than about chronology.

It is perhaps an accident that chronology came to be the first key element. At any rate, its physical position in the National Curriculum document tends to suggest that it is of greatest importance. Chronology is one of the eight overarching concepts of history, part of the substantive structures of the discipline. Historical enquiry is both an overarching concept, and also one of the syntactic processes which define history as a discipline. There is a strong case for historical enquiry being placed first in the curriculum documents. First, it would highlight its central importance in history, its defining nature. Second, it would draw teachers' attentio to it, simply by virtue of the fact that it comes first. Many teachers do not have specialist education in history and may not appreciate its fundamental importance to the discipline. To have it placed first, with perhaps historical interpretation second, would stress its importance. The existing arrangement, with chronology and range and depth of historical understanding coming first, places emphasis inadvertently on part of the substance of history and plays down the importance of enquiry and interpretation.

The final part of the argument against having too great a focus on chronology is the pragmatic (and ironic) necessity of using the time available for history teaching as carefully as possible. Recent trends in the primary curriculum have emphasised the importance of literacy, numeracy and science at the expense of other subjects. The introduction of the Primary National Strategy heralds a possible change in emphasis in the primary curriculum, but one must sound a note of caution here. The strategy may imply a wider curriculum with more time available for other foundation subjects, but the continued national testing and inspection regime is likely to mitigate against new allocations of time to a wider range of subjects in primary schools. Unless the national testing apparatus and punitive inspection system are dismantled, the primary curriculum will continue much as it has done for the past few years, with teachers feeling obliged to teach to the tests in order to protect their schools and their children. Generally speaking history has some 4 per cent of curriculum time, either 45 minutes a week or blocked in half-term or termly units. The crux of the argument is this. With so little time available for history teaching, surely it is better to focus on enquiry, interpretation of evidence and the exercise of the historical imagination than to fritter away precious time on less crucial aspects. There is the additional danger that a major focus on chronology rather than enquiry can lead teachers towards the transmission of historical information rather than the kind of collective collaborative enquiry presented in this book. In an ideal world, with a less crowded primary curriculum, the teaching of time could be highlighted as much as that of enquiry, but this is not an ideal world.

There is a case for teaching an understanding of time across the curriculum, as an ongoing part of literacy, numeracy, science and personal and social education, given its complex nature and the scarcity of time for teaching history. The list below gives some ideas for teaching about time, based partly on the excellent work done by Stowe and Haydn (2000) in this field.

Ideas for teaching about time

- Simulations and games can help to build up 'mini-chronologies' of particular historical events, such as the Cortez simulation in Chapter 9. The structure of this simulation shows the sequence of events, and the decision-making assists an understanding of cause and consequence.

- Storytelling likewise is based on a sequence of events, problems and their resolution. In re-creating stories, children are sequencing events.

- Drama and role-play can help to 'fix' a sequence of events in children's minds.

- Using time language in all its variations consistently and with representations of what the different concepts mean is important throughout primary education, but particularly in the early years. To establish even basic concepts such as 'yesterday', 'today' and 'tomorrow', children in the early years can be asked to draw pictures of themselves and what they were doing, and what they will be doing, on these days.

- Visual representations of time, such as timelines of various kinds, should be used consistently in the primary years as part of outline/background knowledge.

- Using visual evidence, such as art, buildings and artefacts, can help to develop children's associative networks in relation to particular forms of art and architecture, for example, to particular periods.

Outline knowledge: The Ancient Greeks

As well as knowledge in depth, children need some outline or background knowledge about periods in history. Dean (1995) suggests ways of achieving this in all areas of study, either at the beginning of a topic or alongside an in-depth enquiry. Such outline work helps to establish an overview, a chronological framework and a background context for the in-depth topic.

Strategies for outline/background knowledge

- *Topic book blitz*: Using children's topic books (the kinds that often seem to act as a decorative backdrop to history lessons), the children record on to cards between two and five interesting sentences about the Greeks or Romans or whatever. These are pooled and listed. A number of headings are provided and the children sort the facts under the headings, thus revisiting the information and physically organising it. They then circulate with their notebooks, recording one fact from each heading; these are then used in the next strategy. (An example of this is given in Chapter 13.)

- *Concept webs*: The children write the title of the topic (e.g. 'The Tudors') in the centre of a piece of paper, then draw radiating lines, one for each heading,

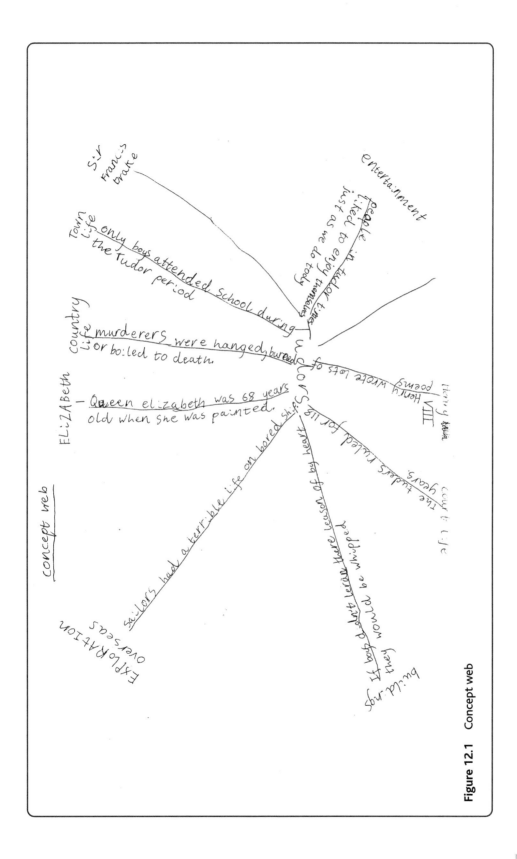

concept web

Figure 12.1 Concept web

containing the one fact which belongs under that heading (see Figure 12.1). Concept webs can also be done without the information collection, purely as an assessment exercise of what the children already know about the topic. If children do this at the beginning and end of a topic it may be used as a form of assessment.

- *Split topics*: The topic can be divided into different aspects such as work, children, education, main events or decades. In groups the children research one aspect or decade, and present their findings to the rest of the class in one of several ways: a poster giving a visual window on that period, or as newspaper headlines.

- *Asking and answering questions*: Children ask questions and other children answer them, looking up the answers in the books. This may also be done as a quiz.

- *Timelines*: These can be created by the children and take many different forms: annotated wall displays; pictures and date cards pegged on lines strung across the classroom; parallel timelines displaying synchronous events in different cultures; a long timeline stretching from one classroom wall right down the corridor outside and into the hall to represent long periods of time.

- *Using pictures*: Here is an example using Greek pots. A teacher is starting a topic on the Greeks with a Year 5 class. Initial questioning has revealed that the children have very little knowledge or understanding of this period and its people, apart from one girl who has been to the Parthenon in Athens while on holiday. The teacher has collected about 16 pictures of Greek pots, which cover all aspects of life. There are enough for one per pair of children. The children have to find out three things about life in Ancient Greece from the pictures on their pots, and report back to the class (adapted from Dean, 1995).

QCA schemes of work and commercial schemes

QCA schemes of work

The QCA schemes are both a blessing and a curse. The thinking behind their creation was sound, but teachers' and schools' responses to them might have been predicted. The basic premise in the history schemes is that for each theme, topic or period from the History National Curriculum there are one or two exemplar schemes, setting out what is to be taught in each lesson. The current list is available on the internet at http://www.qca.org.uk/ages3–14/subjects/history.html.

Note that these schemes are a mere selection from what is to be taught. These are the suggestions for historical content from pages 16 and 19 of the History Curriculum document. The importance of the distinction between black and grey ink in the curriculum document has already been noted in Chapter 1. There is no statutory force in what is printed in grey ink. The content is suggestions only and teachers are free to teach other content if they consider it to be more valuable or of greater significance. In reality, many teachers are unsure of this distinction and try to teach too much content at the expense of teaching historical skills and processes. For teachers with no specialist background or interest in history, the QCA schemes would seem to offer a lifeline, a way through the morass. They obviate the need for selection of material to be taught, for setting learning outcomes, for detailed planning and for selection of resources, since everything is set out and presented as a ready-to-use package for teachers. Above all they remove the need for teacher decision-making, for critical thinking, and for the exercise of the full amalgam of pedagogical content knowledge. The only missing items are the resources themselves. QCA staff involved in the design and making of these schemes never intended that they would be followed slavishly by teachers. Rather they expected that they would be adapted for each school's particular context and range of learners. Instead of this, there has been a tendency to stick closely to them and to make them the basis of planning and teaching in history: an alternative History National Curriculum in fact (Claire, 2002). One can understand this tendency. Hard-pressed teachers, exhausted from literacy and numeracy teaching in the mornings, with the detailed planning which underpins these literacy and numeracy hours, do not have much time to spare for the same kind of planning for other foundation subjects, which in any case have little time allocation or priority in the curriculum. The QCA schemes are a welcome ready-made package which, given their official nature, surely guarantee the blessing and approval of Ofsted inspectors. This is unfortunate.

The trouble is that some of these schemes are simply not very good. They are highly variable in quality. Many of them start with a general activity on time and some of the lesson plans are downright dull (see Chapter 9). They do each have an overarching question which is good, but the early emphasis on chronology tends to play down the leading role which the question ought to have on steering the enquiry of each unit. Having said that, the schemes may be drawn upon for some teaching ideas, but are best not followed slavishly.

Commercial schemes

There are many commercial schemes and packs available for the teaching of history in primary schools. Some seek to offer a complete 'solution' as if the teaching of history were a problem to be solved. They try to encompass subject knowledge, teaching ideas, resources and assessment, and include photocopiable master sheets for use with children. The problem with these schemes is that they deskill the teacher, removing some of the thinking and professional decision-making (Crawford, 1996). Activities are often heavily based on reading and writing, and are very low level: colouring in; cloze exercises; filling in boxes; drawing pictures; cutting and sticking. The best advice that can be given is to evaluate such commercial resources and to take the best aspects of them to use with children.

ICT in history

There are both good uses of ICT in history and poor ones. It is essential that beginning teachers are able to distinguish between the two. ICT is often hailed as a revolutionary set of tools which will completely transform teaching and learning at most and greatly enhance it at the very least. There is considerable investment by government in ICT in schools, and pressure to use ICT in teaching across the curriculum. The reality is probably less extreme than the usual exaggerated claims. Used well, ICT can contribute a great deal to the teaching of history, but it is important to be very clear about the ways in which it can enhance learning and teaching in this subject. In this section, the definition of ICT embraces all technological tools and media, including audio, video, digital and video cameras, computers and software, the internet and interactive whiteboards. The first four will be dealt with first; the second section is devoted to computers and all related aspects.

Audio, video and cameras

Audio tapes can be immensely useful in making stories and written documents accessible to children with literacy difficulties. Stories can be taped and a listening corner established in the classroom with players and headsets to provide the audio channel for children to help with the written word. Likewise, documents can be read aloud on to tape, to enable children working with them to play back several times to help them with challenging texts. Some commercial schemes provide audio-taped versions of the books in the pack. Tape-recorders are also useful for assessment. I have used the technique of having a tape-recorder running while I go around the class asking the children for one thing they have learned from a lesson. This makes a permanent record of the assessment, and gives the teacher access to the wide variety of learning which can result from creative teaching. For example, I used this technique with the Year 6 class who did the work on the 'Story of the Transports'. This was at the end of the first morning, when we did the storytelling, the drama preparation, the drama itself, the writing and the music. Here are some of the children's responses:

'I learned that the concertina and the melodeon are both musical instruments.'

'I learned what a convict is and what happened to them.'

'I learned that tunes went around the world.'

'I learned that poor people had not enough to eat.'

'I learned that punishments were very harsh in Victorian times.'

'I learned that men, women and children were all in one big room in prison.'

'I learned that there are different rhythms in tunes like jig and reel.'

> 'I learned how a concertina is played.'
>
> 'I learned that it took almost a year to sail across to the other side of the world.'
>
> 'I learned that you could be hung for stealing a silver spoon.'
>
> 'I learned that it took weeks to travel across England on the stage-coach.'
>
> 'I learned how Sydney got its name.'

I have also used audio tape to record pairs of children in assessment interviews, probing more deeply into what they learned and how they learned it.

Video, like the QCA schemes of work, is something of a mixed blessing in the teaching of history. There is a great deal of material available of varying quality. Some series are excellent such as the Landmark Series and the Watch Series with Magic Grandad. However, the sheer quantity of video material around, and the ease of planning and teaching which it invites, is something of a problem. I have no systematically gathered evidence on this, but many students on placement tell me that the standard format for each week's history lesson is to have the children watch a video and then set comprehension questions on it. The problem is that there is no historical enquiry, no questioning and interpretation of evidence. In a sense there is some exercise of the historical imagination, in particular in the short drama episodes re-creating past events, but arguably the children should be engaging in the drama themselves rather than watching others do it. Another problem with some video materials is that they tend towards gimmicky presentation, as if this rather dull historical material needs to be dressed up in order to engage children's interest: rather like a children's TV show with wacky presenters, two- or three-minute items to prevent boredom, and silly music or sound effects. This type of programme devalues the intrinsic interest and value of the historical materials. Using other teaching approaches, children can be fully engaged with even challenging material which does full justice to both the historical discipline and their capability as learners. It is easy to understand why hard-pressed teachers who possibly lack confidence in their own knowledge of history and how to teach it turn to video as a fairly easy solution. My own view is that it should be used sparingly, if at all, and it is essential to preview to ascertain whether the material is suitable for one's purposes. Below is a list of suggestions of good uses of video material for different teaching and learning purposes.

Strategies for using video and cameras

- Providing confirmation of interpretations of evidence.
- To teach interpretations of evidence. A class could watch several video clips from recent films about Queen Elizabeth I and discuss the ways in which her character and image are portrayed.

- To examine how characters and events from history have been portrayed in comparison with other sources.
- Use short clips as a springboard to drama and role-play.
- Use video material of artefacts and remains which are otherwise inaccessible for the children (e.g. Ancient Greek remains, remains from far distant cultures).
- Digital cameras can be very useful in making history trails for children to use in towns and villages to investigate buildings, or at historical sites.
- Video cameras may be used to record drama done by the children, so that they can examine their own interpretation of events and characters in the drama.

Computers

According to Haydn (2000), one of the main factors influencing whether or not teachers use computers in their teaching of history is the difficulty of having time to plan worthwhile activities integrating the use of computers. The word 'worthwhile' is important here. Government documentation itself stresses this notion:

> Trainees must be taught how to decide when the use of ICT is beneficial to achieve teaching objectives in primary history, and when the use of ICT would be less effective or inappropriate.

> (TTA, 1998)

The general rule for teachers to apply is that the computer should be used where it enhances the possibilities for learning in history. This isn't always the case. For example, in a software package on the Victorians, one of the tasks was to scroll along a timeline of events in the period and move any anachronistic events. The operation of the scrolling was difficult, and since a timeline is predominantly a visual representation of time, a long horizontal or vertical timeline would be more suitable. Confining it to the limited space of a TV screen seems somewhat inappropriate. Some of the educational software packages have tended to be rather dull and of poor quality, lacking in genuine historical activities. Even the ones which promise more (such as those simulating archaeological digs) have disadvantages. In the ones I have used, the navigation through the chambers of the dig has been so confusing that it has detracted from the historical learning which might be possible. Many of the computer's claimed advantages for learning turn out to be nothing of the kind in reality. It is hailed as a genuinely interactive medium; for example, when children are using CD-ROMs or the internet to search and locate information. However, much of the interaction is at the level of flicking a remote control button. Sparrowhawk (1995) observed 200 primary schoolchildren using CD-ROMs and found that their activity was mostly undirected browsing. History is much more than finding and retrieving information. As Haydn points out: 'The key to developing pupils' historical understanding is their ability to analyse and deploy information after they have accessed it' (Haydn, 2000, p. 103). The most appropriate uses of ICT assist children to do just that. The other centrally important point is that the discipline of history is more than just accumulating information. Genuine enquiry processes should be used, following Hexter's framework (see Chapter 2). Most misused in my experience are CD-ROMs and the internet in purely searching, browsing and locating information. The best and most appropriate uses in my view are as listed below.

Good uses of information technology

- *Word processing*: This is a valuable tool for editing and organising historical information. It is so obvious a use that it is sometimes overlooked, but it is invaluable for a range of purposes. It may be used for sorting information into manageable categories for children to analyse, or to help children construct accounts and explanations. There are facilities for selecting and highlighting text in various ways, moving and deleting information, searching for particular words, sequencing, and making connections. It is not merely for the organisation and presenting of historical understanding, though that is useful, but can also assist with analysis of documents.

- *Data handling*: Databases are excellent vehicles for handling large amounts of information which would otherwise be difficult to sort through. They can help develop questioning skills and refine hypotheses. Many document types can be transformed into databases, including: medical officers' reports, which yield information on what people died of; graveyard information, which can give some idea of life-span; and census returns. Street directories are excellent sources of information about business, commercial and social life in Victorian times. They contain evidence about fairly well-off people: businesspeople, gentlefolk, shop owners and the like. The urban poor and unskilled labourers are not in these documents. As Dean (1995) points out, they are already arranged in the form of a database, and she gives a clear and very helpful account of how to set about making a database from part of a street directory with the whole class, using file-cards to record the information before transferring it on to a database. There are also many databases already set up and available online. For example, there is a database of Spanish ships which sailed in the Armada at tbls.hypermart.net/history/1588armada/database.html. Children can search this database on a number of fields and find out, for example, how many ships made it home to Spain, how many went missing, and how many were wrecked. From this kind of information they can begin to build up an understanding of how great a disaster this was for King Philip II of Spain and what part the weather played in the defeat of the Armada. The Old Bailey site has a database of the proceedings of 45,000 trials from 1715 to 1799 and would make excellent support material for work on the 'Story of the Transports' (see Chapter 7), or crime and punishment in general. The site can be searched in different ways on a range of fields, or it can be browsed for notable trials. The proceedings of some of these trials provide useful documents to assist children to access a wide range of evidence, using techniques and approaches described in Chapter 4. With either a ready prepared database, or one the children make themselves, children will need to ask questions. Databases are thus very useful for developing questioning skills. One technique is to ask the children to compose three statements about the information on the database and ask three questions. A simple question might be 'How many people were hanged for their crimes in the 1720s?' A more complex question might be 'Did crime increase in the eighteenth century?' From questioning and investigating the database, children can move on to testing hypotheses such as: 'Returning from transportation before the sentence was complete was punishable by death.'

- *Simulations and games*: This is an area where commercial games producers have excelled over educational software producers so far, in the scope and complexity of their games, not to mention the graphics. There is a section in Chapter 9 on historical computer games, but the main point about them is that they put children in role as decision-makers in complex and detailed historical situations. Children engage actively and imaginatively with the situation, learning all kinds of factual and conceptual information and experiencing cause and effect.

- *Images*: The internet is an excellent source of images which can be used for historical investigation. For example, after detailed enquiry into Elizabeth I using one of her portraits, children could be set the task of finding and investigating another portrait of her showing her in a very different way. They would carry out the investigation independently, using the skills they had been taught through the whole class work on portraits.

The fundamental point about using computers for history is that it should exploit those aspects and the power of computers to do things which would otherwise be difficult or tedious using other media, for example, databases. It should not be used for unfocused 'finding out', or purely for the presentation of written work, or as a bribe to make an activity seem more palatable. If it is used for finding out information which needs to be preceded by questioning activities and followed by evaluation of the material found, ask questions such as:

- Who produced this website and for what kind of audience?
- Can I trust the information on this site?

- How can I check the truth of this information?
- Is the site trying to persuade or sell something?
- What sort of information is this?
- Is this information or evidence of value for my enquiry?

Typing 'Florence Nightingale' into a search engine will bring up a vast array of sites, which will include all kinds of documents, from teenagers' essays on her to collections of her letters. Children need to be able to assess information and genre types and use this knowledge to decide whether or not the information or evidence is going to be important or valuable to them.

Nowadays we can add the technology of interactive whiteboards which open up a whole range of possibilities in linking the board to the internet. Instead of individual children or pairs working at the computer, activities such as searches or database work may be done with the whole class. Teachers can model how to do these activities, including the all-important questioning and evaluation of information and evidence, or carry out investigations as whole class activities. It will probably be a long time before interactive whiteboards are standard technology in schools, but for those who have them they are a splendid resource.

A final word follows on management of ICT and making sure you are 'covered' for inspections. It is hard to integrate computers into lessons, for if you have two children on a computer doing a task they are not participating in what the rest of the class is doing. Some primary schools have gone down the road of having computer suites as do secondary schools, but these can be a mixed blessing: they are good for database work or document work with the whole class, but I find that, with several computers in one place, time can be soaked up on troubleshooting technical problems. I would suggest having one or two computers in the classroom if space permits, and setting some ongoing tasks which children can do if other work is complete. As for inspection, the broad definition of ICT can be helpful here. If one is using an overhead projector to show a colour image to the class, or a two-minute video clip, or a tape-recording of yourself reading a document, you are using ICT and can safely tick that box.

Assessment

Issues

Some textbooks on teaching history in the primary school almost seem to suggest that assessment in history is relatively straightforward. However, it is likely that it is far from straightforward or easy. Successive Ofsted reports have commented on the poor quality of much assessment in history as a recurrent issue. For example, the Ofsted report for 2002/2003 states that: 'Assessment of pupils' standards and progress remains a weakness in one third of schools' (Ofsted, 2003, p. 2). Previous reports had commented on the tendency of teachers to mark only aspects of literacy, such as spelling and punctuation. The recall of factual information or imaginative writing was likely to have only ticks or smiley faces. Since one of the functions of assessment, in particular formative assessment, is to move children on in terms of understanding what they need to do to improve, the kind of assessment reported on by Ofsted is clearly inadequate. It is clear from the same Ofsted reports that much low-level work is set, involving recall of factual information, colouring in pictures, comprehension work, copying text from topic books, completing cloze exercises and worksheets. Such work is difficult to assess in terms of the level descriptions in the National Curriculum. The problem of assessment is directly related to inappropriate teaching activities, which in itself is caused by a lack of full understanding of the nature of history and its substantive and syntactic structures. Moreover, assessment of history very often has to take second place to assessment in the core areas of English, maths and science.

Another reason for the difficulties in assessment is the nature of the level descriptors themselves. The five key elements (now 'Knowledge, Skills and Understanding' in the latest version of the National Curriculum) are the basis for assessment. They are:

1 Chronology
2 Knowledge and understanding of events, people and changes in the past
3 Historical interpretation
4 Historical enquiry
5 Organisation and communication.

Generally speaking, children in Foundation Stage and Key Stage 1 would be expected to be working at levels 1–3. In Key Stage 2, children would be expected to be working at levels 2–5. Thus in the primary age range we are mainly concerned with levels 1–5. The problem with these key elements is that they do not appear evenly through the level descriptors. For example, Chronology occupies most of level 1, appears in levels 2 and 3 and virtually disappears for the rest of the level descriptors, surfacing only in a part sentence with Organisation and communication in levels 4–8. Historical interpretation does not appear in level 1; only in levels 2–8. As one moves through the levels, much more space is given to Historical enquiry, giving the misleading impression that it is only higher up the age range that enquiry is important. The levels are meant to be used summatively rather than for ongoing formative assessment. Since formative assessment has been shown to be far more central to children's learning than summative assessment, it would seem sensible to focus on formative assessment in history. Bage suggests breaking down the statements in the level descriptors into shorter child-friendly statements, and gives examples in his book (Bage, 2000). While it is a good idea to involve children in self-assessment, it is unlikely that this will solve the whole problem of the difficulties of assessing history using a flawed set of level descriptors which do not map on to the programme of study.

Instead, it is worth considering alternative forms of assessment, with a focus on formative assessment. It seems to me that what is needed is some kind of assessment system which is nearer to individual lesson objectives than to global descriptions of what children might be able to do at the end of each year. It is important to go back to what one actually does with children and to build the assessment from there. To show what is meant by this, the second cameo from Chapter 1 is considered in terms of children's learning and assessment. In Cameo 2, the children are analysing three different source types for jobs and language of time. Thus they are selecting evidence from a range of source types, investigating and interpreting it and presenting their understanding in the written accounts of a day in the life of a housemaid. There is also imaginative engagement and reconstruction of the past in the storytelling, freeze frames and singing activities. In this example of teaching, there is more emphasis on enquiry and interpretation of evidence. It is possible to cross-reference these learning outcomes to the key elements which form the basis of the level descriptors. However, for formative assessment one could use a grid devised from the 'Map of History' (see Chapter 2).

Using such a grid, one can identify which aspects of history a lesson or series of lessons involves, then make a record for individual children. For example, a lesson might give experience in historical enquiry, reasoning and hypothesising. Another lesson might give comparing and contrasting tasks as a way of teaching about change and continuity. A set of drawings of artefacts would yield evidence of children's observational skills. Generating questions about a topic and classifying them into different types of question would show some achievement in the process of questioning.

Carrying out assessment

There are generic methods of assessment which may be used across all subjects. Most books for primary schoolteachers will give some account of these: observation of children; listening to what children say; examining what they write; giving texts and quizzes, for example. This section focuses on a selection of those methods which can be particularly useful in history. It is not intended to be fully comprehensive, since much more research needs to be done into children's historical learning. It also has a strong emphasis on pragmatic realism and recognises the truism that much assessment knowledge is carried in teachers' minds: they simply do not have time to write it all down for all subjects right across the curriculum.

- Oral: When children are reporting back in pairs following a storytelling, or individually during a drama, listen to their contributions and make a note of which pairs are drawing on historical understanding and a sense of period and which pairs do not seem to understand the past context so well.

- Written work: One's exact assessment purposes will vary in accordance with the demands of each written task, but, by using the map of history framework, one can assess individual children's knowledge skills and understanding. For example, using the pieces on the day in the life of a Victorian housemaid, one can look for evidence of selecting from the three sources, interpretation, drawing conclusions and imaginative response to the historical situation. One can also look for the understanding that they are dealing with different kinds of evidence from the past.

- Presentation of historical processes in a variety of forms: drama, freeze frames, songs, board games, drawing, sketches, maps, plans, decisions in simulations. There are many more outcomes of children doing history than oral and written work. Through the accuracy of a child's drawing one can assess observation skills; through the plans for a castle, a child's understanding of the concept of 'castle'. Focus should always be on the learning outcome of that lesson; so that if, for example, one was trying to teach a concept of 'hierarchy', one would look for evidence of having learned about different levels of society. A series of freeze frames telling a historical story in assembly is material for assessment as much as a piece of written work.

- Tape-recording what children think they have learned from a lesson, described earlier in this chapter: This can be very valuable as a means of gaining direct access to children's own perceptions of their learning. It can give teachers insights into both intended and unintended learning outcomes!

- Using writing frames (e.g. Wray and Lewis, 1997) for children to record in their own words what they have learned from a topic: There is not space to go into writing frames in much depth, but they should be familiar to most primary teachers through the materials for the National Literacy Strategy. An explanation frame could be used for children to record their understandings of the reasons for an event. A comparison frame may be used for past and present. The frames are excellent for gaining access to children's understandings in a way that children's history books full of comprehension and cloze exercises, fruits of internet searches, and copied sections from CD-ROMs or topic books will never do.

- Drama for assessment: Children could be asked in pairs or groups to devise a short scene showing the meaning of a concept such as authority or power.

- Self-assessment: Children can compile lists of 'I can do' statements (e.g. 'I can devise historical questions which lead to a worthwhile enquiry') against which to assess their own performance. Such a statement could be the learning objective shared with the children during the lesson.

- Concept webs done at the beginning and end of a topic can be a valuable form of assessment.

Most of these suggested forms of assessment can be built into one's teaching as an integral part of it. For example, tape-recording each child stating what he or she has learned can be a plenary session at the end of a lesson or a series of lessons. The knowledge gained from assessment can be used formatively to 'feed forward' to children what they need to do next, or how to improve their work. For example, to take questioning again, for children who always generate 'trivia'-type questions, activities on devising and sorting questions can be built into most topics. One could take the Nichol framework of question types shown in Chapter 11 and share it explicitly with children, so that they have some understanding of different types of questions. The important point about assessment in history is that most of it should be formative and integral to teaching, moving the teaching and the children's learning forward. Moving children's learning forward should be one's central concern with all the issues addressed in this chapter, which has dealt with some of the thornier areas of history teaching in the primary school and offered some solutions for dealing with these aspects.

Putting it all together
Planning and creativity

This book has introduced a particular view of creative teaching of history in the primary school. It has presented: a concept of creativity and of creative teaching; definitions of history; concepts of learning and teaching; and a wide pedagogical repertoire for teaching history. There are many different teaching approaches and activities, and some examples of short-term planning (i.e. individual lesson plans) to serve as models for teachers writing their own plans. One purpose of this chapter is to pull those strands together in a medium-term plan. It deals with the problem for beginning teachers of how to weave together a series of lessons which make a coherent whole as a scheme of work, yet which meet the requirements of the National Curriculum, the needs of the children and the context in which they are working. This chapter presents: an example of teaching part of one of the compulsory units of study at Key Stage 2; an extended rationale and justification for teaching in that way; and an illustration of the repertoire of the teacher. The second purpose of the chapter is to relate this way of planning and teaching history to notions of creativity.

An example of teaching the Romans in Britain (NC KS2 Unit 9)

The context

This was a Year 5 class in a multicultural school in north-west London. The lessons described below occupied the whole of one afternoon a week for three weeks.

The planning

The statutory requirements of the History National Curriculum are broadly an out-line study of invaders and settlers pre-Norman Conquest and an in-depth study of one of three settling peoples. Thus the scope of what may be studied is very broad. There are also suggestions (in grey ink) in the curriculum document from which teachers can select. I chose the effects of Roman settlement: the Roman Conquest and occu-pation of Britain; Boudicca and resistance to Roman rule; and outline knowledge about the Romans as a background to understanding their impact on the British.

There was also some subject integration with literacy. The lessons are presented in this instance as a narrative account of what I did, rather than as formal lesson plans.

The teaching

Lesson 1

I organised the class with the children seated at their tables and all looking towards the front of the room. I put on the overhead projector a picture of a Roman galley. I then asked the children what kind of ship they thought it might be, pointing out the battering-ram at the bows of the ship. They thought it was some kind of warship. I stated that our question this week was: 'How did the Romans invade Britain with these ships?' I asked them how it was powered and the response was: by oars. I asked the children to count the oars they could see on the side of the ship facing them and I asked how many men to each oar. They thought the oars would be big and heavy and would require two men. I suggested with their help that each pair of men might need a metre of space in which to row, and by counting the oars on one side of the ship we tried to work out the length of the ship. I had a metre rule to show the concept of a metre and I asked for several sensible volunteers to come and stand down the side of the classroom in role as galley slaves. Using the metre rule I demarcated a metre space between each child. They enjoyed this phase of the lesson. There were 24 oars on each side of the ship; through questioning we established that there would have been 96 oarsmen or slaves, 48 to each side of the ship, and other crew in charge of them. The ship would have been between 30 and 35 metres long.

I asked next how they thought the oarsmen would keep in time. One child suggested a drum. We did not have a drum available for the class at that time, but I had a tambour with a drumstick ready. I demonstrated a steady beat, and asked what they might do if they saw an enemy warship. 'Row faster!' was the response. I did this and then asked what if the ship was approaching land. They thought the men would row more slowly as they came towards a beach. I demonstrated this too. I suggested that as well as the drummer there might have been a captain of the galley slaves, whipping those who did not row fast enough or keep in time. This heralded a move into more of a storytelling role for me as the teacher. I asked them to pretend they were Celts, and to imagine what they would do if they saw a fleet of Roman galleys approaching the shore where they were standing. What would they do? A child suggested they might scream with fear or shout loudly. I told them we would try this out: a tiny bit of drama in among the story, discussion and instruction. I counted to three and we all shouted very loudly. This generated a very positive, happy response from the children. I told them that we would go outside and 'draw' the ship on the playground: they would be in role as galley slaves. The children were excited, but, as instructed, behaved well on threat of abandoning this part of the lesson.

We moved outside with the teacher bringing a trundle wheel to measure the sides of the ship, and myself bringing the metre rule and tambour. Once outside I lined the children up at what would be the rear of the vessel, ready to select children as markers for the length and breadth of the ship. This proved to be a mistake and it would have been better to have the children waiting at the 'side' of the vessel, for it was a windy day and hard to make myself heard as I moved further and further away, plotting markers. None the less they were well behaved as I selected a child for each side of the 'ship'. The children were silent, gazing at the sheer size of the ship shown by the children as markers. I asked a girl to play the drum, and another girl to be captain. The last role, that of the man with the whip, I gave to a rather ebullient boy (a mistake) but he did get well into role, rushing up and down the central imaginary 'walkway' in the centre of the ship, making whipping motions and exhorting his slaves.

I moved into storytelling mode. I told the children they were rowing from Gaul to invade England for all the goods and treasure there. They needed to row steadily. At one stage they thought they saw an enemy ship, so the drummer increased her speed and the rowers did too. Then I told them they were coming in to land and had to go more slowly. The drummer and the rowers slowed down their actions. I told them the Celts were waiting on the beach armed to the teeth, and we did the war-cry we had rehearsed in the classroom. I picked one boy to act as standard-bearer and told them that when he leapt into the water, they all had to follow him for the honour of Rome. They leapt off the 'ship' and fought the imaginary Celts. I let this go on for a few moments, then called them back to the ship and home to Gaul. I asked the drummer to beat hard as they pulled away; then steadily as they rowed back. I ended this phase of the lesson by thanking the children for their superb work and lining them up to go back inside the school.

Once the children were seated, I showed them an overhead transparency of the front page of the *Greek Gazette*, a kind of tabloid newspaper published by Usborne Books as part of a series of tabloid newspapers for 'olden times'. These books are highly recommended for a variety of teaching purposes, but in this case I wanted to teach the concept of a front-page story with headlines, subheadings, columns, eyewitness accounts, quotations and interesting detail. I deliberately did not use *The Roman Record*, the book actually produced by Usborne, since part of my medium-term plan was for these children to produce their own Roman tabloid newspaper with a title chosen by themselves. Through question and answer, we examined the front-page story, read it aloud and discussed its elements. I set the task of writing a headline for the invasion of Britain we had just acted out; their homework was to write the newspaper article and illustrate it. An example of a child's work may be seen in Figure 13.1.

Lesson 2

Having caught the children's attention and interest in the Romans with the galley lesson, I wanted them to have some outline or background knowledge of the Romans against which to set the invasion story. I proposed to do this through a lesson that fell into two segments.

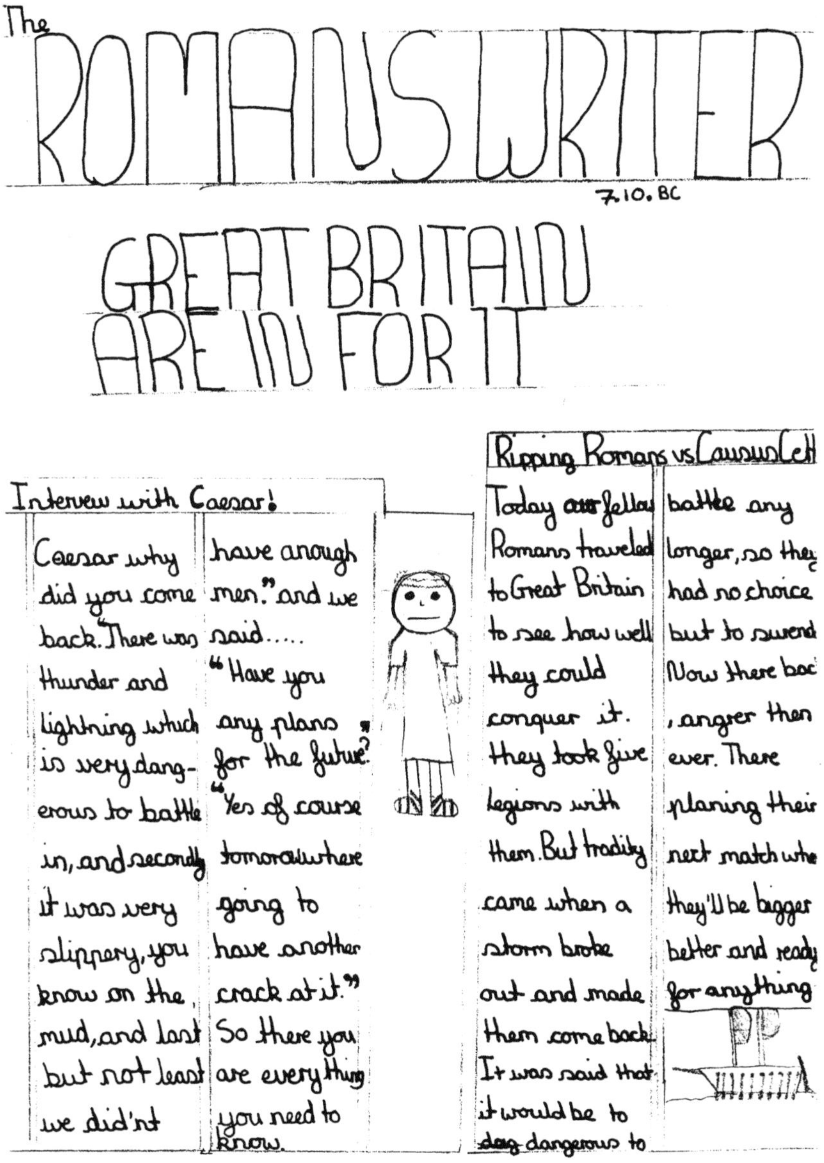

The ROMANS WRITER

7.10. BC

GREAT BRITAIN ARE IN FOR IT

Interveiw with Caesar!

Caesar why did you come back. "There was thunder and lightning which is very dang-erous to battle in, and secondly it was very slippery, you know on the, mud, and last but not least we did'nt have anough men." and we said.....
"Have you any plans for the future?"
"Yes of course tomorow there going to have another crack at it."
So there you are everything you need to know.

Ripping Romans vs Causus Celt

Today our fellow Romans traveled to Great Britain to see how well they could conquer it. they took five legions with them. But tradiky came when a storm broke out and made them come back. It was said that it would be to dag dangerous to battle any longer, so they had no choice but to surend. Now there bac, angrer then ever. There planing their next match whe they'll be bigger better and ready for anything

Figure 13.1 Children's work: The Romans invade Britain!

I started by collecting the children's homework on the newspaper articles from the previous week and praising them for their efforts. I showed two or three which caught my eye as being particularly well laid out and presented in proper tabloid format and style.

I said that our question this week was what were the Romans like and we were going to find out by using topic books. Each child had a card on which I asked them to write a question about the Romans. I gave each child three cards of a different colour and 10 minutes to go through the topic books on their desks (each table had about five or six books). I modelled the process of finding interesting facts about the Romans by looking through one of the books and reading my fact aloud (e.g. 'If a slave ran away he or she could be whipped or thrown to the lions'). They were to write one fact on each card to be shared with the whole class. I asked the slower readers to do one card and helped them with finding their facts.

I then called the class together and went around the class with each child reading out a question and a fact. In this way we pooled a great deal of information about the Romans, including schooling, slaves, towns, villas, food and drink. I then showed them a series of topic headings like the ones just given on larger cards, and told them we were going to sort our information under those headings. I placed the cards at specific points around the classroom, and gave the children five minutes to place their cards with the relevant topic heading. I then asked them to go around again with their jotters, collecting one fact, not necessarily their own, from each topic heading 'station'. The children were mostly engaged during this task but there was some off-task activity and silly behaviour from some of the boys with literacy difficulties, perhaps because of the demands of the task. The next activity planned was to make a concept web of what the children had found out. I modelled on the whiteboard how to make a concept web and gave them 10 minutes to try making their own. (See Figure 12.1 for an example of a concept web.)

I moved on to the second segment of the lesson and showed them an overhead transparency of several advertisements from the *Greek Gazette*. These advertisements serve the dual purpose of communicating much information about, for example, Greek times, and being very humorous as well. The children responded well to these advertisements, laughing at the funny parts and being very interested and engaged. We examined several, looking at different fonts and illustrations, the register of the language and the genre of persuading the reader to buy something (DfEE, 1998, Year 4, Term 3). Their homework this week, which they started in the lesson, was to design their own advertisement to go in the Roman newspaper we were aiming to create. An example of a child's work is given in Figure 13.2.

Lesson 3

For this lesson I wanted the children to have a deep and rich understanding of what it felt like to be the Celts under Roman rule, and the reasons for the Boudicca rebellion. I decided to approach this through storytelling and drama. A detailed account of this lesson is also given in Turner-Bisset (2001). One immediate problem was the classroom context. With the children sitting in groups, their attention might wander to the other children with whom they were making eye contact and I wanted all eyes to be on me. They would have to swivel their chairs to see me. The carpet was a possibility but these were Year 5 children and quite big. They would have been squashed and uncomfortable, and I would not have been able to move around freely. With the teacher's permission, we spent the first few minutes rearranging the classroom

Figure 13.2 Children's work: Advert for Roman newspaper

with the desks stacked at the sides and the chairs in a large circle. I was now ready to begin.

I told them the story of Boudicca and the events leading up to the rebellion. I had read several accounts of the story of Boudicca, including:

- three or four accounts from children's topic books;
- accounts from Roman historians Tacitus and Dio;
- a book aimed at Key Stage 3 by Downton *et al.* (1979);
- Rosemary Sutcliffe's historical novel *Song for a Dark Queen* (1978).

To create my story I used careful editing: for example, even though the rape of Boudicca's two teenage daughters is crucial to the outcome, since these were primary aged children, I did not include it, concentrating instead on the flogging and humiliation of Boudicca herself. (For accounts of how to create stories for the classroom please see Chapter 7.)

I stopped my story at the point at which Prasutagus has died, the Romans have recalled the loan to the Iceni tribe and the tribe, led by Boudicca, has to make a decision about what to do next. I told them we were going to act out the full emergency council meeting of the Iceni tribe, that everyone was to be in role, they could choose to say as much or as little as they wished or nothing at all, and that we would spend a few moments allocating roles. I had ready a set of role-cards: some with large roles such as Boudicca and her royal daughters, several council elders, a poet who tended to make off-the-wall comments but who sometimes spoke great sense (this idea from Sutcliffe's book), and the rest ordinary tribe members. Those keen to speak could put up their hands for the larger roles. Most of the children were keen to take a major role. One boy, Aaron, who had been very silly the previous week possibly because of the literacy demands of the concept web task, begged to be allowed to play Boudicca. I gave him the opportunity, and awarded the role of senior elder to Sophie, a girl with literacy difficulties.

I was in role as chief elder. I explained that I would knock on the table three times as a signal for the council meeting to begin; the same signal would end the drama. I would start the meeting by explaining the crisis situation we were in and invite Boudicca, her daughters and all the elders to speak in turn. Boudicca and I would share the chairing of the meeting. This in fact happened, for as the meeting went on, Aaron in role as Boudicca gained more and more confidence, and ran the meeting very impressively. Sophie showed that she excelled at speaking and listening, and made one or two sensible suggestions. The crux of the problem we were addressing was how to repay the loan to Seneca and avoid trouble with the Romans. The children were not grounded in the historical detail of the time, but they did pick up on information such as the Iceni being rich in horses and minerals, so they suggested selling these to raise money to pay off the loan. In fact many of their suggestions focused on fund-raising (the teacher later explained to me that many of these children sat on the school council, and fund-raising was a perennial concern). Once the children had started to repeat ideas, I gave the signal to end the drama and two minutes to relax and come out of role. I knocked again for silence, and told them the rest of the Boudicca story, to her defeat and death.

I gave the order to put the chairs and tables back. While the children were doing this, I wrote the names of key characters on the whiteboard to assist with spelling. When the children were seated, I explained they were to write an article for their Roman tabloid newspaper on the Boudicca story, either as an eyewitness, a character in the story, or simply in the third person as a journalist reporting on events. We read through the spellings of key names on the board to familiarise the children with difficult names and I asked the children to suggest headlines again. As before the children finished the work for homework. An example of children's work is included in Figure 13.3. It is significant that with one storytelling and the drama, the children were able to write at length about the story. They had no recourse to any secondary sources such as topic books or videos: the writing arose purely from the storytelling and the drama activity. The power of story and drama to generate deep learning has been explored in this book; the children's work here is yet another example of their impact on children's learning.

Rationale and justification

Lesson 1

Some readers will recognise the first lesson as a replication of David (Turner-Bisset, 2001) creating a Roman galley. I described this lesson as an example of expert teaching as a starting point for that book. Enthused and inspired by the lesson, I wished to try it out for myself. Teachers are interested in what works: what kinds of teaching approaches, activities, examples, discourse and feedback encourage children to learn? In observing David, I was struck by the engagement of the children, their learning, the variety of roles and approaches, and the evident enjoyment of all. I wanted to try this lesson for myself to see if it worked as well for a different teacher in a different context.

Rather than a formal lesson plan, I had an agenda of activities and questioning through which I intended to move the children. In the list of activities and approaches used which follows, the chapter in which that teaching approach is discussed is given in parentheses:

- Showing the picture of the galley (Chapter 5).
- Socratic dialogue in which we established the possible size of the ship and how it was powered (Chapter 11).
- The physical representation of part of the ship in the classroom (Chapters 8 and 9).
- Modelling drumming to set the speed (Chapter 13).
- Storytelling of the Roman invasion (Chapter 7).

Creative Teaching: History in the Primary Curriculum

<u>Monday 16th October The story of Boudica</u>

Boudicca was the queen of the Iceni tribe and ruled along with King Prasutagus. The king was older than Boudicca and Boudicca feared that he would die. King Prasutagus had other things on his mind. He had taken a loan from a rich Roman man called Seneca and soon had to repay him. He didn't have enough money to repay him and look after the tribe.

One day he had an idea. He told Boudicca that he would write out his will again and in it he would say half of the money would go to the tribe and the other half than to Seneca. Then Boudicca thought that she was out of her mind to think ~~Tuesday~~ that King Prasutagus would die, because he is only a few years older than her, but a few ~~years~~ days later he did die. Know she had to deal with the situation herself.

She held a meeting for anyone who wanted to discuss what to do. By the end of the meeting she had ~~decided~~.

They went to Colchester. Boudicca riding in her chariot with the rest of the army following behind her. The Romans were not prepared at all and so Boudicca defeated them easily. ~~"On to London."~~

"On to London," Boudicca bellowed and they sped to London. They took Roman London by surprise as well and clobbered them to smithereans. Then they went to St Albums guessed and yes, you ~~guest~~ in the defeated them too.

Then they went to Wales, and chose a sight with trees behind them and open land infront. They asked their friends and family to come along too. They had to ~~go back~~ but the ~~Roman~~ waggons that their family were in were in the way so they were defeated.

Boudicca drank poison, instead of being captured.

✓ What a sad ending to the life of a great leader Excellent work Cyn ③pt

Figure 13.3 Children's work: Boudicca story

- Creating the outline of the ship in the playground (Chapters 8 and 9).
- Further storytelling and the significance of the standard-bearer (Chapters 7 and 8).
- Acting out the battle between the Romans and Celts (Chapter 8).
- Looking at the front page of the *Greek Gazette* (Chapter 13).
- Starting to write headlines and news stories of the invasion of Britain (Chapter 13).

The initial activity of looking at the picture is a powerful way of seizing the children's attention and interest. The overhead projector is an important teaching tool. Its advantage is the size of the image projected. It is an immediate focus for the children's attention. In this part of the lesson I wanted the children to estimate for themselves the size of the ship, guided by my questions and challenges, using the evidence of the picture of the ship.

The physical creation of part of the ship in the classroom was an important precursor to the later full reconstruction in the playground. It acted as an enactive representation of the ship (Bruner, 1970), since, by using children as markers, the class could see how much room just seven oarsmen would occupy. For those learners who find it difficult to understand ideas or concepts through being told, or reading words on a page, acting out through physical movement or positioning can greatly aid understanding of complex concepts. Storytelling is another crucially important teaching approach and has a whole chapter devoted to it (Chapter 7). In this lesson, it became a thread running through which carried the meaning of important concepts such as invasion, galley and standard-bearer. It also captured the children's imagination and helped to hold their interest. Acting out the invasion battle was a drama activity which flowed naturally from the storytelling and was again an enactive representation of an event in the past.

Two of the activities – the drumming and looking at the example of the *Greek Gazette* front page – involved demonstration and modelling of the drumming so that any child I chose later to be the drummer would be able to do it; to speed up and slow down as required. As a class we also modelled the battle-cry which would be used in the drama. For the newspaper stories, the children needed a good example, but not one too close to what I wanted them to write. They needed examples of layout, headlines, subheadings, columns, quotations, and the appropriate style, tone and register of a tabloid newspaper. They also needed an example of an 'ancient' tabloid newspaper to serve as a model for the end-product (in tangible terms) of the unit. The writing task was something of a settling or winding down activity at the end of an afternoon which had involved much varied activity. It served as a consolidation task for the afternoon's work, and as a means for myself and the teacher to assess the children's learning and understanding of ideas about the Roman invasion and Roman ships.

Lesson 2

My agenda for lesson 2 looked like this:

- Topic book blitz using demonstration and modelling (Chapter 12).
- Concept web activity (Chapter 12).
- Writing Roman adverts for newspaper (Chapter 13) (knowledge transfer again).

It is all too easy to take for granted that children will have background knowledge of the period of history or the topic one intends to teach. Background knowledge may vary enormously from child to child, from the child who knows nothing, to the one sitting next to him who has read several 'Horrible Histories' including one on the period you are teaching. I chose to do a combination of a topic book blitz and making concept webs for this class. The sorting of facts under broader headings is an exercise in classifying information. The facts about fish stew, dormice and wine shops are physically grouped under the heading of food and drink. The physical sorting, with moving around the room, is both an enactive representation of sorting facts in the mind, and a respite from sitting still to read and write. The revisiting of each topic heading to collect facts for the concept web serves to reinforce the information. The activity is a collective pooling of information. The final part of making the concept web is another means of revising and sorting facts, this time in a visual or iconic representation (Bruner, 1970). Concept webs may be used in a variety of subjects: their use in history is discussed further in Chapter 12.

The second part of the lesson on designing advertisements for the Roman newspapers as stated previously had the purpose of communicating information about the Romans and enjoying humour. The advertisements in the example newspaper were interesting, amusing and varied. They offered a great deal of information about aspects of Greek life. It is probably true that if one wants to learn about a culture, advertisements for products and services can tell you a great deal about that culture. I wanted now for the children to use their background information in order to produce advertisements. Through doing so, their background knowledge would be revisited and enhanced through working actively on the information to produce it in another form: from information text to persuasion genre (Lewis and Wray, 1995). This part of the lesson carried the secondary purpose of literacy hour work (DfEE, 1998, Year 4, Term 3, p. 43). Finally the activity of designing the advertisements was intended to encourage creativity in the synthesis of different elements to produce their own new texts (Koestler, 1964).

Lesson 3

Here is the agenda for this lesson:

- Telling the story of Boudicca's rebellion (Chapter 7).
- Acting out the Iceni tribe council meeting (Chapter 8).
- Writing out the story of Boudicca (Chapter 7).

For the third lesson I wanted a change of teaching approach and much more emphasis on storytelling and drama. The rationale for this was simply the power and impact of these approaches. In my teaching I have been greatly influenced by the work of the late John Fines. In his teaching there was often a fine line between storytelling and drama, an interface which has been explored in this book (Chapters 7 and 8). I had been very much impressed by his storytelling and by the imaginative response of the children. He frequently used the story as a springboard to other activities, and this I wanted to try here. The proof of the teaching, so to speak, and the children's learning would lie in their imaginative oral responses during the drama and in their written work. The physical layout of the classroom was important. It is worth getting this right in order to create the right atmosphere. The time taken to move furniture around is well compensated for by the ease with which one can undertake storytelling and drama and the quality of the children's work which ensues.

The device of telling a story up to a certain point and moving into drama increases the involvement of the children, which is far from passive during the telling. I find it useful to set ground rules for the drama (e.g. only one person to speak at once) and to have ready a number of small cards with the roles printed on them. Each child, even if she or he ends up with a very small part or a non-speaking role, has a clearly defined role. In some cases I allow preparation time, but in this case none was required for the structure of the council meeting, which I also explained lent a formality and order to the drama. The two-minute recovery period was necessary to give the children time to relax and come out of role. I wanted the desks moved back, since, once I had told the rest of the story, I wanted the children to begin writing immediately while the story was still fresh in their minds. Through the act of retelling in written form, the children add their own interpretation, pick up on details which caught their imagination, and probe aspects of character which may not have been in the original telling or version. The act of retelling in oral or written form helps children to make the story their own, part of their own internal map of understanding these events (see Chapter 2). That the lesson's aims were successful is borne out by the quality of the children's writing (see Figure 13.3). It has to be remembered that these pieces of writing were produced only from the storytelling and the drama: no other written sources were used. The teacher, Kirsty, was astonished to find that so many of them were able to write so well without other support. I would suggest as a hypothesis that it was their imaginative engagement with the events of the past which enabled them to do so.

The repertoire of the teacher

Many of you reading this book will be beginning teachers. I suspect that one reaction to the accounts of these lessons and the rationale might be that this kind of teaching is all very well for experienced teachers, but too difficult or risky for those setting out on the journey of learning to teach. Quite rightly, at the beginning, one tends to want nice 'safe' activities, which don't permit too much movement out of seats or carry with them the possibility of disorder, or worse, mayhem. Order and classroom management are major concerns of beginning teachers. I would argue that being able to use such active teaching approaches is an essential part of a teacher's pedagogical repertoire. It is of central importance to provide learning experiences which allow all children to learn. The strongest argument in favour of the approaches described here is that in terms of children's learning they work extremely well. Since children's learning is our major objective as teachers, we have to be open to the idea that a wide range of pedagogical approaches, strategies and activities is necessary to promote that learning. You will find that the response of the children will be so positive and inspiring that it will encourage you to do more of this sort of teaching and wipe away any doubts you may have.

By way of example, I gave one of my student-teachers a copy of the transcript of David's original lesson on the Roman galley which I later wrote in full in Turner-Bisset (2001). She was so inspired by this that she resolved to try it herself on her second year teaching placement. The interesting point was that she took the central idea of the teaching approach, creating a boat in the playground, and adapted it to the context in which she was teaching. This was a tough primary school on a deprived housing estate in a 'new' town in south-east England. She had one of two parallel Year 3 classes. Her class contained several 'problem' children including twin girls, both elective mutes. The normal teaching approach adopted by the class teacher and her colleague planning in tandem was to watch a video and then give the class a set of written questions. This particular student felt able to go against the constraints and try something different. Her own class teacher would not have tried the mapping out of the ship in the playground, but she was happy to allow the student-teacher to do so. I was privileged to observe the lesson as part of a research project.

The student, Kathy, did use the video prescribed for the week, which was about the Vikings and their ships, their invasion of and settlement in Britain and other parts of the world, and their rowing up the Thames in their attempt to take London. The class watched the video and Kathy gave them each a strip of paper with the same three questions about the ship and what happened when the Vikings reached London Bridge. She then replicated part of David's lesson of working out how much space each oarsman would have to sit in, using children as markers in the classroom, and modelling the drumming. The class then moved outside with chalk, metre rules and the drum. They were very well behaved as she drew the ship in chalk on the playground, and once in position as oarsmen and markers, they rowed as if their lives depended on it. She moved into role as storyteller, letting them know they were approaching London Bridge. At the last minute, they 'saw' Anglo-Saxon soldiers on the bridge. 'Hold back!' she cried and these Year 3 children tried frantically to 'row' backwards, rather than slow the 'boat' by simply dipping their 'oars' in and holding hard. They were evidently deeply absorbed in the story and drama, even the two girls who never spoke. During this activity, children from other classes near the playground were watching from their classrooms. They asked their teachers when they could play with the chalk outline of the ship. The weather remained dry for the rest of the week and at every playtime, groups of children from across the school could be seen using it for their imaginative play. This was an unintended but none the less valuable learning outcome.

The significant points about this example of teaching are the replication and adaptation to another period in history, another culture from the past, and for a different teaching context. It matters not that someone has used the approach before, or that one might be 'stealing' another person's idea. Through the act of adaptation to their own teaching circumstances, teachers can make an approach or an activity entirely their own. These concepts of replication and adaptation are important to the design and purpose of this book, and to its central conception of creativity explored at length in Chapter 1. In this example Kathy was teaching creatively, despite having taken an idea from somewhere else. She replicated the activity but adapted it for her own context, bringing the frame of reference of the Viking invasion and the ramming of London Bridge to the acquired teaching activity of planning out a ship in the playground. Both Kathy and I were eager and enthusiastic to emulate David's terrific lesson, and these emotions are part of the product of creativity. In Chapter 1, following Koestler, I suggested there was a 'rush' of emotion accompanying the moment of creation. For the jester part of the Triptych, the emotion is laughter; for the artist, the emotion is wonder or admiration. This is an explosion of emotions which accompanies the moment of connection. Certainly when I have 'seen' how I can use a teaching approach or a representation to teach someone something, I have been aware of excitement and a feeling of pleasurable anticipation at the prospect of trying it out.

Planning and creativity

It follows that planning for creative teaching can be very pleasurable. It is more usual to conceive of planning as work, but I would argue that in this kind of planning which produces creative teaching there is the kind of pleasure which accompanies any creative activity. I am not thinking here so much of the documentation and recording of planning but of the thinking. When one muses over a range of teaching approaches (e.g. storytelling, drama, music, simulation, pictures or documents) to select teaching activities, one is making connections between the material to be taught and the kind of teaching approaches one might use. In addition, one selects the teaching approach for a particular class of children in a particular context. It is a synthesis, a shuffling of ideas and repertoire to devise the best possible teaching approach for what is to be learned by this group of learners. It follows that the 'teaching approach' should ideally feature on medium-term plans, so that one can see at a glance whether or not one is mixing one's approaches to give the children a varied diet of learning experiences. A further notion I would like to introduce is the rather heretical idea that one should not over-plan, or plan too far in advance. Dean (1995) suggests that it is not worth planning in detail for more than the first few lessons. 'A rolling programme of weekly review and further planning is more flexible, and allows you to adapt to new developments and changing interests' (Dean, 1995, p. 18). Figure 13.4 shows the medium-term plan for teaching the Romans in Britain in this chapter. Like the lesson plans in this book, it offers a good model for medium-term planning, including

Key Question: What happened when the Romans invaded Britain?

Week	Concepts	Skills	Processes	Activities/Approaches	Assessment	N.C. links	Subject links
Week 1	Galley Invasion Ram Slaves Standard-bearer Headline Subheading Eyewitness	Observation Estimation Visualisation Mime Expressive movement	Enquiry Interpretation Imagination	Visual image Modelling Storytelling Planning spaces Drama Writing newspaper article	Understanding of concepts Understanding and recall of content Use of imagination Through oral contributions, how they did the drama, and the written work	N.C. 2a, 2c N.C. 3 N.C. 4a, 4b N.C. 5a, 5b N.C. 9	Literacy Drama
Week 2	Concept web Army Roads Food Entertainment Gladiators Town life Home life	Extracting facts Skimming Scanning Recording information Sorting information	Visiting and revisiting information Mapping information Grouping facts under concept headings	Topic book blitz Organising facts Concept webs Modelling adverts Writing adverts	From their ability to note, collect, record and organise facts From making concept webs From content of adverts	N.C. 2a, 2c N.C. 3 N.C. 4a, 4b N.C. 5a, 5b N.C. 9	Literacy Art Design technology
Week 3	Loan Royal line Rebellion Council meeting	Listening to story Taking on a role Acting out meeting Recalling story Writing story	Imagination interpretation	Storytelling Drama/role-play Writing story Drawing Boudicca from descriptions	From listening and responding to story From role-play and writing	N.C. 2a, 2c N.C. 3 N.C. 4a N.C. 5a, 5b N.C. 9	Literacy Art Drama

Figure 13.4 Medium-term plan for teaching the Romans in Britain

important aspects such as teaching approaches which are often left out. At the end of these three weeks, one would review the work the children had done and plan the next few weeks.

Conclusion

There are several reasons why it is important that teachers should be creative. First of all, teaching is creative in that it is a creative act in which one selects from one's repertoire of teaching approaches activities which are useful for teaching skills, concepts and processes for particular groups of learners in a range of contexts. Second, this planning for teaching is enjoyable, creative behaviour to ensure that every child has the opportunity to connect to the knowledge, skills and understanding of the teacher. The moment of creativity happens when a teacher decides to teach content and processes by a particular approach: Henry VIII's wives as a 'Blind Date' programme; history as a detective puzzle at Key Stage 1; Florence Nightingale – 'This is your Life'; the Ancient Greeks as an invasion and settlement game; or the lives of sailors at sea through a selection of sea songs and shanties. Such planning is a world apart from planning for curriculum 'coverage' and can be very pleasurable. Since teaching is a job with a strong element of altruism, any aspect of the job which has benefits for the teacher can only be a good thing. Teachers who enjoy their work are more likely to create high-quality lessons for their children. There is of course the issue of whether or not teachers should be teaching creatively, or seeking to encourage creativity in children. I would argue that through creative teaching, one is modelling creative activity to children and thus encouraging and facilitating creativity in them. The inspiration and enthusiasm which accompany creative teaching are experienced by the children as well as the teacher.

There are some implications of this way of conceiving of teaching as a creative activity. Teachers need time to create stories for telling, role-play and drama, games and simulations. It is a kind of 'capital investment' which, once made, yields tremendous enhancement of children's learning. This makes the initial investment of time and energy worthwhile. Staff development time and in-service training could usefully be allocated to this kind of preparation and development of teaching activities, rather than the kind of ring-binder-led approach which has characterised some literacy and numeracy training. These folders, full of bullet points and advice, are helpful as far as they go, but they do not go far enough in terms of modelling and explaining how one might teach creatively and in a way which enhances children's learning. In contrast, this book has set out to provide both a wealth of practical examples, and access to the thinking behind them.

Appendix

Simulation: Cortez and the Conquest of the Aztecs

Spanish: Round 1

You are Cortez, leader of the Spanish expedition sent by Velasquez, Governor of Cuba, to explore, trade and search for Christian captives in Yucatan and the Gulf of Mexico. You hear rumours that Velasquez thinks you are too ambitious and plans to have you removed from the expedition.

Do you:

> **1.** Carry on getting your ships ready and not worry about Velasquez?
>
> **2.** Cut short your preparations and sail for Yucatan?

Aztecs: Round 1

You are Montezuma, ruler of the great Aztec empire, composed of several different tribes. You hear stories of many signs and omens that the god Quetzelcoatl is returning to take back the empire from you. A mountain has been seen moving on the waters of the Gulf: a Spanish ship. You believe that the white men are signs that the god Quetzelcoatl has come back.

Do you:

> **3.** Send supplies of food and presents to the Spanish?
>
> **4.** Send a small army to deal with the Spanish invaders?

Consequences sheet: Round 1
Spanish Aztec

1	3	Cortez: You have to deal with a group of soldiers who come to remove you from the ships. This delays you and you lose some men, but you set off. Montezuma: Because you do not attack the Spanish, you weaken your position for the future. Spanish lose 10 men; Aztecs lose 5,000.

1	4	Cortez: You have to deal with a group of soldiers who come to remove you from the ships. This delays you and you lose some men, but you set off. Montezuma: Your army attacks the Spanish port of Veracruz and kills some of the Spanish force. Spanish lose 25 men; Aztecs lose 5.
2	3	Cortez: you sail away early with your eleven ships and avoid Velasquez' men. Montezuma: Because you do not attack the Spanish, you waken your position for the future. Spanish lose 0 men; Aztecs lose 5,000.
2	4	Cortez: you sail away early with your eleven ships and avoid Velasquez' men. Montezuma: Your army attacks the Spanish port of Veracruz and kills some of the Spanish force. Spanish lose 2 men; Aztecs lose 5.

Spanish: Round 2

Cortez: You learn that some of the vassal kings of the empire are ready to rebel against Montezuma. You could march from the coast to Tenochtitlan with the rebel tribes and attack Montezuma. Your troops do not want to march. Food is short and they are torn between their desire for fame and wealth and their fear of defeat and death. They want to sail back to Cuba.

5. You listen to your troops and wait until they have enough food and more promises of help from the rebels.

6. You sink all your eleven ships, so that there is no retreat and they must march on Montezuma.

Aztecs: Round 2

Montezuma: You hear that rebel tribes are marching on Tenochtitlan with the Spanish. Paralysised by indecision (a problem of yours) you seek help from your priests and advisers again.

Do you:

7. Send forces to harass the Spanish on their long march?

8. Thinking the god has returned, prepare a lavish reception to welcome the Spanish as friends and allies?

Consequences sheet: Round 2
Spanish Aztec

| 5 | 7 | Cortez: Some of your soldiers sail away in one ship. This delays the start of the march but the Aztec soldiers do not reach you. |

Montezuma: some of your soldiers fight with rebel tribes and are killed. Spanish lose 50 men; Aztecs lose 100.

5	8	Cortez: Some of your soldiers sail away in one ship. This delays the start of the march but the Aztec soldiers do not reach you. Montezuma: some of your troops from the other tribes, Cempoalans and Tlaxcatans go over to the Spanish side. Spanish lose 50 men; Aztecs lose 5,000.
6	7	Cortez: you lead all your troops on the march to Tenochtitlan, recruiting as many native allies as possible who are hostile to Montezuma. Montezuma: You hear of the massacre of the local nobility at Cholula by the Spanish and begin to think they must be the gods. Spanish lose 0 men; Aztecs lose 100.
6	8	Cortez: you lead all your troops on the march to Tenochtitlan, recruiting as many native allies as possible who are hostile to Montezuma. Montezuma: some of your troops from the other tribes, Cempoalans and Tlaxcatans go over to the Spanish side. Spanish lose 0 men; Aztecs lose 5,000.

Spanish: Round 3

Cortez's procession of his soldiers and Montezuma's procession of the great nobles and priests are about to meet on the causeway to Tenochtitlan: a historic moment.

Cortez:

Do you:

9. Immediately attack Montezuma and proclaim you are the god?

10. Greet Montezuma in peace and wait for a suitable moment to attack later during the feast of Huitzilopochli, where you might be able to kill as many as 10,000 Aztecs?

Aztecs: Round 3

Montezuma:

Do you:

11. Greet Cortez in peace as the returned god, welcome him with gifts and give him and his men palaces to live in?

12. Seeing the number of rebel troops with him, order your soldiers to seize the Spanish and keep them hostage?

Consequences sheet: Round 3

Spanish Aztec

9	11	Cortez: Montezuma is too well-guarded and the men you ordered to attack are killed.

Montezuma: You have been expecting this and signal your guards to kill the men who attack. However, you are still afraid that Cortez might be a god and do not order him taken.
Spanish lose 25 men; Aztecs lose 0.

9   12   Cortez: Montezuma is too well-guarded and the men you ordered to attack are killed. Many more are taken prisoner. You have to plot to break out of prison and attack the Aztecs before you are sent for human sacrifice.
Montezuma: You feel safer now Cortez is captured. Cortez may be a god and you will see if he is when he and his men break out of prison.
Spanish lose 25 men; 200 more are captured; Aztecs lose 0.

10   11   Cortez: The meeting passes off peacefully. Later you and your men kill 10,000 nobles at the religious feast.
Montezuma: The meeting passes of peacefully. Later Cortez and his men kill 10,000 nobles at the religious feast.
Spanish lose 0 men; Aztecs lose 10,000.

10   12   Cortez: You and your Spanish soldiers are taken prisoner and have to escape from the prison, which you do eventually.
Montezuma: Racked with doubts over imprisoning a god, you relax the guard on the prison and make it possible for the Spanish to escape. They take refuge in some of your palaces.
Spanish lose 5 men; Aztecs lose 10.

Spanish: Round 4

The processions of Cortez's soldiers and Montezuma's nobles have met on the causeway to Tenochtitlan: a historic moment. Montezuma recognizes Cortez as a god and surrenders authority to him. The Spanish still worry that they are outnumbered. They ask to be present at a religious ritual, and kill almost 10,000 victims. They take Montezuma hostage and he later dies. The remaining noble leader, Cuauhtemoc, orders the palaces where the Spanish are living to be surrounded.

Cortez:

Do you:

13. Take advantage of a moonless night and torrential rain, flee from the palaces. Meet up with rebel tribes who are now on your side. Prepare an attack on Tenochtitlan?

14. Wait for a better moment to escape, lose time and some of the support of the rebels tribes?

Aztecs Round 4
Cuauhtemoc:

Do you?

15. Attempt to capture the Spanish with Aztec soldiers, failing to enlist the support of other tribes?

16. Persuade some of the rebel tribes to come back to the side of the Aztecs and go after the escaped Spanish men.

Consequences sheet: Round 4
Spanish Aztec

13	15	Cortez: You make a successful escape, but with heavy losses and harassment from the Aztecs. Fighting bravely, you open up the route to Tlaxcala and with the tribes' support, prepare an attack on Tenochtitlan. Cuauhtemoc (Aztecs): You try to stop the Spanish escaping and kill many of them but the rest get away. Spanish lose 100 men; Aztecs lose 50.
13	16	Cortez: You make a successful escape, but with heavy losses and harassment from the Aztecs. Fighting bravely, you open up the route to Tlaxcala and with the tribes' support, prepare an attack on Tenochtitlan. Cuauhtemoc (Aztecs): You try to stop the Spanish escaping and kill many of them but the rest get away. One tribe comes back to the Aztec side. Spanish lose 100 men; Aztecs lose 100, but gain 3,000 more soldiers.
14	15	Cortez: You make a successful escape, but with very heavy losses and harassment from the Aztecs. Fighting bravely, you open up the route to Tlaxcala and with some of the the tribes' support, prepare an attack on Tenochtitlan. Cuauhtemoc (Aztecs): You try to stop the Spanish escaping and kill many of them but the rest get away. Spanish lose 100 men; Aztecs lose 50.
14	16	Cortez: You make a successful escape, but with very heavy losses and harassment from the Aztecs. Fighting bravely, you open up the route to Tlaxcala and with some of the the tribes' support, prepare an attack on Tenochtitlan. Cuauhtemoc (Aztecs): You try to stop the Spanish escaping and kill many of them but the rest get away. One tribe comes back to the Aztec side. Spanish lose 150 men; Aztecs lose 100, but gain 3,000 more soldiers.

Spanish: Round 5

The rebel tribes believe that Cortez will save them from the ruling Aztecs and restore their power. They do not realize that Cortez represented in some ways a more mighty power: that of Spain and Christianity. Cortez has to decide what to do with the help of the rebel tribes. At this point he gains 5,000 more rebel soldiers.

Cortez:

Do you:

17. Retreat to the coastal port of Velacruz and send to Cuba for more troops?

18. Gather several thousand native rebels, construct a fleet of small ships and launch a siege of Tenochtitlan?

Aztecs: Round 5

Cuauhtemoc:

Do you:

19. Send your men after Cortez to finish off him and the Spanish threat once and for all?

20. Seek help of the remaining rebel tribes loyal to the empire and prepare to defend Tneochtitlan?

Consequences sheet: Round 3
Spanish Aztec

17	19	Cortez: Velasquez, angry that Cortez has gone so far beyond his original mission, refuses to send any help. Cuauhtemoc (Aztecs): Your men follow the Spanish to the coast but fall ill with an epidemic of illness brought by the Spanish to the southern American continent. Spanish lose 10 men; Aztecs lose 3,000.
17	20	Cortez: Velasquez, angry that Cortez has gone so far beyond his original mission, refuses to send any help. Cuauhtemoc (Aztecs): you prepare for the siege only to lose many people in the epidemic of illness. Spanish lose 10 men; Aztecs lose 3,000.
18	19	Cortez: For three months besiege Tenochtitlan. The Aztecs are eventually defeated by the repeated attacks, famine and illness. Cuauhtemoc is taken prisoner and hanged on the pretext of a plot. Cuauhtemoc (Aztecs): Your men set off to follow the Spanish but see a great army of natives waiting to attack, the retreat to the city and are besieged. Spanish lose 50 men; Aztecs lose 10,000.

18   20   Cortez: For three months besiege Tenochtitlan. The Aztecs are eventually defeated by the repeated attacks, famine and illness. Cuauhtemoc is taken prisoner and hanged on the pretext of a plot. The Spanish now rule Mexico and the course of world history has changed.

Cuauhtemoc (Aztecs): you prepare for the siege only to lose many people in the epidemic of illness. You are taken prisoner

Spanish lose 50 men; Aztecs lose 10,000.

References

Abbs, P. (1985) *English as an Arts Discipline*, Take-up No 2, National Association for Education in the Arts.

Abbs, P. (ed.) (1987) *Living Powers: The Arts in Education*, Lewes: Falmer Press.

Abbs, P. (1989) *A is for Aesthetic: Essays in Creative and Aesthetic Education*, Lewes: Falmer Press.

Alexander, R.J. (1992) *Policy and Practice in Primary Education*, London and New York: Routledge.

Alexander, R.J. (1995) *Versions of Primary Education*, London and New York: Open University/Routledge.

Alexander, R.J. (2000) *Culture and Pedagogy: International Comparisons in Primary Education*, Oxford: Blackwell, Open University/Routledge.

Alexander, R.J., Rose, J. and Woodhead, C. (1992) *Curriculum Organisation and Classroom Practice in Primary Schools: A Discussion Paper*, London: DES.

Andretti, K. (1993) *Teaching History from Primary Evidence*, London: David Fulton.

Bage, G. (1999) *Narrative Matters: Teaching and Learning History Through Story*, London: Falmer.

Bage, G. (2000) *Thinking History 4–14: Teaching, Learning, Curricula and Communities*, London: Routledge/Falmer.

Beetlestone, F. (1998a) *Creative Children, Imaginative Teaching*, Buckingham: Open University Press.

Beetlestone, F. (1998b) 'Fostering creative development', in I. Siraj-Blatchford, *A Curriculum Development Handbook for the Early Years*, Stoke: Trentham Books.

Bellamy, P. (1977) *The Transports: A Ballad Opera*, Free Reed Records, FRRD 021/022.

Blyth, W.A.L., Cooper, K.R., Derricott, R., Elliot, G., Sumner, H. and Waplington, A. (1976) *Place, Time and Society 8–13: Curriculum Planning in History, Geography and Social Science*, Glasgow and Bristol: Collins/ESL.

Brown, G. and Edmondson, R. (1984) 'Asking questions', in E. Wragg (ed.), *Classroom Teaching Skills*, London: Routledge.

Bruner, J.S. (1970) 'The course of cognitive growth', in B.L. Klintz and J. Brunig (eds), *Research in Psychology*, Glenview, IL: Scott, Foresman & Co.

Bruner, J.S. (1976) 'Early social interaction and language acquisition', in H.R. Schaffer (ed.), *Studies in Mother–Infant Interaction*, London: Academic Press.

Bruner, J.S. (1978) 'The role of dialogue in language acquisition', in A. Sinclair, R. Jarvella and W. Levelt (eds), *The Child's Conception of Language*, New York: Springer-Verlag.

Bruner, J.S. (1983) *Child's Talk*, Oxford: Oxford University Press.

Bruner, J.S. (1986) *Actual Minds, Possible Worlds*, Cambridge, Mass: Harvard University Press.

Burt, C. (1964) Foreword to A. Koestler, *The Act of Creation*, London: Hutchinson.

Central Advisory Council for Education (CACE) (England) (1967) *Children and Their Primary Schools* (The Plowden Report), London: HMSO.

Claire, H. (2002) 'Values in the primary history curriculum', in A. McNully and C. O'Neill, *Values in History Teacher Education and Research*, History Teacher Education Network.

Cockburn, A.D. (1995) 'Learning in classrooms', in C. Desforges (ed.), *An Introduction to Teaching: Psychological Perspectives*, Oxford, UK, and Cambridge, USA: Blackwell.

Collingwood, R.G. (1946) *The Idea of History*, Oxford: Oxford University Press.

Cooper, H. (1992) *The Teaching of History in Primary Schools*, London: David Fulton.

Cooper, H. (1995a) *The Teaching of History in Primary Schools* (2nd edn), London: David Fulton.

Cooper, H. (1995b) *History in the Early Years*, London: David Fulton.

Cooper, H. (2000) *The Teaching of History in Primary Schools: Implementing the Revised National Curriculum* (3rd edn), London: David Fulton.

Copeland, T. (1993) *A Teacher's Guide to Geography and the Historic Environment*, Bristol: English Heritage.

Counsell, C. (1997) *Analytical and Discursive Writing in History at Key Stage 3*, London: Historical Association.

Crawford, K. (1996) 'Packaging the past: the primary history curriculum and how to teach it', *Curriculum Studies*, 4 (3): 401–16.

Davies, I. and Webb, C. (1996) *Using Documents*, Bristol: English Heritage.

Dean, J. (1995) *Teaching History at Key Stage 2*, Cambridge: Chris Kington.

DES (1991) *History in the National Curriculum (England)*, London: DES/HMSO.

DES/QCA (1995) *The National Curriculum For England: History*, London: DES/QCA.

DfEE (1998) *The National Literacy Strategy: Framework for Teaching*, London: DfEE.

DfEE (1999a) *The National Numeracy Strategy: Framework for Teaching Mathematics from Reception to Year 6*, London: DfEE.

DfEE (1999b) *History National Curriculum*, London: QCA/DfEE/HMSO.

DfES (2003) *Excellence and Enjoyment: a Strategy for Primary Schools*, London: DfES.

Dillon, J. (1988) *Questioning and Teaching: A Manual of Practice*, London: Croom Helm.

Donaldson, M. (1978) *Children's Minds*, London: Fontana.

Downton, D., Nichol, J. and Leavitt, M. (1979) *The Romans*, Oxford: Blackwell.

Duffy, B. (1998) *Supporting Creativity and Imagination in the Early Years*, Buckingham: Open University Press.

Durbin, G., Morris, S. and Wilkinson, S. (1990) *A Teacher's Guide to Learning From Objects*, Bristol: English Heritage.

Evans, R. (1997) *In Defence of History*, London: Granta Books.

Fines, J. and Nichol, J. (1997) *Teaching Primary History*, Oxford: Heinemann.

Fox, R. (1995) 'Teaching through discussion', in C. Desforges (ed.), *An Introduction to Teaching: Psychological Perspectives*, Oxford, UK, and Cambridge, USA: Blackwell.

Fryer, M. (1996) *Creative Teaching and Learning*, London: Paul Chapman.

Galton, M., Simon, B. and Croll, P. (1980a) *Inside the Primary Classroom*, London: Routledge & Kegan Paul.

Gardner, H. (1983) *Frames of Mind*, New York: Basic Books.

Gardner, H. (1993a) *Multiple Intelligences: The Theory in Practice*, New York: Basic Books.

Gardner, H. (1993b) *Creating Minds: An Anatomy of Creativity Seen Through the Lives of Freud, Einstein, Picasso, Stravinsky, Eliot, Graham, Gandhi*, New York: Basic Books.

Gruzinski, S. (1992) *The Aztecs: Rise and Fall of an Empire*, London: Thames and Hudson.

Hannington, W. (1977) *Unemployed Struggles 1919–1936: My Life and Struggles Amongst the Unemployed*, London: Lawrence & Wishart.

Hay McBer (2000) *Research into Teacher Effectiveness: a Model of Teacher Effectiveness* (DfEE Research Report 216), London: DfEE.

Haydn, T. (2000) 'Information and communications technology in the history classroom', in J. Arthur and R. Phillips, *Issues in Primary Teaching*, London: Routledge.

Hexter, J.H. (1972) *The History Primer*, New York: Basic Books.

Historical Association (2001) 'Learning to love history: preparation of non-specialist primary teachers to teach history', *Teaching History*, 102 (Feb.): 36–41.

Hoskins, W.G. (1967) *Fieldwork in Local History*, London: Faber and Faber.

Hughes, P., Cox, K. and Goddard, G. (2000) *Primary History Curriculum Guide*, London: David Fulton.

John, P. (1994) 'Academic tasks in history classrooms', *Research in Education*, 51: 11–22.

Kimber, D., Clough, N., Forrest, M., Harnett, P., Menter, I. and Newman, E. (1995) *Humanities in Primary Education, History, Geography, and Religious Education in the Primary Classroom*, London: David Fulton.

Kingston, P. (1982) *The Hunger Marchers in Britain 1920–1940*, London: Lawrence and Wishart.

Koestler, A. (1964) *The Act of Creation*, London: Hutchinson.

Lewis, M. and Wray, D. (1995) *Developing Children's Non-fiction Writing: Working with Writing Frames*, Leamington Spa: Scholastic Press.

Mayhew, H. (1851) 'London labour and the London poor', *News Chronicle*.

Medawar, P. (1969) *Induction and Intuition*, Philadelphia, PA: American Philosophical Society.

Meredith, A. (1995) 'Terry's learning: some limitations of Shulman's pedagogical content knowledge', *Cambridge Journal of Education*, 25 (2): 176–87.

Mortimore, P., Sammons, P., Stoll, L., Lewis, D. and Ecob, R. (1988) *School Matters: The Junior Years*, London: Open Book.

NACCCE (1999) *All Our Futures: Creativity, Culture and Education*, London: DfEE.

Nichol, J. (1979) *Evidence: The Saxons*, Oxford: Blackwell.

Nichol, J. (1984) *Teaching History: A Teaching Skills Workbook*, London: Macmillan.

Nichol, J. and Dean, J. (1997) *History 7–11: Developing Primary Teaching Skills*, London: Routledge.

O'Hara, L. and O'Hara, M. (2001) *Teaching History 3–11: The Essential Guide*, London: Continuum.

Ofsted (2000) *The Teaching of Writing in Primary Schools: Could do better?*, A discussion paper by HMI, London: Ofsted.

Ofsted (2002) *Ofsted Subject Reports 2001–2002 – Primary History*, London: Ofsted.

Ofsted (2003) *Ofsted Subject Reports 2002–2003 – Primary History*, London: Ofsted.

Papert, S. (1980) *Mindstorms: Children, Computers and Powerful Ideas*, Brighton: Harvester Press.

Phillips, R. (2002) *Reflective Teaching of History 11–18*, London: Continuum.

Piaget, J. (1959) *The Language and Thought of the Child* (3rd edn), London: Routledge.

Pluckrose, H. (1991) *Children Learning History*, Oxford: Blackwell.

QCA/DfEE (1998) *A Scheme of Work for Key Stages 1 and 2, History*, London: QCA/DfEE.

Richards, C. (1999) *Primary Education – At a Hinge of History?*, London: Falmer.

Rosen, B. (1988) *And None of It Was Nonsense: The Power of Storytelling in School*, London: Mary Glasgow.

Rosen, B. (1993) *Shapers and Polishers: Teachers as Storytellers*, London: Collins Educational.

Russell, B. (1961) *History of Western Philosophy*, London: Allen & Unwin.

Ryan, D. (1960) *Characteristics of Teachers*, Washington, DC: American Council on Education.

Ryle, G. (1949) *The Concept of Mind*, London: Hutchinson.

Schwab, J.J. (1964) 'The structure of the disciplines: meanings and significances', in G. Ford and L. Purgo (eds), *The Structure of Knowledge and the Curriculum*, Chicago, IL: Rand McNally.

Schwab, J.J. (1978) 'Education and the structure of the disciplines', in I. Westbury and N.J Wilkof (eds) *Science, Curriculum and Liberal Education*, Chicago: University of Chicago Press.

Shulman, L.S. (1986a) 'Paradigms and research programmes in the study of teaching: a contemporary perspective', in M.C. Wittrock (ed.), *Handbook of Research On Teaching* (3rd edn), New York: Macmillan.

Shulman, L.S. (1986b) 'Those who understand: knowledge growth in teaching', *Educational Researcher*, 15 (2): 4–14.

Shulman, L.S. (1987) 'Knowledge and teaching: foundations of the new reform', *Harvard Educational Review*, 57 (1): 1–22.

Sparrowhawk, A. (1995) 'Information technology in the primary school', Conference Address, Manchester BBC, 28 March.

Stones, E. (1992) *Quality Teaching: A Sample of Cases*, London: Routledge.

Stowe, W. and Haydn, T. (2000) 'Issues in the teaching of chronology', in J. Arthur and R. Phillips, *Issues in Primary Teaching*, London: Routledge.

Sutcliffe, R. (1978) *Song for a Dark Queen*, London: Crowell.

Tauber, R.T. and Mester, C.S. (1995) *Acting Lessons for Teachers: Using Performance Skills in the Classroom*, Pennsylvania: Greenwood Publishing Group.

Teacher Training Agency (TTA) (1998) *Using Information and Communications Technology to Meet Teaching Objectives in History*, London: TTA.

Tizard, B. and Hughes, M. (1984) *Young Children Learning: Talking and Thinking at Home and at School*, London: Fontana.

Trevelyan, G.M. (1913) *Clio: A Muse, and Other Essays*, London, New York and Toronto: Longmans, Green.

Turner-Bisset, R.A. (1999a) 'The knowledge bases of the expert teacher', *British Educational Research Journal*, 25 (1): 39–55.

Turner-Bisset, R.A. (1999b) 'History is boring and all about dead people: challenging non-specialist primary teachers' beliefs about history', in R. Phillips and G. Easedown (eds), *History Education: Subject Knowledge, Pedagogy and Practice*, Standing Conference of History Teacher Educators in the United Kingdom.

Turner-Bisset, R.A. (2000a) 'Reconstructing the Primary Curriculum: integration revisited', *Education 3–13*, 28 (1): 3–8.

Turner-Bisset, R.A. (2000b) 'Meaningful history with young children', in R. Drury, R. Campbell and L. Miller (eds), *Looking at Early Years Education and Care*, London: David Fulton.

Turner-Bisset, R.A. (2001) *Expert Teaching: Knowledge and Pedagogy to Lead the Profession*, London: David Fulton.

Turner-Bisset, R.A. (2003) 'On the carpet? Changing primary teaching contexts', *Education 3–13*, 31 (3).

Vygotsky, L.S. (1962) *Thought and Language*, Cambridge, MA: MIT Press.

Vygotsky, L.S. (1978) *Mind and Society*, Cambridge, MA: Harvard University Press.

Wallace, B. (ed.) (2003) *Using History to Develop Thinking Skills*, London: NACE/David Fulton.

Wilson, S.M. and Wineburg, S.S. (1988) 'Peering at history with different lenses: the role of disciplinary perspectives in teaching history', *Teachers College Record*, 89: 525–39.

Wood, L. and Holden, C. (1995) *Teaching Early Years History*, Cambridge: Chris Kington.

Woods, P. (1995) *Creative Teachers in Primary Schools*, Lewes: Falmer Press.

Wray, D. and Lewis, M. (1997) *Extending Literacy: Children Reading and Writing Non-fiction*, London: Routledge.

Wright, M. (1992) *The Really Practical Guide to Primary History*, Cheltenham: Stanley Thornes.

Index